Literature, Religion, and Postsecular Studies

Lori Branch, Series Editor

For Ori at ten years

אם אין אני לי מי לי
וכשאני לעצמי מה אני
ואם לא עכשו אימתי

If I am not for myself, who is for me?
And when I am for myself alone, what am I?
And if not now, when?

—Pirkei Avot 1:14
Jerusalem
Tishrei 5773
September 2012

Victorian Sacrifice

Ethics and Economics in Mid-Century Novels

ILANA M. BLUMBERG

The Ohio State University Press
Columbus

Library of Congress Cataloging-in-Publication Data
Blumberg, Ilana M., 1970–
Victorian sacrifice : ethics and economics in mid-century novels / Ilana M. Blumberg.
p. cm. — (Literature, religion, and postsecular studies)
Includes bibliographical references and index.
ISBN-13: 978-0-8142-5411-0 (cloth : alk. paper)
ISBN-10: 0-8142-1226-3 (cloth : alk. paper)
ISBN-13: 978-0-8142-9328-7 (cd)
1. English literature—19th century—History and criticism. 2. Religion and literature—Great Britain—History—19th century. 3. Self-sacrifice in literature. 4. Altruism in litera-ture. 5. Ethics in literature. 6. Economics in literature. I. Title. II. Series: Literature, religion, and postsecular studies.
PR468.R44B58 2013
823'.809382—dc23
                    2013005436

Cover design by Janna Thompson-Chordas
Cover image "The Visible Madonna" by Frederic Leighton, from *Romola* by George Eliot
Text design by Juliet Williams
Type set in Adobe Sabon

9 8 7 6 5 4 3 2 1

CONTENTS

ACKNOWLEDGMENTS

*J*t is a pleasure to acknowledge those who have encouraged me and improved this work. First, I am grateful to an exemplary scholar and writer, Linda Dowling. Her uncommon standard of excellence and honesty of evaluation have been great gifts. Though she has borne no institutional link to my work since teaching me as a visiting faculty member at the start of my graduate education, she has assisted me at each turn of my scholarly career, offering me the generosity I associate with the Victorian conviction that wisdom is a collective property increased from generation to generation.

I am indebted to my dissertation advisors at the University of Pennsylvania, Nina Auerbach, Erin O'Connor, and Peter Stallybrass, who guided me through my initial consideration of economics and narrative. In my first teaching position at the University of Michigan, Martha Vicinus and Jonathan Freedman responded helpfully to evolving formulations of this study; I am also grateful to the U of M Nineteenth-Century Forum and the First Draft Group where I shared versions of my chapter on Collins. John Kucich, always a model of scholarship for me, has shown himself over the years to be a sensitive and astute reader and advisor. Joe Bristow helped see one of my first essays into print, making the world of scholarly publication seem a navigable and pleasant place to be. His conviction that my subject was relevant was all-important. Rosemarie Bodenheimer and Elsie Michie generously read sections of this manuscript and improved them with their questions and suggestions. Rachel Ablow and Thomas Dixon participated with me at a MLA panel on Victorian Altruism and Egoism, and their work has continued to be highly interesting to me. I am very appreciative that Jan-Melissa Schramm introduced herself to me transatlantically, in order to exchange work on our intersecting topics.

I would be remiss not to acknowledge some of my professors at Barnard College from 1989–1993, who taught me about the nineteenth century, introduced me to literary criticism and theory, and opened the possibilities for interdisciplinary study: Mary Gordon, the late Barbara Stoler Miller, Celeste Schenck, Timea Szell, Mark Carnes, and Nancy Stepan. I am more grateful than I can possibly say to these teachers and to Barnard College, where I learned a usable feminism and experienced the ethical intelligence that can be fostered in the best of classrooms. I strive to produce such results for my students.

I am fortunate to teach now at James Madison College, Michigan State University, under the leadership of Dean Sherman Garnett, who was quick to grant me leave time to work on this book and support to attend conferences that improved it. As a scholar of humanities, I teach among people who work in such diverse fields as forestry and fisheries, international relations, comparative politics, and constitutional democracy; my students come out of their classrooms into mine. The interdisciplinarity I encounter daily challenges me to speak to a wide audience of thinking people and I hope this book has risen to the high level of conversation and commitment I encounter in my workplace. I am particularly grateful to Allison Berg, Lisa Cook, Ross Emmett, Eric Petrie, Colleen Tremonte, and Ken Waltzer, as well as the wonderfully helpful college staff.

I would like to acknowledge the American Association of University Women. The Association supported me with a postdoctoral fellowship that allowed me to concentrate on this book without the necessity of teaching at the same time. I am also grateful to the Jewish Book Council and the Sami Rohr Prize community. While this book is not a Jewish book per se, any book I write has the benefits of their strong support.

I have been gifted with wonderful colleagues and friends, near and far, who have helped in various and vital ways, coming at my subject with what feels like an overwhelming force of super-intelligence! Thank you particularly to Zarena Aslami, Ariela Freedman, Sheila Jelen, John Parker, and Jill Rapoport.

Another dear friend, Lori Henderson, enabled me to finish this book by taking care of our youngest child, Tzipora, with loving enthusiasm and endless resourcefulness.

Sandy Crooms has been a lovely and smart editor and I appreciate the efforts of her entire staff at The Ohio State University Press.

My thanks also goes to the journals *Studies in the Novel, Victorian Literature and Culture,* and *Nineteenth-Century Literature,* where portions of chapters 3, 4, and 5 were previously published.

Finally, I want to thank my parents, Tzivia Garfinkel and Paul Blumberg, as well as my siblings, Jonathan and Naomi, their spouses, Rayli and Joey, and my terrific nieces and nephews: Jessica, Emily, Will, Alyssa, and Simon. I am grateful to the whole of my extended family for their support.

My three children, Priya, Shai, and Tzipora, are the delights of my life. With them, the challenge of balancing the claims of the self and others somehow feels not only manageable, but a blessing.

This book is for Ori who understands that the heart of ethics is not only about the how of action, but the when, which is always now. I am grateful to be in the present with him.

INTRODUCTION

"Many things are difficult and dark to me—but I see one thing quite clearly—that I must not, cannot seek my own happiness by sacrificing others" (*Mill on the Floss* 571).

With these words, Maggie Tulliver, the heroine of George Eliot's 1860 novel, *Mill on the Floss,* steadies herself at a moment of overmastering desire. Confronted with the chance to escape the narrow boundaries of her life with a passionate lover, Maggie nonetheless chooses to turn back because pursuing her own happiness will surely hurt others. As she reaches for the certainty of the medieval Catholic monk, Thomas à Kempis, whose *Imitation of Christ* first taught her to think beyond her own pleasures and sorrows, Maggie tells her lover, "There are things we must renounce in life," and proceeds to do so, at lasting cost to herself and others (571). Maggie Tulliver can imagine no ethical alternative to self-sacrifice.

For Maggie's creator and other major mid-nineteenth-century novel-ists, however, the Victorian imperative of self-sacrifice posed a challenge to the ethical imagination. They sensed in conventional notions of sacrifice an exhaustion and moral inefficacy that frequently bred positive harm. Yet what alternative could there be to a self-denial sanctioned both by ancient Christian tradition and by the latest impulses of evangelical Protestantism? This study will argue that mid-century novelists sought to commandeer the cultural and religious potency of the Christian ideal of self-sacrifice in order to negotiate a transition from the conventionally religious English past to a secularizing but still faithful modernity.[1] In a context shaped by the competing forces of a residual moral demand for selflessness and an emerging laissez-faire economic order understood by many Victorians to enshrine self-interest and individual profit, major novelists questioned and transformed the sacrificial ideal, seeking a new model for the relation between self and other that could stand the double test of moral rectitude and economic realism.

In place of painful, solitary self-sacrifice in service of another's good, these writers narrated an ethical realism suggesting that virtuous action could serve the collective benefit of all parties involved. Believing that this new mode of altruistic action was no mask for a corrupt self-interest, the mid-century novelists sought to portray the genuine, reciprocal good that could flow from it. In a moment of economic optimism and British political ascendancy, novelists worked to transform the ethical landscape by dramatizing the balance between what the theorist of social evolution Herbert Spencer would later call a "proper altruism and a reasonable egoism" (*Principles* 390). From that tense equilibrium, they imagined that communal solidarity and material abundance might follow.

Christian Sacrifice

Lying at the core of the "dominant Victorian moral sensibility," the ideal of sacrifice—especially self-sacrifice—would prompt the alternative ethics put forward by mid-century novelists.[2] In 1854, F. D. Maurice, the Christian Socialist who was to become Professor of Moral Philosophy at Cambridge, attested to the centrality of sacrifice when he charged his readers to recognize it as "no one solitary act . . . but that it lies at the very root of our being; that our lives stand upon it; that society is held together by it;

---

1. The literature on secularization is extensive but, as future chapters attest, the two accounts which have most influenced my thinking are those of the contemporary philosopher Charles Taylor (2007), and the major historian of the Victorian church, Owen Chadwick (1975).

2. I take Stefan Collini's (1991) view that, in naming a "dominant sensibility," we can "suggest, rather than . . . deny, that there were some who did not share it and that there were degrees of sharing it, but . . . that its dominance would be acknowledged by the fact that those who did not share it necessarily stood in some defensive, deferential, or antagonistic relation to it" (63). For an account that explores the place of the anti-social in a culture of altruism, see Christopher Lane (2004), who argues that the emphasis upon fellow-feeling and sympathy indicates the profound difficulty Victorians saw in forging a social life. On his view, Victorian novels "portray hatred in nearly insoluble forms" (xiv).

that all power to be right, and to do right, begins with the offering up of ourselves, because it is thus that the righteous Lord makes us like Himself" (35–36). Maurice described his conviction in religious terms, yet a broad swath of educated Victorians, from devout to agnostic and atheistic, imagined social and spiritual good to depend upon sacrificial virtue. George Eliot had translated the words of Ludwig Feuerbach's humanist creed in *The Essence of Christianity:* "to suffer for others is divine" (60). As all things "divine" were those highest goods that humanity could imagine, so self-sacrifice, according to Feuerbach, was a pinnacle of human achievement. The sacrificial sensibility was promulgated widely: by sermons and tracts, bestselling novels and poetry, published eulogies and biographies of great men and women, accounts of war and empire, self-help manuals and housekeeping guides, treatises of political economy, the history of art, and literary criticism.

The doctrine central to Christianity, redemptive sacrifice—as modeled by Christ's sacrifice on the Cross—had been strongly re-emphasized in nineteenth-century religious belief, from Victorian Evangelicalism to Anglo-Catholicism. I begin with the religious context because, in spite of our tendency to recall the era as one in which faith suffered the challenges of science and modernity, in fact, the mid-Victorian period, as Callum G. Brown argues, reflects the capacity of a "diffusive, rather than enforced religion" to overcome the threats of secularization and successfully "acquire new ways to find social significance" (39).[3] The mid-century witnessed energetic church-building and repair, especially among Dissenting denominations; the establishment of a thriving infrastructure of Sunday schools for adults; large-scale missionary efforts at home and abroad; and an unrivalled output of popular religious literature (Rosman 232). Sermons, both spoken and printed, were so major a force within the public discourse that homes with fewer than six books were likely to count a volume of published sermons among their collections and many educated Victorians not only read sermons, but joined the church-going public to hear weekly sermons with a curiosity and interest that transcended denominational loyalty (Cruse 108). In London, the manufacturing towns, and

---

3. Brown (1992) claims that in the last sixty years of the nineteenth century, religious adherence rose, rather than fell, in mainland Britain. He attributes what has been seen as the "secularization" of social policy in the mid- and late-nineteenth century to "a rising religious fervor for democratic ecclesiastical influence in public policy" (52). Brown dates secularization to the years between 1904 and 1914 when urbanization began to stagnate and Britain "witnessed the rise of truly secular urban policy devoid of moral solutions to urban problems: comprehensive urban redevelopment, housing projects, and welfarism" (54).

even some country parishes, sermons reflected the intellectual ferment of the age.[4]

As Boyd Hilton has comprehensively demonstrated, in the first half of the century, Christians took as their central religious doctrine the Atonement—the exchange whereby Christ had died for the sins of men, redeeming them through his voluntary, guiltless sacrifice. Easter was emphasized rather than Christmas; Christ as lamb, rather than man. Atonement theology, Hilton suggests, fit well the pessimism and anxiety that had arisen in the aftermath of the French Revolution and the massively influential *Essay on the Principle of Population* (1798), where Thomas Malthus suggested that scarcity and competition, misery and poverty, were inescapable conditions of life. The theology of the Atonement emphasized humanity's depravity and refused the notion that anything but Christ's singular sacrifice could redeem fallen souls.

While Atonement theology was critical to Anglicans and Scottish Presbyterians who formally identified as Evangelicals, evangelical emphases informed the beliefs of Christians from Broad Church to High Church and Anglo-Catholics, and all forms of Dissenters. In the chapel of Rugby School, headmaster Dr. Thomas Arnold described Christ's death—his "sacrifice for sin"—as "the central point of Christianity": "we are forgiven for his sake; we are acquitted through his death, and through faith in his blood" (Arnold 260). And when the major nonconformist preacher and hymnist Thomas Binney (1798–1874) preached his famous "Gethsemane" Sermon at King's Weigh-House Chapel in 1850, he enlisted a collection of scriptural verses that described Christ's status as a "sacrificial victim" merely as prelude to the more original and nuanced part of the sermon (159). Binney depended on his audience to know well the following catalogue of verses that, indeed, were common currency for mid-century Christians immersed in a theology of Atonement:

> "His soul was made an offering for sin." "He bore our griefs and carried our sorrows." "He was wounded for our transgressions and bruised for our iniquities; the chastisement of our peace was upon Him." "It pleased the Lord to bruise Him and to put Him to grief; Jehovah laid on Him the iniquity of us all." . . . "He suffered, the just for the unjust." . . . "By His stripes we are healed." (159)

---

4. See Doreen Rosman (2003) 142–45; Amy Cruse (1962) 121–41, 76–80, 108–19 for helpful pictures of the intellectual and spiritual commitments to preaching among the Victorians and especially for Cruse's description of cross-denominational influences.

Binney ended his sermon with an emphasis on the unique efficacy of Christ's atonement; Christ's sacrifice saves humanity from the despair it must otherwise face when confronted by the "deep sense of unpardoned sin":

> Happy will it be for every one of us, at every return of recollected guilt, to cling to the hope provided for us in the vicarious sufferings of the Christ of God. "The Blood of Christ cleanseth from all sin." Pardon, in the Gospel is promised *for a reason;* that reason is the great redemptive act of the sacrifice of Messiah, which is to be confided in and pleaded by the contrite man. That reason never failed, and it never will fail, so long as there is a sinner to believe and a God to hear. (164)

Christ's sacrifice was the sole source of salvation available to believing Christians, ever-mindful of their sinful nature.

From chapel to church, from parish to city, preachers instructed listeners in their dependence on Christ. Charles Haddon Spurgeon, the Baptist preaching phenomenon, exclaimed before thousands of listeners in 1856:

> [I endeavor] . . . to commend God's love to you, as much as ever I can, and [invite] as many of you as feel your need of a Saviour, to lay hold of him and embrace him now as your all-sufficient sacrifice. Sinner! I can commend Christ to thee for this reason: *I know that thou needest him.* Thou mayest be ignorant of it thyself, but thou dost need him. ("Love's Commendation" 421)

While evangelicals like Spurgeon held fast to an understanding of Christ's "all-sufficient sacrifice" as vicarious expiation, by 1854, as Jan-Melissa Schramm has recently detailed, the precise mechanism of redemption had become the central theological debate of mid-century, a debate which had lain quiet since the turn of the century when Joseph Priestley and the Unitarians had questioned the true nature of atonement and the doctrine of Original Sin (142). Following on the heels of Maurice's controversial *Doctrine of Sacrifice,* religious works on sacrifice in the form of sermons, pamphlets, tracts, and scriptural commentaries poured forth from 1856–1860 (years which also saw the publication of the first three literary works of this study). The controversy concerned the move of Broad Church thinkers such as Maurice and Benjamin Jowett, Professor of Greek at Oxford, away from the idea that Christ's death was literally 'in place of' a humanity condemned by Original Sin, redeemed only through Christ's exchange. Maurice instead stressed the metaphorical nature of sacrifice and approached the Gospels under the influence of Coleridge and the German Higher Criticism, alive to the human element in Christ, seeking in Christ not a vicarious victim, but a model, a "supreme example of self-abnegation and submission to the perceived will of God"; likewise, in 1855, Jowett described the crucifixion as neither "the sacrifice, nor the satisfaction, nor the ransom, but the greatest moral act ever done in this world" (Schramm 149).

Given the degree of controversy that attended the redemptive nature of Christ's sacrifice in the 1850s, it is notable—and central to this study, which is not one of theology—that widespread *consensus* attended the matter of *personal* Christian sacrifice, among lay Christians as among theologians. At mid-century, British Christians were largely agreed in understanding personal suffering and sacrifice in imitation of Christ as critical elements of genuine religious experience. While evangelicals, like all Protestants, rejected the idea that salvation was achieved by works, nonetheless, they insisted on its harmony with the works God willed, particularly those which required the renunciation of individual desire or temptation: "any act of obedience by which we give up our own will to God's will may be regarded as an act of self-denial, or what the Bible terms a spiritual sacrifice" (Chalmers *Posthumous Works* 21). Thomas Chalmers, the greatly influential Scottish evangelical and Professor of Moral Philosophy at St. Andrews, understood such spiritual sacrifice to be the hallmark of a pious life on earth:

> The utter renunciation of self—the surrender of all vanity—the patient endurance of evils and wrongs—the crucifixion of natural and worldly desires—the absorption of all our interests and passions in the enjoyment of God—and the subordination of all we do, and of all we feel, to his glory—these form the leading virtues of our pilgrimage. (Chalmers "Introductory Essay" 21)

The totality reflected by the term "utter," and the quadruple recurrence of the term, "all," testify to the rigor of the evangelical demand conveyed to the reading and listening public.

Many sermons sought to address the practicalities of such a lofty demand, seeking to translate it to the realm of everyday action.[5] The

---

5. See Robert H. Ellison (2010) for his discussion of the particularly Tractarian emphasis on "practical application" (20).

famous verse in Luke, "If any man will come after Me, let him deny himself, and take up his cross daily, and follow Me," allowed John Henry Newman to recommend to his many eager listeners and readers, High Church and beyond, a regular practice of discerning and creating opportunities for self-denial (Lk 9:23). From that verse, Newman preached, "a rigorous self-denial is a chief duty. . . . [I]t may be considered the test whether we are Christ's disciples, whether we are living in a mere dream, which we mistake for Christian faith and obedience, or are really and truly awake, alive, living in the day, on our road heavenwards" ("Self-Denial" 91). Small acts of daily self-denial were to be moments of evidence, otherwise unavailable, that one's Christian faith was more than mere words or the desire for worldly approval and reward. This sermon, among others Newman preached between 1825–1843, was republished and circulated to a broad audience in the 1860s, even after his conversion to Roman Catholicism.

Working against Egoism

While the force of the sacrificial ideal was felt keenly by religious Victorians, it extended as well to those Victorians who were not conventionally devout. As Owen Chadwick notes, when agnostics imagined that they could drop the creed linked with inherited morality, they nevertheless assumed that the morality itself was "absolute and must be preserved" (*Secularization* 231). George Eliot, who had left behind Christian dogma, praised evangelicalism as having "brought into palpable existence and operation . . . that idea of duty, that recognition of something to be lived for beyond the mere satisfaction of self, which is to the moral life what the addition of a great central ganglion is to animal life" (*Scenes of Clerical Life* 320). The "mere satisfaction of self," as Eliot called it, or "egoism," was anathema for mid-Victorian writers concerned with sustaining, consistently improving, and striving finally to perfect human civilization. The Christian "being right and doing right," that F. D. Maurice described and the humanist "moral life" that Eliot envisioned both explicitly depended on moving beyond the self.

Just as Christian writers naturally understood the ethical imperative to be self-sacrifice in imitation of Christ, the more secularized Victorian notion of "duty" also retained at its core a sense of painful, self-lacerating sacrifice. When Maggie Tulliver asserts to her lover that "there are things we must renounce in life," she understands that painful renunciation not to be an act of unusual generosity or sensitivity to others, but to be simply her duty, an equation we can see reflected in her rhetorical question, "If the past is not to bind us, where can duty lie?" (602). The frequent assimilation of duty to sacrifice was a hallmark of Victorian moral thought, one so regular that John Stuart Mill saw fit to correct it in *Utilitarianism* by distinguishing the free offering of what he called "generosity," which no one was bound to offer his fellows, from the just payment of the debt of "duty," which could be exacted rightfully from every human being (454). Later, Henry Sidgwick, too, sought to unravel "duty" and "virtue," but noted the difficulty that "in some sense, [it is] a man's strict duty to do whatever action he judges most excellent, so far as it is in his power" (219). The distinction between duty and what moral philosophers call "supererogation," or going beyond the call of ethical duty to do an act of moral good that is not required, perplexed Victorians who sought to celebrate unusual virtue but, at the same time, worried that its absence might be ethically culpable.[6]

How can we explain the Victorian tendency to collapse praise for the commission of virtuous action with the condemnation of omission? Why is it that Maggie Tulliver imagines the call of duty to encompass that which might fairly be considered beyond the call of duty? When we consider the paradox of Victorian renunciation coming to be both commonplace and exemplary, it is useful to consider a long history of Christianity. The contemporary philosopher Charles Taylor argues that from ancient times Christianity was tensed between the often exclusive imperatives of human flourishing and renunciation. At first, this tension was resolved by a hierarchical system in which an elite population served the imperative to renounce, as if on behalf of the masses who could not be expected to meet such standards. When radical Protestantism opposed this division and abolished the allegedly higher, renunciative vocations in favor of an egalitarian model focused on the sanctification of everyday life, it preserved the imperative of renunciation by building it into ordinary life. However, Taylor notes, this shift in paradigm risks "loading ordinary flourishing with a burden of renunciation it cannot carry. It . . . fills out the picture of what the properly sanctified life would be with a severe set of moral demands. This seems to be unavoidable in the logic of rejecting complementarity,

6. See Sidgwick, "Virtue and Duty" (217–30) and "Ethical Judgments" (23–38). There is a large and fascinating recent literature on supererogation, including many discussions of heroes and saints that could be—but has not yet been—usefully applied to considerations of Victorian culture. Susan Wolf (1982) and Edith Wyschogrod (1990) are among the most influential accounts. For a helpful introduction, see David Heyd (2008).

because if we really must hold that all vocations are equally demanding, and don't want this to be a leveling down, then all must be at the most exigent pitch" (82). The intensity of "ordinary" Christian renunciation may be understood, then, as a direct inheritance of the Protestant resolution of this ancient tension, with its anti-elitist drift having raised the sacrificial standard for all believers.

Yet it is fair to say that mid-nineteenth-century people experienced the renunciatory imperative with a special intensity that was inseparable from their sense of the conflict and competition that divided the self from others. The intellectual historian Stefan Collini has offered the insight that Victorians of the educated classes habitually thought in terms of a "sharp and sometimes exhaustive polarity" between egoism and the new notion of altruism first made available by the positivist philosopher Auguste Comte (65).[7] At its most extreme, altruism meant positively "living for others," *vivre pour les autres*, as Comte taught: setting others as the motivation and end of all moral action.[8] The social ethic of altruism made its demands as Victorians sought to compensate for the accelerating loss of the transcendental basis of religious belief. Whereas in the second half of the century both Christians and secularizing thinkers accepted the idea that *individuals* might be able to maintain their moral standards if they lost religion, they also agreed that the standards of *society* were likely to suffer in the absence of religious faith (Chadwick *Secularization* 230). William Gladstone, for instance, expressed his fear for public morality when he wrote in 1840 that "egoism . . . is sure to prevail whenever the pressure of high Christian motives is removed" (463). Yet by mid-century, egoism did not recognizably appear to have prevailed any more than in any other period. Instead, among the educated classes, the *fear* of egoism had prevailed and it was repeatedly singled out for mention by those thinkers who newly felt the world to be inhabited solely by human selves bound to ethical standards by nothing more powerful than their own frail and fallible wills. Historians are generally agreed that "even as religion became progressively more attenuated, as the public became more relaxed in its faith and the intellec-

---

7. Taylor also describes the nineteenth-century ethic of altruism as maintaining a "polar opposition between the obligation of benevolence, on one hand, and selfish desire on the other" (395). For a strong recent consideration of the "invention" of altruism, see Thomas Dixon's (2008) wide-ranging "word history," which considers political, social, philosophical, and evolutionary contexts for the term.

8. See Chadwick on the centrality of Comte to nineteenth-century moral thought. Chadwick argues that Comte's proposals were "nearest to a popular theory of ethics, not religious, that the middle classes of the nineteenth century achieved" (*Secularization* 236). See also Dixon for the relation between altruism and Comtean positivism (41–89).

tuals more openly skeptical, the social ethic did not become correspond-
ingly attenuated or relaxed" (Himmelfarb 289).

As evangelicals had emphasized self-control and discipline as a way
of following and glorifying God through beneficent action, secularizing thinkers such as J. S. Mill and Leslie Stephen re-wrote those ethics
in an anthropocentric turn. As they appealed to "inner sources" rather
than divine grace to bring out the beneficent side of human nature, they
imagined the work of building and defending the human will from selfishness to require great and persistent effort. For believers and un-believers
alike, the anthropocentric turn narrowed down the spectrum of Christian vices in such a way that selfishness or egoism was imagined to be the
root of all moral failing while selflessness or altruism came to be defined
as the "heart of moral virtue" (Collini 65–66).[9] In a world without grace
to redeem Original Sin, altruism alone could assume a redemptive power
proportionate to the destructive power of the egoism which was humanity's fallen condition.

Yet this altruism bore the same parabola-effect of Christ's sacrifice on
the Cross, that is to say, one could approach it but never attain it. Further,
the everyday was filled with opportunities for altruism that demanded but
consistently eluded fulfillment. We have long known of the pre-eminence of
morality in Victorian culture. What this meant in practice was the tendency
"to give evaluative priority to [the category of] morality," and "to evaluate
nearly all action from a moral lens" (Collini 63). In expanding the range of
actions considered morally meaningful and then judging such actions from
an exclusively moral point of view, Victorians found themselves bound by
a set of extreme definitions for both egoism and altruism. An action that
had not hurt a second party but had neither actively assisted him or her
might be considered egoistic because it had failed to make central another's
needs. By the same token, an action that had benefited another substan-
tially but had simultaneously benefited the actor him- or herself might not
be understood as authentically altruistic because the self had not yielded
decisively to the other. In such a schema, egoism was not only a commission—a consideration of the self, however slight and seemingly innocu-
ous—but the momentary forgetfulness of others. Such extreme definitions
made it nearly impossible to imagine acts of genuine altruism and, ipso
facto, nearly inevitable to imagine such acts as tainted by egoism. How

---

9. Dixon, too, argues that Comte and Lewes used the terms altruism and egoism in
ways that mapped "the distinction between moral badness and moral goodness . . . onto that
between devotion to self and devotion to others," thus "enshrining the distinction between
self and other at the heart of . . . ethics" (196).

were Victorians to find a standard of unselfishness that could avoid, as Sidgwick wrote, "making exaggerated demands on human nature"? (87).

Against a Maximalist Altruism, toward an Economy of Mutual Benefit

At mid-century, novelists constructed their alternative ethics in response to the troubling sense that all human actions might be divided into two categories—egoistic or altruistic—to the exclusion of a morally meaningful or a morally neutral middle ground. Maggie Tulliver's equation of duty with self-sacrifice offers us a clear example of what I will be calling "maximalist altruism," the tendency to strive for an altruism purified of any speck of self-interest, as if only such altruism might be ethically justifiable and as if the lack of such an effort would be ethically culpable. If Herbert Spencer's *The Data of Ethics* (1879) would later seem to the philosopher and proto-psychologist Alexander Bain to have constituted "a definitive rebuttal of 'popular exaggerations of altruistic duty,'" mid-century novelists were deeply enmeshed in this problematic decades earlier (Dixon 184). While the philosophers J. S. Mill, Leslie Stephen, and Henry Sidgwick were concerned by the impossibilities of a maximalist altruism, some of the century's most popular moralists—Charles Dickens, George Eliot, Anthony Trollope and Wilkie Collins—narrativized such concerns, providing memorable refractions of its lived experience to a wide and growing audience.

These novelists faced a challenging project: to offer, first, a compelling enough critique of the shortcomings of this prevailing ethical standard and second, a compelling enough articulation of its potential alternative for a conscientious ethical subject to accept. Continuity would be critical to this new ethic; it could not break entirely with what appeared recognizably virtuous to Victorians if its authors wanted it to be a genuine alternative. Sacrifice would have to be renovated, but its dimension of social generosity could not be dispensed with.

In their critique, mid-century novelists sought to reconstruct the notion of costly, self-punishing sacrifice by reconceiving the basic social unit as communal, rather than individual. From Charles Dickens' historical melodrama *A Tale of Two Cities* (1859) to George Eliot's pastoral *Adam Bede* (1859); from Anthony Trollope's fable-like *The Warden* (1855) and his psychologically realist *The Last Chronicle of Barset* (1867) to Wilkie Collins' sensational mystery *The Moonstone* (1868), novelists explored the way that self-sacrifice resulted from and intensified not social cohesion, but a breakdown in social ties. As we will see, in each of their novels, sacrifice reveals itself in morally ambiguous, even reviled terms such as suicide or self-destruction; unnecessary or useless waste; vanity or hidden pride; greed; selfishness itself. Rather than stemming from benevolent impulses, self-sacrifice often comes from anti-social impulses and weakens the social whole.

Only by setting aside a vision of human beings as isolated individuals who would rise or fall alone could these novelists define an ethics responsive to both the self and others.[10] In place of social atomism, the novelists imagined a world where human beings were mutually dependent. In such a world, costly self-sacrifice could no longer set the ethical standard because it would be recognized as equally destructive to others as it was to the self. Sacrifice would then yield to the pursuit of benefits that would be truly collective: constructive for others, constructive for the self. Loss and gain might then no longer divide people, but instead unite them in shared, enriched experience. I will suggest here that the novelists glimpsed this model of collective benefit in the transformative energies of Victorian capitalism.

Until fairly recently, when scholars have considered the relation of novelists to the emerging industrial capitalist order and to the discourses of political economy, we have imagined it to be largely antagonistic—and for good reason.[11] Dickens' portraits of the under-classes have left indelible images of those ground under by poverty, greed, and competition. His novels emphasized the eerie way in which, as Marx described, capitalism seemed to turn people into abstractions and, inversely, to animate corpo-

---

10. In her recent study of ethics and the English novel, Valerie Wainwright (2007) has argued that in Victorian novels, virtue is "anchored to conceptions of rewarding lives" (3). Consequently, she traces the development of an ideal of personal cultivation and flourishing in the work of Victorian novelists, whom she sees as heralding modern forms of identity. As my final chapter argues, this conception does not seem to me to characterize the mid-century period. While I find convincing the accounts such as those of Taylor or Alasdair McIntyre who stress certain fundamental continuities between Victorian identities and our own, this study does not emphasize the already richly discussed subjects of selfhood and identity. I work here with the assumption of Tobin Siebers that "the heart of ethics is the desire for community" (qtd. in Davis and Womack x). "Purely private or non-collaborative forms of self-cultivation or self-assertion" are interesting to me here only insofar as they provide a heuristic against which to measure the challenges Victorians faced in distinguishing themselves from others, in limiting the claims others could exert upon them while still preserving a coherent and cohesive social life (Collini 66). I suggest that the drive toward Victorian individualism took much of its force from the strength of the prevailing forces against it.

11. For Victorian critiques of capitalism, see Elisabeth and Richard Jay (1987).

rate bodies and commodities.[12] Likewise, the multifaceted costs of a new socioeconomic order were made vivid in Elizabeth Gaskell's life-and-death dramas of the conflicts between workers and manufacturers, George Eliot's nostalgic paeans to a simpler agrarian past, William Thackeray's satiric visions of the vanity of consumption, and Anthony Trollope's insistence on the besetting sin of dishonesty. Novelistic portraits of egoism and altruism have seemed to flow directly from the overwhelming temptations of the commercial ethos toward egoism and its disincentives toward altruism.

In the last fifteen years, it has become more common for critics to acknowledge the ways that novelists themselves were inside commodity culture even as they functioned as its critics. As Andrew Miller puts it, "adopting a moral stance against the commodification of the world, novelists simultaneously understood that literary work was itself commodified; they were, as a result, required to negotiate between their moral condemnation and their implication in what they opposed" (*Novels behind Glass* 7). Leading scholars have turned as well to the points of contact between political economy and aesthetics.[13] Catherine Gallagher, for instance, has demonstrated that although Victorian novelists often positioned themselves as antagonists to the doctrines of political economy, the discourses of literature and political economy developed in tandem over the course of the century, with mid-century novelists influenced by the logic of political economy even when they criticized it. Kathleen Blake has suggested that middle-class Victorian novelists were, in fact, often proponents of political economy and utilitarianism, drawn by the democratic, reformist, and pleasure-seeking elements of these schools of thought, elements that have been all but lost in most contemporary scholarly accounts. My own point of entry is to propose that novelists responded to and transformed a central discourse of political economy as they sought to restore a moral dimension to the order of mutual benefit that was coming to characterize a modern, secular age.[14]

---

12. The classic critical account of this literary phenomenon in Dickens is Dorothy Van Ghent (1953). See also John Kucich, "George Eliot and Objects," and Karl Marx, "The Fetishism of Commodities."

13. See Regenia Gagnier, (*Insatiability*) and Mary Poovey (*Genres of the Credit Economy*). Jennifer Ruth (2006) and Bruce Robbins (2007) offer timely commentaries on the conjunction between aesthetics and economics in Victorian times and in our own.

14. Here, I bring my findings together with Taylor's description of a modern, secular age as one in which the economic dimension takes on a larger explanatory power and the order of mutual benefit comes to dominate lived experience. Whereas Taylor retains the sense of mutual benefit as part of the "impersonal order" that displaces a providential sense, my analysis works to explore mutual benefit as an element of immediate human relations.

Can Self-Love and Benevolence Go Hand in Hand?:
Political Economy Meets Christian Morality

When Victorians confronted the daunting prospect of unbelief, they faced
a related hazard: the need to recast an account of social relations that had
made sense to their eighteenth-century predecessors but no longer seemed
convincing. Much eighteenth-century social and economic thought—from
the Third Earl of Shaftesbury to Adam Smith—had portrayed a harmonious world in which the relation between self-love or self-interest and
benevolence or charity was undergirded by a divine or natural order guar-
anteeing the common welfare. But this harmonious picture had been constructed by the eighteenth-century writers only after a fierce struggle with
the challenge posed by Thomas Hobbes's *Leviathan* (1651) and Bernard
de Mandeville's materialist satire *The Fable of the Bees; or, Private Vices,
Publick Benefits* (1723). Mandeville had provocatively proposed that it
was precisely the vices or self-regarding actions of individuals pursuing
luxury and pleasure which ultimately produced wealth and social progress to the benefit of all. His corrosive attack was steadily countered in
such literary works as Alexander Pope's "Essay on Man" (1733)—"Thus
God and Nature linked the general frame/ And bade Self-love and Social
be the same/ . . . Self-love forsook the path it first pursued,/ And found
the private in the public good"—and contested at length in Bishop Joseph
Butler's *Fifteen Sermons* (1726) where Butler portrayed self-love as not
only a Christian duty but one entirely consistent with the Christian duty
of benevolence. By the end of the eighteenth century, then, Mandeville's
challenge had been met and modified sufficiently that the notion of an
enlightened self-interest as serving the common good had become quite
orthodox.

Victorians inherited this comforting moral orthodoxy only to find it
undermined in turn by the consequences flowing from Malthus' *Essay.*
Placing scarcity at the center of his economic paradigm—the apparently
inescapable fact that population would increase geometrically while food
supplies could increase only arithmetically—Malthus at a stroke divided
the discipline of theology from the science of political economy, darken-
ing any hope for an economic order based on benevolence and harmonized
interests.[15] Though Christian thinkers such as William Paley, J. B. Sumner,
and Bishop Edward Copleston would work to reconcile Malthus' economic science with a theology that could account for misery and poverty,

---

15. This is A. M. C. Waterman's (2004) convincing argument. See 107–42.

nonetheless, Malthus' vision of a world where competition for scarce, finite resources characterized social relations would profoundly shape Victorian imaginings of the present and defer any previously felt sense of harmony far into the future. In the Malthusian world where population outstripped resources, basic tenets of eighteenth-century moral and economic thought could no longer be assumed. Wealth might not be fundamentally good; wealth-creation might not always be feasible; and measures to increase the wealth of nations might not be consonant with or belong to Christian religion (Waterman 109).[16] Anglophone economic thought that had been, as the major historian of economics A. M. C. Waterman argues, "congenial to, and to some extent intertwined with," Christian theology was no longer easily reconciled with it (108).[17]

For classical political economists, it was competition rather than a model of Christian benevolence that was understood to serve the social good. Writing in 1833, an alarmed Thomas Carlyle described the self-centered rapaciousness of those who should be Christian brothers:

> "Fellow, see! thou art taking more than thy share of Happiness in the world, something from *my* share: which, by the Heavens, thou shalt not; nay I will fight thee rather."—Alas, and the whole lot to be divided is such a beggarly matter, truly a "feast of shells," for the substance has been spilled out: not enough to quench one Appetite; and the collective human species clutching at them! (259)

The difficult decades of the thirties and forties pitted brothers against each other for mere subsistence in a zero-sum game which Carlyle described as necessarily divisive. Such competition was no abstraction. As Harold Perkins reminds us, the competition that characterized capitalism in the first half of the century was personal and individual: "competition was not the bloodless competition between material products and between abstract corporations of the modern 'free enterprise' economy: it was *individual* competition, the competition of flesh-and-blood men for wealth, power and social status" (221–22).

----

16. Hilton describes England's unprecedented economic growth as greeted by "a general uncertainty in which a mood of 'change and decay' vied with exhilaration and patriotic optimism" (65). Britain was perceived to be the only industrializing country, and as such, its situation might not be natural; time, too, was seen as cyclical and might just as likely be leading backward than forward (66).

17. For a theological reading of Smith that convincingly argues an affinity between *Wealth of Nations* and Anglican theology, see Waterman 88–106.

Reconciling traditional ethics with a new economic science was not a simple task for educated Victorians or for working-class aspirants. John Ruskin's denunciation of profit-seeking described it as thoroughly incongruous with the professed beliefs of Christian Englishmen:

> I know no previous instance in history of a nation's establishing a systematic disobedience to the first principles of its professed religion. The writings which we (verbally) esteem as divine, not only denounce the love of money as the source of all evil, and as an idolatry abhorred of the Deity, but declare mammon service to be the accurate and irreconcileable [sic] opposite of God's service: and whenever they speak of riches absolute, and poverty absolute, declare woe to the rich, and blessing to the poor. Whereupon we forthwith investigate a science of becoming rich, as the shortest road to national prosperity. (*Unto This Last* 61)

Playing upon the double scriptural sense of riches and poverty, Ruskin refused Malthus' narrower demarcation of wealth as a purely material measure. If Ruskin was one of the most vociferous critics of mammonism and the dehumanization and aesthetic poverty brought about by industrialized labor, he was nevertheless not alone in his worries. As the historian G. R. Searle has shown, even in years of "innocent optimism," the "practical application of market values proved capable of arousing disquiet, controversy, and genuine perplexity" among the educated classes who had grown up schooled in Christian morality (vii–viii).

Contemporary objections and anxieties regarding Victorian money-making may seem too familiar to bear rehearsing. Yet in the wake of Max Weber's account of the shared ethos of the Protestant ethic and the spirit of capitalism (1905), it has become difficult to see conflict rather than mutual responsiveness between two major systems that recommended labor, self-control, and self-denial in pursuit of a deferred, increased reward. Boyd Hilton's history has also stressed the convergence between spiritual and worldly aims in the first half of the century, as evangelicals such as Chalmers underwrote laissez-faire economic policy by articulating for it a religious basis that emphasized a purifying series of temptations and punishments. Smith's invisible hand was re-imagined as a hidden hand that "held a rod" which responded to human behavior; now, "enlightened self-interest meant not that private vices would conduce to public good," but that calamitous public and private punishments for vices such as the excessive pursuit of wealth "might . . . conduce to future virtue" (Hilton 114).

This virtue was self-denial. Spiritual wealth was made in the early capitalist marketplace.[18]

Yet, as Ruskin's example indicates and as Hilton himself acknowledges, the ideological homologies between the Protestant inheritance and capitalism were not universally apparent to many Victorians who felt a powerful tension between religious truths and the rules that governed their everyday experience of the marketplace.[19] Ruskin's critique and the ambivalence of many educated Victorians (including the novelists of this study) were conditioned by the traditional Christian antithesis between virtue and wealth. Some of the most familiar scriptural teachings stressed the ephemerality and insignificance of material wealth: "Lay not your treasure on earth, where moth and rust doth corrupt, but lay up for yourself treasures in Heaven" (Matthew 6:20–21). The profit motive directly contradicted such teachings, offering in their stead a system of value that was understood by its critics to undermine faith and generosity. Preachers often referred to the snares of worldliness and avarice, with Spurgeon, for example, warning vividly of the risks of dining at "Satan's Banquet": "If your God is this world, depend upon it you shall find that your way is full of bitterness. Now, see that table of the worldly man . . . who lives for gain. Satan brings him in a flowing cup, 'There,' says he, 'Young man, you are starting in business. . . . Get money—get money—honestly if you can, but, if not, get it anyhow," says the devil (280).

Spurgeon would not have frightened George Eliot, and Dickens would happily have caricatured him, yet both these novelists shared with Spurgeon a dread for the temptations of self and an equally strong admiration for the discipline that put others before the self. Only a political economy that convincingly demonstrated its generosity would speak to thinking Victorians who recognized the accomplishments and efficiency of industrial

---

18. See also Waterman's largely complementary account of the Christian political economy: "Original Sin and redemption by Christ imply that human life on earth is a state of 'discipline and trial' for eternity. . . . Private property, together with the competition produced by scarcity results in the market economy. *The efficacy of the market in organizing human action for wealth creation is evidence of divine wisdom and mercy in turning human frailty to socially beneficent ends.* Though the market produces some poverty and inequality, these may be regarded, for the most part, as a deliberate contrivance by a benevolent God for bringing out the best in his children" (205).

19. Christopher Herbert has explored the way that Victorian thinkers experienced the claims of Christian and capitalist ideals as irreconcilable, with poverty and riches mutually sustaining each other in a sort of zero-sum game ("Filthy Lucre"). See also George Levine's argument that money is the primary motif that embodies the tension between the religious and the secular in Victorian novels (*Realism* 185–244). See Hilton 116–21.

capitalism and market philosophy, but worried about their morality (Searle 7, x). Competition and profit-seeking needed redemption by a discourse that would make them indispensable to modern social good.

Laissez-Faire: A Vision of the Common Good

Mid-century prosperity, made most visible by the Great Exhibition, set the stage for mid-Victorian novelists to consider the ethic of mutual benefit in place of painful sacrifice.[20]

Novelists were not alone in this shift of perspective. A new Victorian discourse of self-interest as a form of public interest began to flourish, working at the intersection of moral-religious and economic registers. According to Hilton, at mid-century, Christian economists moved away from their earlier recommendations of self-denial and "the elusive goal of economic conscience" to embrace a market mechanism capable of maximizing public benefits derived from individual profit-seeking (265). Meanwhile, the shift by 1870 away from a theology based on Atonement to one that emphasized the Incarnation—Christ's human life, rather than his death—played a major role in recasting the value of worldly experience.

In more secularized portions of the population, the argument that political economy was not hostile to morality gained traction as reformers sought to popularize its teachings among members of all classes, arguing that the basic tenets of political economy could solve social problems rooted in poverty and crime. In 1858, the headmaster of the Manchester Model Secular School and Birkbeck Schools, Benjamin Templar, claimed that schoolchildren could be taught lessons that merged moral and economic ends: personal "industry, sobriety, and economy" would contribute to the "common good" (18). Central to the moral redemption of self-interest was the claim that its consequences inevitably benefited others; self-interest was thus not selfish. As Templar put it, children should learn to appreciate "the beneficence which has so ordained man's social arrangements, that the pleasure and benefit arising therefrom shall be mutual; that man does not, and cannot, 'live to himself alone'" (18–19).

---

20. As Thomas Richards (1990) puts it, "As every child in England knew, the innovation of the Great Exhibition was that it announced the long-awaited arrival of a millennium of prosperity" (66). Richards argues that the Great Exhibition embodied the "*myth* of the achieved abundant society" (66); in fact, he suggests, it "actually helped to create the sense of surplus that it is often cited as evidence for" (28–29).

Templar's moral education translated Smith's economic wisdom that described the "invisible hand" of impersonal market forces taking an individual who "intends only his own gain" and leading him "to promote an end which was no part of his intention. . . . By pursuing his own interest he frequently promotes that of the society more effectually than when he really intends to promote it" (*Wealth of Nations* 32).

The period I treat in this study, the decades of the fifties and sixties, marks the moment at which English economic policy had begun its decisive turn toward a laissez-faire model that embraced "free trade" and largely unfettered competition. Years of serious contention and social unrest over the protectionist Corn Laws which benefited landowners came to an end with their repeal in 1846. The Sugar Bill was passed in 1848 so that preference was no longer given to British planters in the West Indies. In 1849, the Navigation Acts were repealed and foreign shipping, before prohibited, now began to take a central and lucrative role in trade between England and its colonies.

The 1850s then inaugurated what we may generally consider two decades of economic and social optimism in Britain. Updating a discourse that had originated in the late seventeenth century to distinguish the sweet and gentle nature of commerce ("Le doux commerce") from violent and coercive forms of transaction, the Victorian proponents of market forces re-emphasized their social and moral uses (Hirschman 61). The ethos of laissez-faire was, as historian Martin Daunton says, "about visions of peace and prosperity, of providence and harmony" (7).

Yet the Victorian version of "laissez-faire" hardly meant an end to state intervention. Instead, as Daunton puts it, the Victorian period was characterized by "an attempt to create a society where free market relations were not undermined by interests or monopolies" (6). Disinterestedness was a central feature of the thinking of leading politicians who sought to dismantle monopolies and remove protectionist measures in order to "creat[e] a sense of balance in the economy and politics so that the state was not favouring one group over another through tax breaks or privileges" (4).

Anti-monopolist "free trade" promised great material rewards, as well as a new stability among classes whose divisions had been emphasized in the Hungry Forties. If taxes were reduced and the prices of utilities—gas, water, electricity, telecommunications—regulated, more members of society could share in the benefits of economic growth. The social order that had been threatened by radical labor movements might be preserved if the working classes recognized a legislature concerned with equity and justice

(Daunton 8). When, in 1839, James Wilson, later to found *The Econo-mist*, recommended the much-debated repeal of the Corn Laws, he epito-mized the sense that laissez-faire policy would bring wealth to all classes. "The only true theory on national interests," he argued, was one in which "nothing can possibly be favourable to the whole that is detrimental to the part . . . nothing can be detrimental to one portion that is favourable to another portion" (Edwards 9).

In the world of political economy, "free trade" was thus seen to hold out the democratic promise of benefit for all. As Taylor notes, the idea of a natural order characterized by a harmony of interests slowly displaced a rival model of order that had been based on "obedience, hierarchy, belong-ing to, even sacrifice for a larger whole" (414). Free trade instead assumed, as Daunton describes it, "a world of active participation in a commercial economy" (107): "a removal of barriers to free association by all mem-bers of society in a world of small firms and voluntary societies designed to generate moral and civic virtue and not merely individual self-interest" (114). Clubs, charities, churches, chapels, friendly societies, trade unions, and cooperatives flourished in early Victorian Britain while, in the second half of the century, a municipal and urban associational life thrived in the form of parks, art galleries and museums, and universities (22). Free trade was a new vision of community.

Economic Alterity: A New Critical Conjunction

If Victorian novelists actively participated in the new commercial econ-omy of "free trade," they also understood their vocation to serve the social interests of harmony and mutual benefit.[21] In her 1856 review of "The Nat-ural History of German Life," George Eliot famously argued that the social work of realist art was to depict the poor and working classes honestly and vividly, with details garnered from painstaking observation and "concrete knowledge," so as to extend the sympathies of readers (108). Sympathy, or fellow-feeling, required a recognition of what ethicists and literary critics today call alterity—the notion that there are others beside the self—accom-panied by what Eliot described as a yielding of egoism to the appreciation of another's circumstances.[22] Eliot believed that by surprising readers into

21. See N. N. Feltes (1986) on the relation of novelists to their labor and to its products, and on changes in the field of publishing as the forces of industrial capitalism transformed 'books' from petty-commodities to commodity-texts in the second half of the century.

22. There is a large literature on sympathy and novel studies from which this study has benefited, particularly the studies of Rachel Ablow (2007), Gallagher (*Nobody's Story*), and

moments of amplified experience and extended contact with "what is apart from themselves," art could encourage social and political reform as no other form of representation—statistics, sermons, dissertations—could do (110).

Eliot's description of the capacity of realist art to create the "raw material of moral sentiment" has survived nearly true to form for over 150 years (110).[23] Scholars focused on the ethics of literature have set at the very center of their work the discourse of alterity which was, in its own terms, so meaningful to Victorian novelists of sympathy. Describing the demands of alterity, Geoffrey Harpham writes,

> The other does not simply exist; it imposes responsibilities, obligations, constraints, regulations: it claims its rights. Taking the forms of Reason, God, the injunction to care, objectivity, the unconscious, communal norms, or the Good, the other impinges on the subject from the outside, or from some interiority so profound as to escape the control of the *cogito*. The appearance of the other marks an 'ethical moment' even in discourses not obviously concerned with ethics. Have we attended to the voice, the face, the law of the other? Have we been faithful to its dictates? Have we permitted the other to be itself, to retain its autonomy? Have we taken proper care, proper responsibility? The answers to such questions form the center of ethical self-awareness." (*Getting It Right* 7)

The discourse of alterity has been particularly appealing for readers trained on poststructuralist assumptions, for psychoanalytic and cultural critics, as well as for scholars working in multicultural studies where differences of race, class, and gender are central.[24] If the field of ethics had once seemed to presuppose an exclusionary narrative of universal humanism with an autonomous, unified, liberal, male subject, the demand to recognize the Other challenged such limits.[25]

Jaffe (2000). See Levine for an analysis of sympathy in relation to epistemology: he argues that the necessity of working against the "insistent self" and attempting to know what is not the self served as the basis for a Victorian ethics with sympathy at its center (*Realism* 4).

23. See Suzanne Keen (2010) for her pre-history of contemporary ideas that link empathy, altruism, and novel-reading.

24. Harpham describes the centrality of the discourse of alterity to philosophical, psychoanalytic, aesthetic, sociological and political approaches. In a wide-ranging argument about the nature of ethics, he argues that ethics itself is "consistently 'other'" (9) to the major discourses listed above which repudiate ethics only to end by embracing it (*Getting It Right* 13).

25. Feminist ethicists, for instance, have revitalized the field by challenging the ethics of justice with the ethics of care and by questioning whether ethics can be the sort of principled

Though the notion of alterity has a broad appeal across disciplines, literary scholars have inherited from the Victorians the sense that literature is a privileged site for studying and cultivating the ethics of alterity.[26] This sense has prompted many to focus on the ethics of literature itself, that is to say, the ethics of reading and interpreting, of form, practice, performance and audience.[27] From the work of J. Hillis Miller, *The Ethics of Reading* (1987) and Wayne C. Booth's *The Company We Keep* (1988); to the work of Tobin Siebers, Derek Attridge, Adam Zachary Newton, Geoffrey Galt Harpham, and Dorothy Hale, among others, the ethics of readerly and writerly activity has taken center stage.[28]

In this study, I seek to broaden the field of "ethics and literature" by moving away from a concern with alterity and literary praxis to consider the search for a livable equilibrium between ethical and economic imperatives as refracted by mid-nineteenth-century novels. If we return to that influential Victorian text—Eliot's theory of sympathetic reading—we may note that the element that has most frequently dropped out of its analysis is its context. Eliot offers her most extended, important statement on realist art while considering the relation between the working classes and those who "theorize" on them and "legislate" for them (Eliot "Natural History of German Life" 108). True sympathy, based on empirical knowl-

---

"science," which moral philosophers from Henry Sidgwick forward imagined it should be. Margaret Urban Walker proposes as an alternative to an ethical science a new form of "moral understanding": a "collection of perceptive, imaginative, appreciative, and expressive skills and capacities which put and keep us in unimpeded contact with the realities of ourselves and specific others" (170).

26. As Dorothy Hale (2009) has argued, the "revival of ethics" has led to a "new celebration and defense of literature" across a surprisingly wide theoretical spectrum (896). Hale points out that the focus on alterity as literature's special province oddly bridges the approaches of those poststructuralist literary theorists writing the "new ethics" and the "pre-Barthesian" moral-philosophical approach of Martha Nussbaum. For a sustained, trenchant critique of Nussbaum to read alongside Hale, see Harpham, *Shadows of Ethics*, "Philosophy Looking for Love," 220–42.

27. For a concise history of the work of putting literature to ethical service, see Adam Newton (1997). All such claims for literature occasioned or responded to counter-claims about its ethically dangerous possibilities. Novels, especially, were said to unsettle the social order; they would teach young girls an indelicate worldliness; they were anti-social and prompted unhealthy solitary habits; they worked against empathy by encouraging readers to invest in the fates of fictional figures rather than real people. On the dangers of reading, see Patrick Brantlinger (1998) and Kate Flint (1993).

28. Here, the range is great. While Booth asks the following sorts of questions—"Should I believe this narrator and thus join him? Am I willing to be the kind of person this storyteller is asking me to be?" (39)—Newton's *Narrative Ethics* argues in a Levinasian strain that the very act of being exposed to the immediacy and demands of another's narrative or exposing someone to one's own is an ethics of its own.

edge, is what the upper classes are supposed to feel for the lower classes, in order to provide an appropriate moral education for both groups. Thus the Victorian sense of alterity that has shaped 150 years of thinking about the sympathetic effects of reading comes from a very particular kind of difference: economic.

The fact that much work in "ethics and literature" has not been concerned explicitly with economics may help explain why a number of theorists writing in *The Turn to Ethics* (2000), expressed anxiety that the focus on ethics threatened "a turn away from politics." As Nancy Fraser has noted, for progressives, the recognition of the difference of the other has often seemed to conflict with the "redistribution" orientation, that is, the focus on a "more just allocation of resources and goods" (95). This study thus aims to mimic a particular habit of mind and pen that became elusive in the twentieth century but still flowed naturally in the mid-nineteenth century: the habit of considering ethics and economics as one field of ideas.

It seems to me significant, but rarely noted, that the recent, identifiable turn of literary critics to ethics has coincided with a particularly rich and ongoing turn to economics, particularly in Victorian novel studies.[29] Like ethics, economics is so fully the "medium" of Victorian novels that it is difficult to imagine Victorian novel studies without this focus, yet it is only in the last fifteen to twenty years that we have benefited from a critical mass of studies that have been termed the "New economic criticism."[30] That the "turn to ethics" has overlapped with the "New economic criticism" is not, to my mind, a coincidence but an as-yet unfulfilled promise, one to which we are just beginning to attend.[31] My own critical trajectory took me through economic criticism to ethics. By way of considering excessive or non-reciprocal exchanges that structure Victorian novels, exchanges such as theft, gift, debt, and sacrifice, I found myself considering novelistic representations of economic and social relations; ethics seemed the

---

29. Important studies of ethics in relation to literature preceded the last few years of the century, but they tended to position themselves as embattled or marginal, in part because in the wake of New Historicism, ethics was seen to be falsely universalizing. For two examples, see Booth and Siebers. Even Miller's recent *The Burdens of Perfection* (2008) addresses such anxieties.

30. On the "New economic criticism," see Mark Osteen and Martha Woodmansee's influential anthology (1999). For more recent subdivisions of the field, see Poovey (*Genres* 10–14). Major texts from this critical orientation will be referenced throughout this study.

31. I have already noted major exceptions. The work of Blake, Gagnier, Gallagher, and Poovey obviously merge the fields, however, their studies tend rarely to be classified under the category of "ethics."

most obviously inclusive category for such a project. I take my own path
not as merely idiosyncratic, but as reflecting both Victorian and contemporary concerns against the respective backdrops of industrial and global
capitalism.

My hope is that it will prove useful for us today, as we witness and participate in the phenomenon of global capitalism, to go back to a novelistic
moment in which ethics and economics were being explored in tandem,
sometimes in hope and curiosity, other times in despair, but always with
the sense that ethics is not immaterial. Ethics concerns the distribution of
resources and, at the same time, such material considerations cannot be
made absent ethical thought. As Regenia Gagnier suggests, we can indeed
see signs today of a welcome return to the Victorian "epistemic pluralism
and diversity"; for the first time in 150 years, disciplinary divisions in the
sciences have begun to yield to a recognition of our shared concerns in the
complex experiences of being human ("Uneasy Pleasures").

Economics and ethics, likewise, can speak to each other. The role of
the liberal state in organizing an ethical distribution of goods is a subject
of its own. My own interest has been drawn recently by the contemporary
American entrepreneurial impulse, increasingly visible, to promote profit-
making initiatives that simultaneously benefit needy individuals, nations,
and continents. This trend prompted me to return to Victorian novels and
consider the notion of "mutual benefit" as an ethical innovation made
available and likely to emerge under the new conditions of industrial capitalism.[32] Cynicism is not hard to come by—and is often merited—but I
contend that it is worth looking seriously both at Victorian approaches
to mutual benefit and at new versions of cosmopolitan ethics in our own
time—from large-scale "philanthrocapitalism" to the work of clear-eyed
"social entrepreneurs" who seek entrepreneurial strategies to redress problems wrought by business strategies and, in response, to maximize "social
impact" rather than profit."[33] (If the language sounds utilitarian, its effects

---

32. See Bill Clinton's *Giving* for examples of the ways contemporary American entrepreneurs frame their projects with relation to the social good. While it is easy to be cynical
about the motivations and methods of millionaires and billionaires, not to mention upper-
middle-class Americans aware of their relative good fortune in the world, I think we are
seeing a phenomenon that demands more than casual dismissal. For a recent cultural and
materialist defense of historical and contemporary forms of capitalism, see Deirdre N. Mc-
Closkey (2006). Though my project is not a defense of industrial capitalism, McCloskey's
work helps clarify the history not only of defenses of capitalism, but of proleptic optimism
about their possibilities.

33. There is an abundance of contemporary work in ethics that is relevant here. For two
important examples that diverge significantly on the relation between haves and have-nots,
see Kwame Anthony Appiah (2007) and Peter Singer (2009). In the specific works I have

make their own case.) Victorian fiction may help us interpret our own historical situation more creatively and effectively; at the same time, we may be in an unusually advantageous position to read the ethical-economic contents of Victorian fictions written by novelists seeking an ethics adequate to the hopes and fears of a new economy whose outcome they could not foresee, but whose arrival they could not ignore.

Sacrificial Best-Sellers: Yonge, Dickens, Eliot, Trollope, Collins, and Ward

The novels under discussion in this study are organized to constitute what I hope will prove an innovative teaching paradigm as well as a coherent unit of research. Self-sacrifice is so fundamental a feature of Victorian literature that it would be difficult to find a novel that does not take it up in some form. I have chosen to focus on a limited number of novels that foreground the dynamics of self-sacrifice and prompt analyses whose terms can be applied to other contemporary works. Further, I have chosen to work with texts that were commercially and critically successful by Victorian standards (some extraordinarily so) in order to describe materials that reached a broad audience. Because all the major canonical texts I treat originate from the same quarter of a century, even a fifteen-year period, I have ordered them less to follow a linear chronology than to constitute a progressive spectrum of secularizing thought, with Dickens at the least secularized end and Collins at the most. Since this assessment is surely debatable, I seek to define and explore modes of secularization within my analyses.

Though my roster of novels focuses on major canonical texts whose appeal is still strong, especially among scholars, it begins and ends with texts that are no longer widely read or taught today. Charlotte Mary Yonge's *The Heir of Redclyffe* and Mary Augusta Ward's *Robert Elsmere* are explicitly concerned with religious faith and doubt, subjects central to Victorians but often gestured to only in the most general terms by contemporary Victorianists or treated in isolation by specialists in religious culture and history. I aim to show that these two culturally central novels of faith and doubt do not depart as dramatically as we might have imagined from the representation of social, exchange or sacrificial relations that we find in the Victorian novels I survey in the middle of the study. Rather than

cited, the former is committed to programs of education and nation-state activism while the latter has long advocated individual acts of giving and renunciation. See also David Bornstein and Susan Davis (2010).

reinforcing our sense of the division between "religious" novels and "secular," these two bookend novels have the opposite effect of revealing how
religiously inflected are the ethical structures we see in novels considered
more secular. Much of what we have taken for the psychological realism
of Victorian fiction, I suggest, can be traced to the religious inheritances
explicitly considered in novels of faith and doubt. Perhaps, then, what we
have understood as accessible—thus, teachable with more ease—we have
partially misrecognized and imagined as more familiar than in fact it is.
Reading Dickens, Eliot, Trollope, and Collins in between Yonge and Ward
may, I hope, make both more intelligible and, at the same time, more challenging, the social, exchange, and sacrificial relations we witness in the
wide range of Victorian novels. Yonge's novel, in particular, offers us a rich
ground for analyzing and teaching the gender politics of Christian self-
sacrifice, an ideal unusually egalitarian at the middle of the nineteenth
century and thus a provocative point of contrast with other religious and
economic structures.

Any study of Victorian sacrifice will also be a study of Victorian notions
of heroism. Yonge's and Ward's novels, both massive best sellers, feature
the least compromised heroes of this study. *The Heir of Redclyffe* is a
story of Christian heroism embodied in the figure of Sir Guy Morville who
strives successfully to discipline and deny himself, then dies self-sacrificially
as a result of tending in sickness his rival, the very man who has persecuted
him over the course of the novel. Sir Guy's death offers spiritual uplift to all
who survive him. *Robert Elsmere* also ends with the self-sacrificial death of
a young hero, a Church of England minister who gives up his country living and his family happiness to found a New Brotherhood of Christ among
the London working classes when his scientific learning unsettles his orthodoxy. Elsmere's tireless labors on behalf of the poor and suffering drive
him to an early, tragic death. The arc from Yonge to Ward traverses evangelical faith and modern thought, surveys the distance in rank and lived
experience from country gentry to the urban poor, and describes the space
of domestic leisure and the stage of public work. Yet the novels, dramatically different in tone, scope, and matter, written thirty-five years apart,
both feature heroes whose stories are wholly shaped by the self-sacrificial
ideal and model of Christ. Most simply, these "bookend" novels record
the Christian roots and resonances of the self-sacrificial ideal and demon-
strate its powerful hold on the Victorian imagination. In so doing, they
also highlight the risks taken by novelists who sought to modify the ideal.

Yet if Yonge's exploration of sacrifice provides us one Christian "base-
line" against which to measure secularizing alternatives, it also offers us a

vital corrective to the notion that mid-century popular Christian thought required of its adherents utter self-abasement. In *The Heir of Redclyffe*, the meaningful claims of the social world challenge an ascetic sense of Christian self-denial. When Yonge seeks to limit rather than endlessly expand the claims of self-sacrifice, she appears surprisingly close to the critical positions I trace in Eliot, Trollope, and Collins. Whereas it is straightforward that a hedonistic egoism would be sin to the Christian, it is far less clear that what we might call a moral egoism should be equally sinful: "'it is as easy to be selfish for one's own good as for one's own pleasure'" (Yonge 1: 165). Like Trollope, Yonge examines and limits the self-sacrificial requirement on the basis of intercollective subjectivity: one's own good cannot be separated from the best intentions of others; further, one's own good is no more significant than another's good. Thus at times, when it serves others, pleasure becomes its own Christian obligation while sacrifice becomes a kind of obstinate egoism. If self-sacrifice in its purest form is still for Yonge the ethical ideal, nonetheless, her novel paves the way for its critique.

The Heir of Redclyffe was written in 1853 and belonged, as Kathleeen Tillotson claims, to an era of Victorian chivalry, not the era of common sense (*Mid-Victorian Studies* 55). Dickens' *Tale of Two Cities,* published in 1859 and set on the eve of the French Revolution, stands oddly in between the two "ages." Slatternly Sydney Carton is hardly the chivalrous hero, yet he is no more a man of rational common sense. All structures—from chivalry to utilitarianism—seem empty to Carton. Still, Carton becomes the novel's moral hero, giving up his life for Lucie Manette and her family. Carton's last-minute heroism reflects a terrible anxiety about the motivations and meanings of self-sacrifice. Carton's depiction as "self-flung away, wasted, drunken, poor creature of misuse," evokes a haunting image of the Victorian suicide (138). Dickens, often associated in his time as in ours with extreme, caricatured versions of virtue and vice, here explores a borderline. By making Carton not a paragon of virtue, but instead a suicidal figure, saved from despair and dissolution only by voluntary death, Dickens challenges the deepest logic of the sacrificial demand. Whereas suicide was considered a Christian sin from Christianity's earliest history, Christ's self-sacrificial death was distinguished as a model and an imperative. Carton thus forces the question of what constitutes the difference between culpable suicide, on one hand, and honorable self-sacrifice, on the other hand. At what point does selflessness become an inexcusable violence against the self rather than an act of heroic concern for the other?

Carton's final salvation is routed through the fundamentally religious concept which so seized Dickens' imagination: the notion that Christ was a substitute, guiltless among the guilty, paying their ransom and redeeming them from sin. Dickens merges a humanist sense of collective ethical responsibility with a Christian sense of transcendent morality to resolve the anomie that brings about suicide and to motivate a worthy self-sacrifice. Dickens thus stood between a religious past and a secularizing modernity as he transformed sacrifice of the most intense Christian sort into a humanist act of temporal preservation and confined the category of anomic modern suicide to meaningless violence directed not only at the self, but the other, too.

Yet even as Dickens redeemed the dangerous but critical interchangeability of suicide and sacrifice, he could offer no lessons for living, only for dying. While chivalrous nobility of character is rendered in the novel as an exercise in futility, common sense devolves into the pursuit of self-interest at the expense of others. Sacrificial substitution is all there is left, yet once it has taken place, ethics is again left unprescribed and threatened. The dilemma between common sense and the claim of self-sacrifice is at the center of George Eliot's English novel of the same year, *Adam Bede*. George Eliot had thought deeply and diversely on the subject of self-sacrifice, trained as she was in evangelical Christian thought, Feuerbachian humanism, and a Comtean positivism that put 'living for others' at its heart. *Adam Bede* stands apart from other novels of Eliot's that deal directly with the imperative of self-sacrifice because the ethical dilemmas in *Adam Bede* arise among witnesses rather than actors in a tragedy of self-indulgence, as they face the personal benefits they may realize out of the victims' losses.

When the protagonists, Adam Bede and Dinah Morris, turn to the prevailing Victorian ideal of self-sacrifice as the appropriate response to their own pleasure, the novel suggests that guilty self-sacrifice may be mistaken and useless in a modern world. Eliot rejects unreasonable guilt at good fortune in this world and sketches a new moral economy in which the inherited Christian ideals of brotherhood, poverty, debt and guilt come under critical scrutiny while a measured personal benefit begins to seem justifiable, even in a world where others will continue to suffer. *Adam Bede* thus constitutes a singular critique of maximalist altruism from the novelist most deeply associated with the Victorian ethic of fellow-feeling.

Yet Eliot's critique is limited by the fundamentally moral orientation of her heroes. Especially when read in company with her other novels, *Adam Bede* stops short of questioning the basic logic of the ideal of self-sacrifice. It takes Trollope to imagine a world of social relations that undercuts the necessity for sacrifice. Examining the first and last novels of the Barsetshire series, *The Warden* and *The Last Chronicle of Barset,* I take Trollope's novels as systemic challenges to maximalist altruism. If sacrificial logic suggests that one party suffers to prevent another's suffering, Trollope exposes the fundamental divide between parties posited by such a logic. If two parties care deeply for each other, then one's sacrifice on behalf of the other cannot please or help the latter since it depends upon the pain of the former. If the pain of one is the pain of the other, and the pleasure of one, the pleasure of the other, then the sacrificial structure ceases to operate effectively. Sacrifice for Trollope is praiseworthy only insofar as it re-aligns human interests, rather than pursues a further divide between them.

Though Trollope does away with the drama of glorious self-sacrifice and its implied division between parties, he nonetheless holds to an idea of sympathetic, generous behavior. His fiction transforms a major Victorian ideal into the anticlimactic stuff of everyday living. The novels reconceive morally desirable action as mutually beneficial rather than purely altruistic; as automatic and unconsidered rather than deliberate or self-conscious; and as normative rather than extraordinary or impossibly idealistic.

Trollope's resolution of the sacrificial problem is appealing in its utopian sense of the possibilities of social harmony and the unity of personal interests that so many Victorians could see only as divided. Yet this study would be false to its subject if it ended on Trollope's class-limited social vision. From Trollope, my study moves to Wilkie Collins' popular mystery *The Moonstone,* which considers sacrifice as a system of nineteenth-century social relations. *The Moonstone* reflects the way that the least advantaged members of society make the costliest sacrifices while those who possess economic or ideological advantages seek out opportunities for self-sacrifice but inevitably reward themselves. When given by the powerful, the "free gift," absent all self-interest, tends to reveal itself as theft, bribery, or assignment of debt. At once a critique of traditional Christian morality in practice and the self-interest of contemporary political economy, of waning aristocratic privilege and waxing imperial greed, *The Moonstone* turns to the emerging profession of novel-writing to imagine a form of ethical exchange.

Text, suggests Collins, is the only gift that can escape demanding a return on its investment; it is the sign of selfless sacrifice. The writer insured the ethics of his offering by laboring under the risk that his labor might go unread and unrewarded. The uncertainty of literary commerce hallowed the work of the middle-class Victorian novelist. Unlike the structure of promise and automatic reward that Christianity offered its adherents, the mutual benefit granted to author and readers in the case of a book's success was so fraught with contingency that self-interest alone could not motivate professional writing. Collins' remarkable innovation was to turn to the culturally recognizable vocabulary of self-sacrifice and then to fulfill a compromised Christian faith by reconstituting its claims in the literary marketplace. Where Dickens could unabashedly make a redemptive Christ-figure of Carton; where Eliot could draw characters already so schooled in Christian self-sacrifice that her work was to make them less so; where Trollope could wish for a nominally Christian world so harmonious it no longer needed sacrifice, Collins' novel premised a purity of contemporary exchange more "Christian" than Christianity.

It is not surprising that the novelist who offers us the most secular vision of ethics also seems most devoted to preserving a sacrificial ideal in a world he perceived as caught between discredited religious teachings and self-interested economic structures, themselves indebted to Christian theology. While Collins' novel responds to the Arnoldian problem of "Wandering between two worlds, one dead / The other powerless to be born," the final novel of this study has crossed over. In *Robert Elsmere* (1888), a transformed sacrificial ideal finds expression at the hand of Mary Augusta Ward, a writer who many contemporaries saw as the late-century disciple and inheritor of George Eliot. The drama of Elsmere's life is the recognition of Jesus as a historical figure who suffered and gave his life to teach humanity by his example. When Robert resigns his ministry to find his place preaching this new gospel among the East End's working classes, Ward enshrines her hero as an "altruist" of a new stamp, working at social reform until his fragile constitution consigns him to a spiritually heroic death, having devoted his best energy to those less fortunate.

If, at first glance, *Robert Elsmere* seems to maintain an orthodox self-sacrificial rigor even as it transforms its source, I suggest at the end of this study that Elsmere's self-sacrifice cannot be assimilated to the mid-century model of divided experience in which one party suffers that another may profit. Elsmere, positioned against his devoutly orthodox wife, Catherine, embodies the value of mutual benefit that we have seen articulated in the third quarter of the century. Whereas both Catherine and Yonge's mid-century hero, Sir Guy Morville, are described as figures linked to the past by an "ascetic temper," Robert Elsmere is a man of the present and the future, firmly rooted in the passions, politics, and promises of this world (Yonge 1: 59; Ward 139). Committed to his own sacred development as a scholar and human being, Robert is equally devoted to realizing the potential of his fellows—of all classes and belief systems. Thus Ward, deeply influenced by the Oxford idealist philosopher Thomas Hill Green, suggests that the only viable means of advancing humanity is in fostering a widespread self-devotion to a life of mutual service. Ward makes Elmsere a new brand of hero whose search for self-fulfillment is justified and celebrated because it is rooted in the fulfillment of others. Dramatizing a new approach to altruism, one that focuses not on the virtue of the individual actor but on the enduring and shared good of a social world, *Robert Elsmere* enshrines the synthesis of benevolence and self-love which had been so elusive for mid-century novelists but for which they had nonetheless reached.

It would take until the end of the century for the self-sacrificial ideal to find bold detractors who would challenge, as Oscar Wilde famously put it, the "sordid necessity of living for others" ("Socialism"). Until that time, modern ethics found one resolution in the earnest pursuit of mutual benefit.

CHAPTER 1

The Heir of Redclyffe
and the Heiress

Men, Women, and Christian Self-Sacrifice

𝓘n 1853, Charlotte Mary Yonge published what was at least the twelfth of the two hundred or so books she would publish before her death in 1901, all, as she said, for the Church of God: *Pro Ecclesia Dei*. Yonge's church was the Anglican one of the early John Henry Newman, Edward Pusey, and the poet John Keble, Yonge's neighbor and close personal mentor in Hampshire. Yet even as Yonge's novels can leave no doubt of her powerful adherence to Tractarian ideas, they were spiritually meaningful to thousands of novel-readers who were not themselves followers of the Oxford Movement. *The Heir of Redclyffe* shared the season's limelight with Charlotte Brontë's *Villette* and Elizabeth Gaskell's *Ruth* and, by 1876, had seen twenty-two editions to seven editions of *Ruth* and two of *Villette*.

While the well-studied texts of Brontë and Gaskell—from *Jane Eyre* (1847) to *Villette*, from *Ruth* to *The Life of Charlotte Brontë* (1857)—have afforded critics ample opportunity to consider female self-sacrifice, we need only consider Yonge's popularity to recognize that any deep understanding of Victorian self-sacrifice will have to reckon with the influences of avowedly Christian fiction upon a much wider spectrum of readers than we might have expected.[1] Likewise, we need to reckon with

---

1. See Giles Gunn (1987), on the necessity for a conjoint analysis of the Western literary and religious heritage. Gunn suggests that critical studies have generally treated literature as a valorization of religion, a criticism, or an alternative to or substitute for

images of self-denying men, as well as the women we have been used to studying. In this chapter, I read Yonge's bestselling novel closely in order to particularize our knowledge of one coherent and successfully disseminated version of Christian self-sacrifice. The obvious methodological benefit to this analysis is that it allows us better to detect the ways in which the secularizing novelists of this study distinguished their approach to ethics from an important religious approach at mid-century.

But equally valuable is giving the measuring stick of "Christian self-sacrifice" its due. Without a rich and accurate sense of what a believing novelist such as Yonge was offering her readership (an approach that reflects both differences and similarities from some influential religious writings we will consider), it is all too easy to posit an inflexible, even unintelligent, religious morality, unsupple in its application and unresponsive to contemporary concerns. On the contrary, Christian self-sacrifice was not only an elusive moral ideal for those who earnestly pursued it but also a demanding and complex *idea* for those, like Yonge, who sought to understand it. Dogma, in such cases, can be just as complex as the challenges to it.

Sir Guy Morville's sacrificial death was the heart of the novel for its immense and diverse body of mid-century readers. From William Morris, Edward Burne-Jones, Birkbeck Hill and Henry Sidgwick, to nameless soldiers fighting in the Crimean War, readers affirmed the spiritual charisma of Yonge's selfless hero and heroine: "'How glorious would be such a deathbed as Guy's and how glorious for the survivor to be such as Amy!'" (Hill, as quoted in Tillotson 49–50).[2] The clarity of this climactic moment has made it more difficult to see that *The Heir of Redclyffe* reflects a deeply faithful Christian novelist overlapping with her more secularized counterparts as she sought to limit and refine the everyday practice of sacrifice, rather than to expand and popularize it. Showing herself to be cannily aware of the risks of misguided self-sacrifice among Christians seeking to transcend the worldly, Yonge dispelled stereotypes of an ascetic, self-lacerating Christian heroism and delineated a version of self-sacrifice alive to immediate social responsibilities. Finally, Yonge offered her readers an

religion (188). This study considers the relation between literary texts avowedly religious and those more ambivalently linked to religious faith. To my knowledge, there has yet to be a serious study of the relationship between best-selling Christian and the more secularized fiction of the nineteenth century; a phenomenology of the Victorian reading experience of such literature would also be invaluable in helping us understand how readers responded to dogma in fiction.

   2. Tillotson tells us that Yonge's hero and heroine "magnetized youthful aspirations in the 1850's and at a wide range of brow-levels" (49–50). See also Cruse 42–64.

ideal that was, in its way, surprisingly more egalitarian than that which was offered by many more secularized writers, posing an ethical and literary challenge to her contemporaries and to her readers.

While Yonge sought to limit sacrifice, her limitation worked from a different cause and to a different effect than the other writers of this study. Yonge restricted self-sacrifice because she glorified it and she glorified it by restricting it. Yonge saw the *right* to sacrifice oneself as reserved for the spiritual elite: those who had struggled and suffered to attain their moral knowledge. One was not a sacrificial victim, in Yonge's novels, but a sacrificial agent, informed, practiced and tested. We can see Yonge's bestselling *Heir of Redclyffe* laying out the troubles of self-sacrifice in a realist key, then imagining their transcendence in idealized terms that Dickens, Collins, Eliot and Trollope would all counter as they took up this most central Victorian value in their own work.

Yonge's notion of sacrifice as a form of great spiritual achievement also cast her into a culture-wide debate over the gender of heroic sacrifice. Did sacrifice belong to impressively self-disciplined men or did it belong to women, praiseworthy in their natural capacity to subordinate themselves to others? Yonge's contemporary Gaskell embraced women's self-abdication in many of her works, allowing figures such as Ruth and *Mary Barton*'s fallen woman, Esther, to serve as holy scapegoats for an imperfect and unjust social world; their hard-won moral authority and their prophetic voices are inseparable from their sacrificial status.[3] Brontë also considered self-sacrifice through the prism of gender, though she responded quite differently. In her first major novel, troubled by the risks the ideal posed to women, she handed over martyrdom to men in the figure of the missionary St. John Rivers with whose death she ended the novel. By contrast, she refused the independent Jane Eyre to the pyre, dramatizing a different form of spiritual heroism in pursuit of truth and loyalty to a self well-known rather than the holiness of high discipline and extreme self-denial. For Brontë, the complications of self-sacrifice—it could be consciously sought only by people somewhat maimed, less than fully human—were especially dangerous for women who were afforded fewer choices in life and often pressured or coerced into sacrifice.[4]

---

3. As Christine L. Kreuger (1992) argues in a discussion of the "vexed feminism" of female writers who took up the preacher's role, Gaskell's social problem novels reflect a writer who could "explain women's roles in a male culture," but they could not "articulate a thorough rejection of the exploitive world or imagine Ruth's, Mary Barton's and Margaret Hale's existence apart from it" (226).

4. I have treated *Jane Eyre* limitedly and intermittently in this study because it seems

By contrast to both Gaskell and Brontë, Yonge's response to the problem of gender was not to define sacrifice as the particular province of men
or women but to assert a competing binary division between divinity and
an aspiring humanity. In a culture, as Mary Poovey has argued, organized
by "articulating difference onto sex," Yonge articulated difference in religious terms (*Uneven Developments* 201). By sidestepping Victorian England's central social division between men and women, Yonge challenged
the more secularized novelists of her day with an ethics that transcended
what she perceived as limited local and temporary conditions. Offering an
aspirational ethics, uncompromising in its standards and rich in its promised reward of Christian salvation, Yonge's work helped to set in relief the
special task that lay before secularizing Victorian novelists.[5] This task was
to define an ethics that responded precisely to that specificity of local and
temporary conditions; to the changes in social, economic, and intellectual
life that seemed to consign resolution by traditional Christian self-sacrifice
to literary romances and determined more realist novels as the most appropriate site for compelling alternatives.[6]

Sacrifice and the "Trivial Round"

The Heir of Redclyffe tells the story of two contrasted characters and cous-
ins, as Yonge put it, "'the self-satisfied'" Philip Morville and the "'essentially contrite'" Sir Guy Morville who dies saving his rival Philip, returning
good for positive evil (as qtd. in Tillotson 51). While the framing plot of

---

to me to bear the ethos of the "hungry forties," and thus to require different parameters
than the novels of the third quarter of the century. Obviously, it offers rich opportunities for
analyses of sacrifice.

    5. Andrew Miller's study of moral perfectionism (*The Burdens of Perfection*) rightly
emphasizes the centrality of the ideal of perfection for Victorians. My work analyzes the
literary labor of novelists seeking an escape from the "burdens of perfection."

    6. The "realist novel" is a heuristic category since all the novels I consider here mix
genres, drawing upon features from literary romance, sensation fiction, fable, the gothic, and
so on. I use the term to indicate novels that move toward a psychological realism in their
depiction of character. See Christine Sandback-Dahlström (1984) for a developed account of
the merging of genres in Yonge's work. For discussions of Yonge's realism, see the Victorian
critic R. H. Hutton, who disparaged Yonge for allowing her realism to yield to her doctrinal
allegiances. Gavin Budge (2003) argues, however, that Yonge did not "feel the need to be
a didactic novelist . . . because in her view the very process whereby a novelist represents
human experience linguistically is a guarantee of the religious truth of her works"; see his
analysis of the realist form's "intrinsic tendency to steer the reader in direction of Tractarian doctrinal correctness" (214). On the relation between realism and parable, see Susan E.
Colón (2010).

the novel concerns Philip's deceit to others and to himself as he attempts
to discredit Guy, the extensive middle of the saga concerns Guy's battle to
conquer himself. Yet Guy is an unusual penitent because his is "the repentance of an apparently blameless character" (Mare and Percival 133). As
Yonge's foremost biographical critics put it in 1947: "we are most struck
by his readiness to accuse himself of sin, and his habit of repenting where
we can see little or no blame" (Mare and Percival 134). Guy believes himself to have inherited the family curse of quickness to murderous anger, yet
as all readers must immediately note, his goodness and moral seriousness
are more than a match for any inherited character flaws. Upon the death
of the grandfather who raised him in puritanical strictness, Guy comes to
reside with the Edmonstones where his Christian education, shepherded
mainly by Mrs. Edmonstone, begins in earnest.[7] Guy's self-doubting and
self-searching tendencies mark him as the hero of the novel, especially
since they stand him in contrast to Philip's self-congratulatory satisfaction
and obscured self-knowledge. Yet without the aid of the maternal Mrs.
Edmonstone, we are led to see that Guy would make a mess of things, sacrificing himself in ways that range from the socially inappropriate to the
morally wrong. The drama of the novel resides less in Guy's problematic
proclivity for anger and quick temper, and more in his indiscriminate incli-
nations toward self-denial and sacrifice.

Perhaps what makes Yonge's work especially helpful to a study of sacrifice is its novelistic commitment to dramatizing the domestic life not only
at its high watermark points of crisis and drama, but in the ebb and flow
of the everyday. Thus as a Christian value, sacrifice, too, becomes a consideration of ordinary, but sanctifiable, life. As John Keble famously wrote
in the opening hymn to his *Christian Year* (1827), no Christian needed to
bid farewell to neighbor or work and retire to a cloistered cell, but instead,
"the trivial round, the common task, / Would furnish all we ought to ask;
/ Room to deny ourselves; a road / To bring us daily, nearer God." If the
Christian were in the right state of mind (this subjunctive condition repeats
in the poem), God would continuously offer opportunities for sacrifice: "If
on our daily course our mind / Be set to hallow all we find, / New treasures still, of countless price, / God will provide for sacrifice." Treasures
which are typically rare, infrequently encountered, sought-out commodities become in Keble's hymn a description of "all we find" on our "daily
course." And, in a kind of closed circuit, the opportunity to sacrifice such
everyday treasures *for* God is nothing other than a gift *from* God.

---

7. As Talia Schaffer (2000) notes, Yonge's novels of the 1850s depict "youths struggling
toward emotional and spiritual maturity with the help of wise, guiding parents" (246).

The idea of the trivial round and common task characterized many teachings on sacrifice. In the 1830s, John Henry Newman returned to it when he argued that "although the Mosaic rituals of sacrifice might have passed away," they "are still evidence to us of a fact which the Gospel has not annulled,—our corruption"; Newman went on to say that "an expiation is needful in all the most trivial circumstances of our conduct" ("Sins" 96). In another sermon, he suggested that one means of such expiation was self-denial:

> It is right then almost to *find out* for yourself daily self-denials; and this because our Lord bids you take up your cross daily, and because it proves your earnestness. . . . Rise up then in the morning with the purpose that (please God) the day shalt not pass without its self-denial. . . . Let your very rising from your bed be a self-denial; let your meals be self-denials. . . . Make some sacrifice, do some distasteful thing, which you are not actually obliged to do. . . . Try yourself daily in little deeds, to prove that your faith is more than a deceit. ("Self-Denial" 93–94)

Yet this habitual devising of trials comes under critical scrutiny in Yonge's novel of everyday Christian life, exactly where we would imagine it to be most meaningfully dramatized.

Uncalled-for Sacrifices: "And yet what a pity"

Yonge's treatment of sacrifice is most prominently characterized by the anxiety that the ideal might be misapplied and carried out in ambiguous circumstances that do not call for it. In *The Heir of Redclyffe,* the uncalled-for sacrifice constitutes waste; Yonge's domesticating but nevertheless not wholly sympathetic term for this waste is "a pity." We first encounter such wasted sacrifice in Philip's past. Upon the death of his father five years before the novel's action opens, seventeen-year-old Philip gives up his well-founded hope of university honors and obtains a commission in the army in order to enable his sisters to go on living in their home and to marry well. Guy's response when he hears this story upon his arrival among the Edmonstones is to cry, "'Noble! . . . and yet what a pity! If my grandfather had but known it—'" (1: 23). While the two branches of the family have been at odds, Sir Guy suggests that if money was all that had been wanting, it might easily have been supplied. The grammar of uncalled-for sacrifice indicates the counterfactual wish—"if only," "if my grandfather had but"—that merges past with present: if only something then had been different, as it so easily might have been, how many other things might now be better. And so, "what a pity!" In Yonge's uncalled-for sacrifice, we might note the reversal of her teacher Keble's subjunctives: his "if"s and "were"'s all point to the human task of finding opportunities for sacrifice whereas Yonge imagines undoing a sacrifice mistakenly undertaken.

For Yonge, uncalled-for sacrifice results from inappropriate independence, a derivative of pride. Mr. and Mrs. Edmonstone both confirm that Philip acted quickly, without their consent or advice: Philip "'never said a word . . . till the thing was done. I never was more surprised in my life'"; "'it was done in a hasty spirit of independence'" (1: 23).[8] Philip's secrecy, haste, and independence in this matter of sacrifice presage the secret, hasty, independent engagement that he will later contract with the Edmonstones' oldest daughter, Laura. This engagement comes quite unambiguously to no good. In fact, alongside Philip's defaming of Guy, it is the other major sin in the novel.

Like all decision-making in Yonge's High Church world, sacrifice cannot be simply an act of the will or follow from an intuitive sense of right and wrong, but must acknowledge the superior authority of one's models and elders, and the teachings they represent: "some standard of right besides himself" must guide the one who is to act (2: 315). The critic R. H. Hutton rejected this mode of intellectual repression in no uncertain terms: Yonge's heroes, he wrote, "must fit into the hierarchical order of society which Miss Yonge has been taught to accept. . . . [S]he represents her most intellectual heroes as perfectly content under repressions which would, by any mind of more speculative faculty than her own, be felt as intolerable" (216).[9] Yet Yonge was extremely consistent in her demands that the young consult their elders and follow their recommendations. Her heroine, Amabel, embodies this value of submission perfectly.

When it comes to mistaken sacrifices, the motivating vanity that is pride is answered in Yonge's work by the resulting vanity that is futility. The clearest mark of uncalled-for sacrifice in Yonge's work is the absence of its desired effects. Yonge held such a strong conviction that the uncalled-for sacrifice was morally wrong that she was willing to abandon her realist

---

8. A synonym here is "self-will," as when Guy, having made a damaging, uncalled-for sacrifice, accuses himself of acting against Mrs. Edmonstone's instructions in a "'fit of self-will in managing myself . . . yet I thought it a positive duty;—wrong every way'" (1: 161).

9. See Elisabeth Jay, "Women Writers," for her suggestion of Yonge's insubordination as a successful writer and her guilty compensation in the content of her fiction.

mode to depict a providentially didactic reversal of the hoped-for results. Philip's ostensibly noble sacrifice of his education misfires not only by association with his engagement to Laura, but also by result. Yonge engineers the nearly immediate death of Philip's "sweet" sister Fanny, who might have benefited from the sacrifice (1: 63). Meanwhile, the eldest, Margaret, marries a man morally her inferior for the sake of an establishment, quickly becoming one of the novel's most reprehensible characters. Much later in the novel, when Philip comes to understand his own sins, Margaret serves to torture him with her self-complacency which he recognizes as the mirror image of his own past self. Yonge's decision to demonize Margaret renders Philip's sacrifice itself as painful as his sister's presence finally becomes to him. The sense of waste and "pity" that Guy spontaneously invokes when he first hears of Philip's sacrifice repeats at the contemplative end of the story, when Mr. Edmonstone comments that, with the sisters as they are, "'there is all his expensive education thrown away, and all for nothing'" (1: 23).

Mrs. Edmonstone's more thoughtful response to Philip's sacrifice echoes the chime of pity—"'It is a great pity, for his talent is thrown away, and he is not fond of his profession'" (1: 23)—but adds the waste of talent and a third, new element here related to talent: the lack of pleasure where there might have been innocent delight. Philip is at his least self-conscious, his most natural and likable in the novel, when he is translating, reading, and otherwise involved in the very pursuits his sacrifice required him to give up. Philip's uncalled-for sacrifice and its painful results embitter him unnecessarily, since the pleasure he has given up has not been dangerous, but harmless to others and good in its own right.

Yonge's critique resonated with major preachers, ranging from the liberal Anglican F. W. Robertson of Brighton to the "Archbishop of Nonconformity," the Congregationalist Thomas Binney, both of whom were sounding a different note than the influential High Church voices of Newman and Keble. Like Yonge, Binney and Robertson help us see that Christian thinkers were not immune from the more general move away from a version of self-sacrifice emphasizing self-punishment and denial. When we encounter theologians and preachers moving toward a more selective application of the ideal, we can see initial elements of the theological shift in emphasis Boyd Hilton has dated to the second half of the century, from the centrality of Christ's sacrifice to the centrality of his living example. Thus Victorian Christian voices such as Binney's and Robertson's remind us that critiques of what I have termed maximalist altruism were indeed not necessarily secular and that some arose out of a multifarious religious framework.[10]

In 1853, Binney published an extended version of a lecture he had delivered to the London Young Men's Christian Association at Exeter Hall in the previous year titled, "Is It Possible to Make the Best of Both Worlds?" This lecture, which reached a circulation of 30,000 copies within a year, took up the risks of sacrifice. Although it was greeted in some more high-minded quarters with irony, it was nonetheless a highly popular work that went into ten editions by 1856. Even as Binney acknowledged that he did not "deny the reality or the duty of self-denial as a Christian virtue" (118), his aim was to take up "the ethics of common life," "the ways and means of ordinary happiness" and associate these with "religious faith, Christian ideas, and a future world" (236). His main premise was that "in general, great sacrifices and predominating suffering are what is *exceptional*" (19). In a world where the necessity for great sacrifice was rare, the impulse to self-sacrifice most often reflected a misconstrual of Christian teaching:

> Voluntary martyrdom, unrequired sacrifices, "running without being sent," playing the hero when your proper part is just quietly "to abide in your calling," and to do, there, such duties as God has made yours—these things often bring misery and wretchedness to those whom they seduce, and disgrace on religion which *seems* to be the thing that leads them astray. The blame should fall, however, on the men themselves, not upon that whose impulse and objects they misinterpret. (115)

Moving to a point that Yonge, too, would treat, Binney defended the place happiness and self-preservation might assume for the Christian:

> Admitting the principle that happiness is not to be thought of as *the* aim of life, nor the desire of it made the aim to virtue; that expediency and calculation are to give place to the simple and august idea of duty; still, don't you think that a prudential regard to results,—self-preservation, the thought of our own future well-being, the desire of happiness in fact as related to all the capacities of our nature, and to the whole extent, or probable extent, of our existence—don't you think that this, though not *the* motive—the regal and predominating motive to action, may be one of the motives? May it not be fairly allowed and justified? (19–20)

---

10. I am indebted here to an anonymous reader for OSUP who helped me formulate this idea more clearly than I had been able to do on my own.

While Yonge is less interested than Binney in a "prudential regard to results," and the practical reconciliation of this world's pleasures and the next, we will see that her attention to happiness is, like Binney's, an antidote to sacrificial thinking. If "pleasure-hunting" is an evil, Yonge nevertheless insists on its distinction from the good—even the duty—of certain pleasures.

Unacceptable Sacrifices: When Pleasure Is a Duty

The relation between pleasure and sacrifice finds its fullest exploration in Yonge's depiction of the anxiously self-searching Sir Guy, whom the irreverent young Charles Edmonstone at first describes as "'puritanized till he is good for nothing'" (1: 26). Charles comes around to recognize Guy's deep kindness and compassion and to be himself transformed by its example, yet, at this early moment, Charles' throwaway comment, "good for nothing," expresses one of Yonge's truths: a goodness that comes out of too-thorough a self-restraint, too entire a rejection of pleasure, does makes one good for nothing human. Goodness, for Yonge, does not equal asceticism.

Guy has a powerful conviction that whatever is pleasant must be harmful. His "serious, ascetic temper" becomes evident when he seeks forms of self-discipline, telling Mrs. Edmonstone, "'your own home party is enough to do me harm; it is so exceedingly pleasant,'" to which she replies, "'Pleasant things do not necessarily do harm . . . there are duties of society which you owe even to us dangerous people'" (1: 59). This lesson is especially important for someone in Guy's preeminent social position; it is and will be his duty to live among others, visibly and actively. Yet Mrs. Edmonstone's remonstrance merges what might be a class-specific social lesson with the wider Christian lesson, democratizing it in the process. Self-denial cannot impinge on one's responsibilities to others, whatever the nature of those responsibilities; when it does, self-denial becomes a form of self-indulgence. Yonge offers a clear and positive answer to a set of Victorian concerns that Herbert Spencer expressed in the following way:

> Is each person under duty to carry on social intercourse? May he, without any disregard of claims upon him, lead a solitary life, or a life limited to the family circle? Or does positive beneficence dictate the cultivating of friendships and acquaintanceships to the extent of giving and receiving hospitalities? And if there is such a requirement, what constitutes proper discharge of it? (*Principles* 2: 411)[11]

---

11. Spencer answers in utilitarian terms that such social participation should be encour-

Yonge's anti-ascetic, Christian answer is that all people owe themselves to each other and cannot seclude themselves in self-protecting gestures. Sin, her main concern, may come easily in social life, but not for that can social life be avoided.

Yonge's novelistic treatment of Guy's "egoism" is extraordinary in the way that it ratchets up the classic Victorian contest between one's own needs and others' from a matter of narcissistic pleasure to moral pleasure. Guy's initial "selfishness" is in service of his soul and yet it is still selfishness. Guy's first lesson in the duty of accepting pleasure (one he learns multiple times) is that "'it is as easy to be selfish for one's own good as for one's own pleasure'" (1: 165). He feels "'the duty of giving up, wrenching oneself from all that has temptation in it'" (1: 60), yet is instructed by Mrs. Edmonstone that no *duty* can ever be given up, even if it bears temptations: "'It is pleasure involving no duty that should be given up, if we find it liable to lead us astray'" (1: 60). In this early case in the novel, Guy must submit to the social intercourse that so "unsettles him" and learn to deny himself in "'the trivial round and common task,'" as Keble preached, rather than in dramatic renunciations or self-mortifications (1: 60). When Guy expresses a wish for "'something unpleasant to keep me in order,'" Yonge depicts the wish as exaggerated, even childish in comparison with the man Guy later becomes: "'Something famously horrid,' repeated he, smacking the whip with a relish, as if he would have applied that if he could have found nothing else" (1: 59). Guy learns from Mrs. Edmonstone that the pleasures linked to duties must be accepted and that any associated temptations must be battled "from within" (1: 60).

Yet Guy never fully accepts Mrs. Edmonstone's idea that pleasant things need not harm. Yes, pleasure may be a duty and Guy accepts that he must tolerate it for the sake of others even against his own moral self-interest, but he still finds it impossible to believe that what he enjoys or finds pleasant can be meritorious. As we have seen, Guy's very form of understanding the social duties he owes others is expressed in terms of the opposition between moral good, on one hand, and pleasure, on the other: "'it is as easy to be selfish for one's own good as for one's own pleasure'" (1: 165); this statement comes *after* he has absorbed Mrs. Edmonstone's lesson. Guy's suspicion of pleasure resurfaces when, much later in the novel,

---

aged to the extent that it tends toward the "general happiness" (*Principles* 2: 411). He makes a special category for the social duties the rich can tender the poor and suggests that "social beneficence" does "enjoin . . . bringing rich and poor together" as well as voluntary teaching (2: 413). For a more recent treatment of whether it is a duty to live among others, see Samuel Scheffler, "Morality's Demands."

Guy allows himself and Amy, newly married, only those things which elude the category of "mere pleasure-hunting" (2: 121): "it did not seem to him to come under the denomination of pleasure-hunting, since they had not devised it for themselves. . . . " (2: 95). Pleasure is only acceptable de facto; tolerable, but not a good.

Finally, the economy of pleasure pits it against merit or reward. Guy's pleasure appears to him to sap an activity of the merit it would otherwise have held: "'I enjoyed it too much to have anything to say for myself,'" Guy protests after his courageous, life-threatening rescue of shipwrecked sailors (2: 14). When Guy and Amy marry, Guy notes, "'it does not seem like merit to feast one's poor neighbors rather than the rich. It is so much pleasanter'" (2: 76). Guy's "serious, ascetic temper," his deep sense that pleasure and merit work in opposition to each other, challenge the reader to reckon with the evangelical conviction that suffering and the good are naturally linked. Mrs. Edmonstone's moderations notwithstanding, pleasure for the novel's radical hero remains only a duty.

The No-sacrifice Zone: Pleasing Oneself to Please Others

Guy learns early on that it is his social duty to participate in activities even if they give him pleasure. But, in a way, this dutiful pleasure is hardly pleasure. If Guy participates in it against his own initial wishes, it becomes but another, more abstracted form of self-denial.

As we will see throughout this study, the complex interaction between self and other can make the logic of self-denial and sacrifice incredibly convoluted at times. To begin to follow it, one must enter into the self-suspecting habits of mind that would try to search and root out a hidden devotion to self in its least obvious as well as its most obvious forms. Yonge is an expert at anatomizing the different forms such moral calculation can take.

Once Guy makes his peace with accepting dutiful pleasures that serve the narcissistic pleasures of others, Yonge takes him on to the even more intricate contest between his moral self-interest and now the higher, altruistic (rather than narcissistic) pleasure of others. In the pursuit of his own moral safety, Guy absents himself from a ball, inadvertently giving offence. Reviewing the situation with Amy (in a parallel to the episode with Mrs. Edmonstone and in anticipation of Amy assuming the guiding role), Guy explains that he set aside Mrs. Edmonstone's advice and remained at home because he thought her advice was purely in his own service: "'I thought it her kindness in not liking me to lose the pleasure'" (1: 164). In fact, his participation—and his pleasure—would have brought pleasure to many. As Amy says, "'We all thought you would like it. . . . Is it not sometimes right to consider whether we ought to disappoint people who want us to be pleased?'" (1: 164).

Amy's complex formulation bears two assertions phrased interrogatively as their opposites. "Is it not right" and "Whether we ought to disappoint" mean, really, that it is right and we ought not to disappoint. The tentative register suggests Amy's modesty in making a correction to Guy whom she sees as having achieved a "'great piece of self-denial,'" but it also conveys the increasing complexity of moral reasoning that requires constant, fluid shifts in subject position and often results in conclusions opposite what we might expect (1: 164). Amy reminds Guy that the higher, altruistic pleasure of others depends on Guy taking the "lower" pleasure, the enjoyment that he wished to avoid. Thus *Guy's* higher pleasure must now encompass allowing others to give him precisely the pleasure that he has previously avoided. Guy quickly sees the right of things: "'I had no right to sacrifice your pleasure! I see, I see. The pleasure of giving pleasure to others is so much the best there is on earth, that one ought to be passive rather than interfere with it'" (1: 164). Guy now sees that he must accept his own pleasure in order to support other people's best intentions and best selves. Here, we witness a final merging of narcissistic pleasure with moral, on both sides. Guy's "passivity," his willingness to acquiesce, facilitates both his own and others' selflessness, their awareness of the other as a form of moral excellence.

We witness also an important equality between parties, where Guy is not pretending to enjoy himself or submitting to enjoy himself simply to please less morally developed others. Instead, he is recognizing that others seek his pleasure out of their own virtue, which is as important as his own. The other's "equivalent centre of self," to use George Eliot's crucial phrase, comes into clear focus in the *absence* of self-sacrificial thought. The morally nuanced lesson of the novel is that sacrifice cannot automatically be the rule of the day. Of course, it is worth recalling that we deal here with a protagonist heroically devoted to rooting out selfishness, rather than a moral neophyte who must learn the basic need for self-denial and sacrifice. Still, that Yonge saw such morally nuanced deliberations as accessible and necessary for her broad audience suggests that refining the call to sacrifice seemed to her relevant cultural work.

Likewise, the liberal theologian F. W. Robertson whose early death occasioned a great posthumous readership in the 1850s and beyond, understood self-sacrifice to require clarification, particularly with respect to its cause. In his sermon at Brighton of 23 June 1850, "The Sacrifice of Christ," Robertson, who had moved away from the evangelical Calvinism of his youth, sought to distinguish self-sacrifice "for its own sake" from "self-sacrifice, illuminated by love." Noting that "self-denial, self-sacrifice, self-surrender" seem "hard doctrines, and impossible!," Robertson turned for explanation to the text "the love of Christ constraineth us":

> Self-denial, for the sake of self-denial, does no good, self-sacrifice for its own sake is no religious act at all. If you give up a meal for the sake of showing power over self, or for the sake of self-discipline, it is the most miserable of all delusions. You are not more religious in doing this than before. This is mere self-culture, and self-culture being occupied forever about self, leaves you only in that circle of self from which religion is to free you; but to give up a meal that one you love may have it is properly a religious act—no hard and dismal duty, because made easy by affection.

For Robertson, love alone made self-sacrifice proper: a "positive enjoyment as well as ennobling to the soul." Without love, self-sacrifice was fundamentally a form of egoism, an occupation "forever about self," in precisely the sphere that was meant to transcend self. When Guy learns to focus on others, he approaches the state in which he can, Christ-like, save Philip's life at the cost of his own, a form of self-sacrifice that leaves behind his earlier "moral self-interest" and religiously childish masochism. As Robertson noted, and as the novelists of this study would have agreed, self-sacrifice bore remarkably distinct possibilities:

> So sacrifice, bare and unrelieved, is ghastly, unnatural, and dead; but self-sacrifice, illuminated by love, is warmth and life; it is the death of Christ, the life of God, the blessedness and only proper life of man.

This refined sacrifice is aspirational, heroic, but human: precisely the sort of sacrifice that could inspire Victorian readers who in the second half of the century would more and more often encounter representations of a Christ whose divinity was inseparable from his humanity.

Happiness: "Not an earthborn fancy"

The altruistic pleasure of others is, as Guy describes it, "the best there is on earth." If pleasure here overlaps with Yonge's hallowed category, happiness, this overlap is not simple since typically, these two terms stand in opposition.[12] Guy and Amy are the characters most strongly associated with happiness and, as we have seen, most troubled by "mere" pleasure. Guy's love for Amy is never described in terms of pleasure which is why Guy allows it himself: "sternly as he was wont to treat his impulses, he did not look on his affection as an earthborn fancy, liable to draw him from higher things, and, therefore to be combated; he deemed her rather a guide and guard, whose love might arm him, soothe him, and encourage him" (1: 222).

Happiness, unlike impulses, fancies, and other forms of narcissistic pleasure, does not find its ground in the workings of the social world but in the world beyond the earthly one. Its appearances in this world are ephemeral, hints of what is present elsewhere. Early in the novel, as part of a word game, Amabel impresses Guy by describing happiness as something that "gleams from a brighter world, too soon eclipsed or forfeited" (1: 45). And after Guy's death, Amy describes him with the highest praise, saying that "no one else had such a power of making happy" (2: 364). Happiness, for Yonge, is always Christian; it is the force of feeling that recognizes the true order of things, the true hierarchies and relations of human beings in God's world, even at moments that would otherwise be terribly painful. Perhaps the deep affiliation between happiness and goodness is Yonge's most carefully guarded orthodoxy.

Guy, closer than any other figure in the novel to an accurate perception of those true realities, is also most out of step with earthly business. Suffering under false accusations leveled by Philip, Guy is separated from his beloved Amy. Guy's seclusion and denial at Redclyffe over Christmas lay the ground for his final battle with himself, which culminates on Easter:

> Easter day steadied the gaze [beyond the earth] . . . and as the past week
> had nerved him in the spirit of self-sacrifice, the feast day brought him
> true unchanging joy, shining out of sadness, and enlightening the path that
> would lead him to keep his resolution to the utmost, and endure the want
> of earthly hope. (2: 33)

Eventually, Guy's name is cleared and the Edmonstones accept him back into their family as Amy's fiancé. Almost immediately Guy is exonerated. He has not been guilty of debt or profligacy, as Philip has supposed. On

---

12. When Guy expresses a wish for a limited wedding journey, it is because "he could not see that happiness was a reason for going pleasure-hunting" (2: 95).

the contrary, he has secretly pledged aid to help establish a charitable sisterhood and discreetly supported his needy uncle's innocent child. Not only has Guy lived in some privation to aid these causes but he has done nothing to defend himself against Philip's imputations. Though it "cost him all he held dear," Guy remains silent, mistrusting his own motivations and wary of hurting those whom he has attempted to help (2: 33).

Just when this story most palpably strains the realist imagination, transforming Guy from a struggling character into a perfect and thus death-bound hero, Yonge clarifies that such a problem has been her subject all along. Guy's unrealistic goodness is not so much an artistic challenge, but a real-world, Christian challenge represented in her novel. Guy has gotten himself into trouble not only because Philip has made a target of him but because, on the whole, self-sacrifice is too good to be believed. People misconstrue it because it runs so contrary to good sense, as well as to the self-important and self-defensive stance ordinary people tend towards.

We see an instance of this risk much earlier in the novel, when the stakes are much lower, and Guy has offended by not attending the ball. In conversation with Mrs. Edmonstone, Guy reveals his inability to understand his worth to others and Mrs. Edmonstone remonstrates with him by holding up a general standard of human behavior against which Guy is abnormally good. Against this standard, Guy will appear to be intensely self-important rather than the opposite. After recognizing that his mistake had been "in forgetting that his attendance did not concern only himself," he goes on to say that he "could not see what difference it made except to their own immediate circle. 'If it was not you, Guy, who made that speech,'" says Mrs. Edmonstone, "'I should call it fishing for a compliment'" (1: 166). Much later in the novel when Guy seeks to defend Philip when the Edmonstones are angry with him on Guy's behalf, Mrs. Edmonstone reprises this comparative sentiment, saying, "'My dear Guy, if we did not know you so well, we should almost accuse you of affectation'" (2: 64). And when Guy's name is partially cleared, Charles exults, "'I knew it would come out that he had only been so much better than other people that nobody could believe it'" (2: 44).

In Yonge's novel, true self-sacrifice is often marked by such misunderstanding and the concatenations of punishment that follow. Guy is regularly misunderstood because egoism and self-satisfaction are so much the rule of the world. When Philip ascribes caprice or temper to Guy's renunciations, he is voicing a judgment that might well be true if Guy were not Guy (1: 154). Self-imposed sacrifice happens in this novel when Guy seeks

to do good, but guiltless Christian suffering begins when others misconstrue what he has done. Small matters like forgoing a desirable horse or
the ball, or his habit of living modestly, give rise to the near or temporary
loss of the most consequential matters: his good name, his love for Amabel, and his immeasurably valuable family life with the Edmonstones.

Initial self-sacrificial acts thus pale in comparison with their effects in
the social world; these effects require a far fuller abdication of control.
Authentic self-sacrifice demands that one renounce control not only over
one's actions but over one's image, as well. When, at the novel's end, Philip
becomes the heir to Redclyffe and initially seeks to give it up, he is taught
by Amy that he must accept it. He gives up the "great renunciation and so-
called sacrifice, with which he had been feeding his hopes," Yonge's narrator intones, "and in this lay the true sacrifice, the greater because the world
would think him the gainer" (2: 288). A small circle of intimates will know
and recognize sacrifice, and, as Yonge firmly believed, He who knows all
things and sees into all hearts will know and reckon.

Sacrifice and Opportunity: Time and Space

Thus far, I have suggested that in *The Heir of Redclyffe,* Yonge offered her
readers an alternative to the stereotype of an ascetic, self-punishing Christian heroism. As she narrated a form of self-sacrifice responsive to the just
demands of a Christian social life, Yonge reflected the difficulties of indiscriminate self-sacrifice among naive Christians.

But Yonge distinguished herself in a second way in this most popular
novel when she offered her readers an ideal that bypassed the limitations
upon women—and upon men—inescapable in fiction confined to representing Victorian realia. As we have seen, *The Heir of Redclyffe* dramatizes
the difficulties of finding opportunities for meaningful self-sacrifice; when
the opportunities are scrutinized appropriately, they tend to disappear. This
problem appears to be particularly true for men. Very early on, Guy suggests that the openings for sacrifice are few and Guy's reaction to Philip's
renunciation sets the note for much of what follows: "'One would almost
envy him the *opportunity* of making such a sacrifice'" (1: 23, emphasis
mine). Later, when Guy hears the details of Philip's losses, he says of him,
"'he is as near heroism in the way of self-sacrifice as a man can be in these
days'" (1: 62).

While Yonge speaks here in temporal terms ("in these days"), space
seems equally essential, particularly given the gendered subject, "a man."

What can a man do here and now, or now and here—in the bosom of the family—to be a self-sacrificial hero? The fact that Philip's sacrifice succeeds only in wasting his potential undermines Guy's assessment and reinforces the sense that good men are looking for sacrificial opportunities at home and not finding them. Yonge seems to strain against the limitations of the trivial round and the scope of the domestic novel as the appropriate setting for self-sacrifice.

When Yonge's novels move beyond the domestic sphere, it is often by gesturing to the arena many mid-Victorians associated strongly with self-sacrifice and personal valor: the battlefield. *The Heir of Redclyffe* circulated well beyond the space of the home and family, and was read and honored by English soldiers fighting in the Crimean War. Yonge, whose father was a decorated military man in the Oxford Light Infantry in the Peninsular War, valorized England's fighting men and followed their pursuits closely, while also immersing herself in English history for past instances of military heroism. As Susan Walton has chronicled, Yonge faced challenges in bringing together the image of the Christian chivalric hero with contemporary militarism and the realities of modern warfare. Still, by the time she wrote *The Heir of Redclyffe,* much of that difficulty was overcome.[13]

Spiritual and martial heroism seemed primarily to heighten each other in the image of the Christian chivalric soldier who brought to the battle the same qualities that distinguished him at home. Upright, honorable, unfailingly courageous and quick to sacrifice himself for others, this sort of soldier participated in warfare as a noble pursuit, rather than a violent, morally ambiguous one.[14] The Church Militant, as John Keble called it,

---

13. The violence of warfare and, specifically, the mandate to kill rather than to be killed, posed the greatest problem to the image of the Christian chivalric soldier. Walton describes a positive shift in English attitudes toward the military at mid-century, stemming from causes including the threat posed by Napoleon, the heroism on display at the sinking of the HMS Birkenhead in 1852, and the death of the Duke of Wellington (35–38). Such a shift set the stage for Yonge to merge nationalist and religious ideals in the figure of the modern Christian soldier. Only later would Yonge shift her admiration from fighting men to rest more exclusively upon missionaries who could live lives of valour without the taint of violence (21).

14. Analyzing representations of Florence Nightingale, Poovey notes what she calls the "two narratives about patriotic service that were culturally available at mid-century—a domestic narrative of maternal nurturing and self-sacrifice and a military narrative of individual assertion and will" (*Uneven Developments* 169). Claiming that the domestic ideal "always contained an aggressive component," she understands the domestic to encompass the military (170). While her notes explore the Christian imagery applied to Nightingale, she does not see the problem of Christ's gender as central to the mix of militaristic and maternal descriptions.

could take great pride in its military soldiers since they were understood to
be spiritual soldiers as well.

With such shining images of war and soldiering, it is not surprising that
The Heir of Redclyffe sometimes strains against its domestic setting. In
concert with the way the novel frequently relies on military metaphor to
illustrate spiritual achievement, it reflects the difficulty of forging a compelling manhood at home, without the defining tests of war or adventure.
This lack may explain why the novel shifts genres to include features such
as Guy's dramatic rescue of men at the scene of a shipwreck. Guy's success
in that scene is the redemption of an earlier, homelier story that he tells
about witnessing an old ram floating away in a powerful stream. By his
own account, Guy "foolish[ly]" jumps in to save the ram: the stream is too
strong, the beast is too heavy "'and not at all grateful for my kind intentions'" (1: 47). When finally both Guy and the beast are rescued, Guy's
faithful servant Markham says, "'if you do wish to throw away your life,
let it be for something better worth saving than Farmer Holt's vicious old
ram'" (1: 48).[15] Guy spends the novel looking for a canvas grand enough
for his character. Markham's complaint—"'You'll never be content till you
have got your death'" (2: 13)—is, of course, the truth, for Yonge, as much
as for Guy.

Yet that earlier episode is important because it reflects the refining of
Guy's capacity for self-sacrifice, his self-sacrificial style, so to speak. When
the shipwreck does come about, Guy's heroism is distinguished from the
bravery of another, less "steady" young man who does it "'for the lark,
and to dare the rest; but Sir Guy does it with thought, and because it is
right'" (2: 10). Guy's heroism—his "thorough contempt and love of danger one reads of"—is a "courage based on that foundation" (2: 16) of faith
that transforms it from a mere "exploit" to an expression of his "steady
perseverance in well-doing" (2: 27). Such steady perseverance leads directly
to his final sacrifice: his life for Philip's. We can see here Yonge working to
distill the sort of Christian courage that Thomas Hughes would later define
and praise in *The Manliness of Christ* (1879). Manly courage encompassed
"tenderness and thoughtfulness for others" (as qtd. in Gay 105). Manliness was not merely contempt for death, but the motive of serving others,

---

15. This episode pre-dates the Trollopian episode of Johnny Eames saving the earl from
the bull in *The Little House at Allington,* an episode both comical and heroic, reflecting
Eames' general decency, but in no way transforming him or setting out an arc that will move
beyond realist detail or anecdote to transcendent action or meaning. The rewards for this
self-sacrificial action are notably worldly, marked too by the distinction between farmer and
earl. For further discussion of Trollope's ethics, see Chapter Five.

distinct from "animal courage."[16] This form of manliness is continuous with action and judgment in the domestic sphere, rather than opposed to it.

Yonge's particular challenge was to fashion virtuous male heroes that a general reading public could perceive as manly. The difficulty of avoiding priggishness in a character seeking a morally immaculate life was one Yonge acknowledged. Nonetheless, she does not solve the problem by situating Guy's death at the shipwreck or a like adventure. Instead, Guy (like Gaskell's Ruth in the eponymous novel of the same year) contracts an illness from nursing another, stronger man and then succumbs to his weak constitution. Such a death shapes a version of heroism removed from the fields of battle and adventure. In this way, Yonge addressed a question that concerned many Victorian writers and thinkers: what was the relation between gender and sacrifice?

The Gender of Sacrifice

Twenty-first century readers often have abundant differences with the world-view of Yonge who feared unwomanly and unchristian self-assertion and believed she should write no books that did not serve the needs of family and Church.[17] Within Yonge's books, we can find a systematic repression of ambitious female characters, a reduction of such ambition to mere cleverness, and a tacit acceptance of narrow definitions of femininity evident in such ordinary descriptions as Mary, "though perfectly feminine, had an air of strength and determination" (1: 43).[18] These features in Yonge's writing have made it more difficult to see that in *The Heir of*

---

16. On the basis of John Tosh's studies, Walton suggests that Victorian "manliness" was predominantly defined by moral qualities such as courage, determination, readiness to work, rather than the "physical shows of strength previously regarded as proof of manly vigour" (6–7). Militarism post-mid-century combined the two.

17. Yonge confided to Keble the worry that her personal passion for writing might blind her to its necessary Christian aims, to which he responded, as she said, in both a "soothing and guarding way," that "a successful book might be the trial of one's life" (Coleridge 192). He also reminded her that the book was a form of offering up her talents. Yonge donated its proceeds to George Augustus Selwyn, then Bishop of New Zealand, in order to outfit the schooner Southern Cross which served the Melanesian Mission of the Anglican Church and the Church of the Province of Melanesia. See Schaffer for a useful discussion of the challenges faced by today's scholars, especially feminists, when reading Yonge.

18. Sandback-Dahlström argues that Yonge's response to the constraints of gender is evident in the mutilation of various characters. Their burden, or "share of the cross," represents the situation of the writer who lets dogma limit her imaginative vision (7).

Redclyffe, the moral standards she teaches are often uniform with respect to gender.[19]

Scholars of Victorian literature have been diligent in delineating the claims of the self-sacrificial imperative upon women. Feminist scholarship made us aware in the first case of the repressive norms governing and seeking to contain women's lives.[20] Fiction offers countless examples, from Dickens' long-suffering Angels of the House to Eliot's frustrated St. Theresas. Victorian non-fiction testifies to women's place, from Ruskin's prescriptive statements in *Sesame and Lilies* (1865): "She must be enduringly, incorruptibly good; instinctively, infallibly wise—wise not for self-development, but for self-renunciation" (78), to John Stuart Mill's descriptive critique in *On the Subjection of Women* (1869):

> If women are better than men in anything, it surely is in individual self-sacrifice for those of their own family. But I lay little stress on this, so long as they are universally taught that they are born and created for self-sacrifice. I believe that equality of rights would abate the exaggerated self-abnegation which is the present artificial ideal of feminine character, and that a good woman would not be more self-sacrificing than the best man. (166)

Maternity was often figured in terms of self-sacrifice. August Comte worshipped at the shrine of the selfless Madonna-mother while traditional Christian writers, for example, Sarah Stickney Ellis, described motherhood as "that which is strong enough to overcome the universal impulse of self-preservation" (2); the child was the mother's "object . . . for which to suffer" (4). Breastfeeding, too, was evoked by writers such as Spencer and Leslie Stephen in discussions of biological altruism.

Yet, as we saw in the sermons treated in the introductory chapter, self-sacrifice was a fundamental Victorian value, apart from considerations of gender. Across genre, we encounter earnest praise for male self-denial. In fiction, Thackeray's hero Henry Esmond sacrifices his claim to a title, vowing "never to deprive that family which he loved best in the world. Perhaps he took a greater pride out of his sacrifice than he would have had in those

---

19. Andrew Miller has recently noted that Yonge's moral perfectionism includes women as well as men and argues that his subject—moral exemplarity in narrative—is no less a female phenomenon than a male one (*Burdens* 13).

20. See the early, path-breaking literary studies of Victorian femininity, such as Martha Vicinus' edited collection *Suffer and Be Still* (1972) and Sandra M. Gilbert and Susan Gubar's *The Madwoman in the Attic* (1979). Notable accounts of the subversion or negotiation of prescribed gender roles in history and literature include Nina Auerbach (1978), Seth Koven (2006), and Vicinus (1985).

honours which he was resolved to forgo" (235). George Eliot's Reverend
Farebrother quietly gives up the woman he loves for the sake of her happiness, as Dickens' Jarndyce likewise brings together his beloved Esther Sum-
merson and the man she prefers; and, as we will see, Sydney Carton offers
his life for the woman he worships. *Jane Eyre* ends by singling out from
among all other characters the austere St. John River: "Firm, faithful, and
devoted. . . . His is the exaction of the apostle, who speaks but for Christ,
when he says, 'Whosoever will come after Me, let him deny himself, and
take up his cross and follow Me'" (477).

In the writing we have come to know as "Victorian sage writing," John
Ruskin repeatedly linked the value of sacrifice to male vocation, in *Unto
This Last,* where he described the necessity for soldier, pastor, physician,
lawyer and merchant to be ready to give up their lives under the appropriate circumstances, "as a father would in a famine, shipwreck, or battle,
sacrifice himself for his son" (27). Likewise, in the "Lamp of Sacrifice,"
he imagines sacrifice operating as, among other things, a social tonic that
binds men across class:

> It is not the church we want, but the sacrifice; not the emotion of admira-
> tion, but the act of adoration; not the gift, but the giving. And see how
> much more charity the full understanding of this might admit, among
> classes of men of naturally opposite feelings; and how much more noble-
> ness in their work. (19)

Thomas Carlyle's discussion of work and duty relied heavily upon the
notion of self-sacrifice: "It is only with Renunciation (*Entsagen*) that Life,
properly speaking, can be said to begin" (257). In the emerging field of
social science, Spencer went so far as to describe the "sympathetic self-
sacrifices required of men to women in general, and especially required of
husbands in their behavior to wives," suggesting that husbands owed their
wives more beneficence than wives owed husbands (*Principles* 2: 356).

My point here is not to argue for a "moral androgyny" of sacrifice,
but to note what James Eli Adams has called the potential "openness" of
the value in a culture that prized it (*Dandies* 7). In his profound study of
Victorian masculinity, Adams describes asceticism as a virtue that became
gendered around mid-century as middle-class intellectuals sought to define
and defend their maleness as a form of "virtuoso asceticism," in contradistinction from female forms of influence and domestic activity (2).[21] Yet the

---

21. Male self-sacrifice has been most obviously recognized in the form of the self-

very struggle for the cultural authority accorded to asceticism reflects its initial ideological availability to both genders.

Phenomenological features of asceticism dovetailed with Victorian assumptions about men and women to open it to both groups with different emphases. As Geoffrey Harpham notes, all asceticism is ambivalent because self-denial can itself serve as a "strategy of gratification or empowerment" (*Ascetic Imperative* xiii). And as Adams puts it, "Because self-discipline perplexes the binaries of active and passive, of self-assertion and self-denial, tributes to it frequently confound traditional assignments of gender" (8).

As we might expect, it was often the case that Victorian feminine self-sacrifice was rendered less valuable by deeming women naturally self-sacrificial. With no desires to overcome, they amassed no moral capital through self-denial. Adams describes the way masculine and feminine praise could divide in terms of "masculine self-discipline . . . represented as an ongoing regimen of aggressive self-mastery, and a feminine self-denial . . . represented as a spontaneous and essentially static surrender of the will to external authority" (Adams *Dandies* 9). And feminine self-denial could meet punitive limits when women used it toward the end of self-determination.

Yet the salient point for this study is that the ambivalence of self-sacrifice begins in its most impressive avatar: Christ. Investigating the ethic of self-sacrifice means investigating Christ's own gender position as Victorians imagined it, as well as the implied gender of the religious devotee imitating him.

The Gender of Christ?: Humanity and Divinity

In 1837, Sarah Stickney Ellis claimed that Christ was the only man to have displayed the "'self-sacrifice and pure devotion'" of women (as qtd. in Adams *Dandies* 8). Ellis' analogy between Christ and women might well be read as a bid for female power, yet it also draws our attention to the other side of the ambivalence that Harpham argues is central to asceticism. If the

---

discipline necessary to the capitalist enterprise. By the 1830s, especially in the discourse of political economy, "self-discipline is increasingly claimed as the special province and distinguishing attribute of middle-class men, as both manhood and masculine labor are constructed in increasingly agonistic forms" (Adams 7). See Nancy Armstrong, *Desire and the Domestic Novel*, for her discussion of female self-regulation forming the basis for male accumulation.

drive to sacrifice can function as a strategy for gratification or empowerment, Harpham tells us that it also bespeaks "the urge for [worldly] transcendence" (xiii). In light of that urge, I want to suggest that in reading
Yonge, we might construe gender as a secondary category, not nearly so
meaningful as the distinction between humanity and divinity.[22]

At mid-century, the figure of Christ confounded many accepted notions
of gender, challenging a strict ideology of separate spheres and distinct values for men and women. As Norman Vance has noted, the manly Christian hero was meant, like Christ, to combine "entertaining and healthy
activism" and "the less vivid religious imperatives: patience and heroic
martyrdom, self-abnegation and the discipline of the will" (7). The challenge to contemporary gender ideology is evident in the efforts expended,
for instance, in the sermons of Spurgeon. Witness his dramatic rhetorical
efforts to marry marvelous strength, on one hand, and the final infirmity
that is death, on the other:

> Do any of us know what is contained in that great word 'die'? Can we
> measure it? Can we tell its depths of suffering or its heights of agony?
> "Died for us!" Some of you have seen death. . . . [Y]ou have seen the
> strong man bowing down, his knees quivering; you have beheld the eye-
> strings break, and seen the eyeballs glazed in death; you have marked the
> torture and the agonies which appal men in their dying hours; and you
> have said, "Ah! it is a solemn and an awful thing to die." But, my hearers,
> "Christ *died for us*." All that death could mean Christ endured; he yielded
> up the ghost, he resigned his breath; he became a lifeless corpse, and his
> body was interred. . . . "Christ died for us." . . . I beseech you regard the
> Royal Sufferer. See him, with the eye of your faith, hanging on the bloody
> tree. Hear him cry, before he dies, "It is finished!" ("Love's Commenda-
> tion, 414–15)

Even after Spurgeon renders Christ passively "yielding up," "resigning,"
becoming a "lifeless corpse," and finally "interred," he returns Christ from
beyond the grave to cry out, "It is finished!" so that death's demand for

---

22. I am cautious of the real-world political costs to setting aside concerns of gender, especially in analyzing the religious world which has often addressed the institutional realities
of sexism more slowly than the secularized. At the same time, literary criticism has been so
used to examining the sociological stage of identity that we do not have nearly as developed
an apparatus for evaluating the notion of transcendence. Even if, as Harpham notes, the
urge for transcendence cannot be separated from the world which needs transcendence, the
urge needs our analysis.

keen endurance and active suffering trumps the silence and glaze of life's end. For Spurgeon, the "strong man's" strengths, dramatically categorized, only make the reduction of death more stark.

Yet Spurgeon's emphasis on the "manliness" of Christ met up in the second half of the century with more descriptions that gave "unexpected scope to the positive value of what is usually called the 'feminine element' in a manly man's character" (Vance 109). Muscular Christianity's most popular writers described the subordination of personal will as a critical feature of male socialization. Thomas Hughes' 1857 bestseller, *Tom Brown's Schooldays*, for example, portrayed Dr. Arnold's public school as one that taught the lesson of self-sacrifice to its boys when they learned to work and play not for individual success but for the common cause. "Giving up" is a phrase that recurs commonly in this story that dramatized a thorough Christian education: cricket, for instance, was praised because it is such "an unselfish game" (Hughes 354). The story valorizes Tom Brown's final recognition of his debt to his old school-master in a picture of gentle humility which might easily sustain a change of pronouns to female: "the grief which he began to share with others became gentle and holy . . . and while the tears flowed freely down his cheeks, [he] knelt down humbly and hopefully to lay down there his share of a burden which had proved itself too heavy for him to bear in his own strength" (375). From a loyalty to his human master, Hughes suggests, Tom Brown will learn "the knowledge of Him who is the King and Lord of Heroes," a heroism characterized as much by "love," "tenderness," and "purity," as by "strength" and "courage" (375).

Good Christian men had to be as willing as women to give up their autonomy and sacrifice their will. In *The Heir of Redclyffe*, Yonge dramatizes this gender-inclusive imperative by criticizing Philip's unwillingness to accept a rule beyond his own necessarily limited rationality and, by the novel's end, finds him a teacher in Amabel, who is the novel's paragon of submission to the authority of her elders, Guy, and God. It is Amabel whom Philip earlier in the novel describes as the "victim" of a "sacrificial" marriage to Guy (2: 79). Yet her submission is her strength and the novel follows her well beyond the death of Guy, testifying to her Christian fortitude. It also follows Philip closely through his broken repentance and lasting regret. As Catherine Wells-Cole writes, "The reducing of Philip provides *The Heir of Redclyffe* with a surprisingly sharp critique of authoritative manhood" (77).

Still, Yonge knew as well as writers such as Charles Kingsley and Thomas Hughes that any recommendation of Christianity that did not

present a compelling vision of masculinity would fail in its aims.[23] Against
Philip's decline, Guy's elevation suggests one contemporary strategy that
addressed the problem of Christ's "double gender." While mid-century
Christian writers often turned to the aristocratic trope of chivalry and its
code of generous feeling and action—"dedicated courage, loyalty, unselfish devotion and protection of the weak"—to characterize the gentleman,
Yonge may have worried that recourse to the chivalric mode would not do
enough to assure Guy's manliness, especially against the invalid Charles,
the weak Mr. Edmonstone, and the encompassing domestic sphere (Vance
17).

Yonge combats the risk that Guy will seem a "milksop" by giving Guy
a strong temper (1: 26). Wells-Cole argues cogently that "Guy's strong
assertion of feelings, and in particular his anger, is the novel's principal
means of representing his masculinity" (74). Consequently, the great part
of the novel details the struggle to conquer his anger and by extension, his
fallible humanity. By the time he tames that anger—no small feat—he has
transcended body and gender, and is ready for death.

Guy's struggles do not have a female analogue in the novel and thus it
might be argued that Yonge de-values or naturalizes female sacrifice. Even
in Amy's most painful hours of separation from Guy, before his name is
cleared, her submission to her parents' judgment and to providential justice seems to come with minimal struggle. She appears, like the heroines
of Dickens, to have so deeply internalized submission to others' wills that
sacrifice no longer figures as an especially apt descriptive term, since she
possesses little independent will or agency that must suffer to submit. If
Amy's sacrifice is rendered mainly effortless and thus possibly less morally
valuable (certainly less valuable in terms of narrative possibilities), neither
does Mrs. Edmonstone's maternal sacrifice on behalf of Charles become a
model. Her habit of "giving up everything for his sake, and watching him
night and day" may be well motivated but serves no good end and, at the
same time, turns the sisters into "slaves," a loaded term that partakes of
none of the praise of self-denial (1: 14). The other significant female character, the eldest daughter, Laura, denies herself for the sake of Philip but
that choice is judged in purely negative terms as the service of an idol and a
refusal of the truer hierarchies of demand and denial.

---

23. Gay and Vance agree with Adams in claiming that male writers who wanted to define
appealing forms of Victorian masculinity in the second half of the century felt compelled to
defend ascetic virtues as non-feminine. Vance's larger argument concerns muscular Christianity's social activism and its negotiation of the growing divide between secular and sacred
realms.

In short, the narrative possibilities of struggle, temptation, self-discipline and sacrifice all fall to Guy, with an opening at novel's end for Philip to join the program. Does this effectively work against my suggestion that we experiment with reading the "urge for transcendence" as a move beyond gender? I think not. The ending of Yonge's novel depends on a fairly conventional feature of plot that is nonetheless suggestive with respect to this question.

The novel's title, *The Heir of Redclyffe*, wraps both Guy and his rival Philip within the same identity, at the same time emphasizing that there can be but one heir of Redclyffe at a time. In the end, Philip takes Guy's place, assuming his longed-for role as heir of Redclyffe while also reflecting Yonge's tendency to "punish her worldly and self-sufficient characters by giving them what they once wanted" (Tillotson 55). Yet the novel's title also foregrounds a less discussed element of the plot. At Guy's death, his widow Amy is pregnant. Should the baby be a boy, he will inherit Redclyffe. Should the baby be a girl, she will not. The "heir of Redclyffe" will be male, no matter what: either Philip or Guy's son. Yet the unknown sex of the child Amy bears within her and Philip's penitential desire for renunciation raise the shadow of a female "heir of Redclyffe."

With this shadow, we can see Yonge evoking an alternative reality in which inheritance indicates spiritual possession and power, and men and women may be equals.

The Heir/ess of Redclyffe

Yonge amplifies the alternative of male and female equality by drawing out the narrative suspense of the child's sex over the course of nine chapters, the length of a pregnancy. For nine chapters, *The Heir of Redclyffe* refers to an unsexed being, that the novel will later call "a morsel of a creature"; a "specimen of humanity" (2: 265); "'infant humanity'" (2: 266); a "little unconscious creature"; "the creature that was only his and hers"; and finally and repeatedly, "'Guy's baby'" (2: 265). Yet the baby is not actually without a gender for the nine chapters in which the audience and characters wait to hear it. Assuming the mimeticism of the novel, the baby has a gender; we simply don't know it. At the same time we are asked to recognize that *Yonge* does know it. The novel clarifies both the omniscience of the narrator and the design of the author in a few critical instances, for example, when the narrator asserts, "One short year after, what would Philip not have given for that quarter of an hour" (1: 309). Such a prolepsis disturbs the verisimilitude of the novel and introduces a didactic, moralizing strain that Yonge generally avoids. Yet such a sentence defines and stabilizes the status of the storyteller in such a way that at points when the narrative withholds information, readers can recognize intention.

The narrative suspense here is heightened by the natural phenomenon it represents: pregnancy, in which even the woman whose body holds the child does not know its "sort" (2: 264). A contrast here with *David Copperfield* may clarify Yonge's interest in limiting the consequences of gender for the believing Christian. As compared with Yonge's relative silence on the subject of the infant-to-be's sex, the comedy and pathos in Chapter One of *Copperfield* reside in Aunt Betsey Trotwood's stubborn certainty that her sister-in-law's baby will be a girl and her irrational refusal of the unknowability that pregnancy imposes upon its observers. On the other hand, Betsey Trotwood's certainty that David will be female merely makes explicit the imaginative, projective processes so often erased in the aftermath of a child's birth. In retrospect, it seems impossible—and critical—that David could have been anything but a boy. Meanwhile, the absent father in *Copperfield* registers the imaginative possibility of David's own non-existence even as it evokes the irreducibility of David's life, his memorable, "I am born," as he leaves the same "land of dreams and shadows, the tremendous region whence I had so lately traveled," at the same time as he considers "the mound above the ashes and the dust that once was he, without whom I had never been" (18).

In *The Heir of Redclyffe,* by contrast, the absent father (Guy) does not occasion serious meditation on the daughter's irreducibility or the consequential alternatives that might have been. Instead, I suggest that both Guy's absence—his transcendence of the body in death—and the prolonged suspense as to the sex of his child assert a distinction between the realm of economic and political life, on one hand, and spiritual life, on the other hand. As Poovey has argued, "the model of a binary opposition between the sexes, which was socially realized in separate but supposedly equal 'spheres,' underwrote an entire system of institutional practices and conventions at mid-century, ranging from a sexual division of labor to a sexual division of economic and political rights" (*Uneven Developments* 8–9). Yonge knew well that sex made all the difference in economic and political life where matters of inheritance and entail seriously disadvantaged or altogether excluded women. (In *The Heir of Redclyffe,* the entail excludes females [2: 285].)

Yet her novel suggests that in the realm of spiritual life, sex determines little with respect to possession and power because in that realm the very terms possession and power are impossible to fathom without recognizing them as the coincidents of intentional dispossession, abdication or denigration of worldly power. If, as Harpham says, there is no transcendence without a world to transcend, for Yonge, the truer statement works in the opposite direction: one comes to know the nature of the world by measuring it against its transcendent alternative. Yonge's spiritual world often functions as an inverse of the economic-political reality that hosts it, as when Amy refuses Philip's offer to restore Redclyffe to her daughter, stating, "'what a misfortune to her, poor little thing, to be a great heiress'" (2: 286).

Yet Amy and her daughter, Mary Verena, clearly are the novel's great heiresses. While others in the novel also respond profoundly to Guy's example, Amy and Mary are Guy's primary spiritual heirs. Both are described as looking in some ineffable way like Guy, in spite of the difference of sex. At the precise moment of Mary Verena's baptism, Amy first perceives the baby's resemblance to her father: "She had earnestly and often sought a resemblance without being able honestly to own that she perceived any; but now, though she knew not in what it consisted, there was *something* in that baby face that recalled him more vividly than picture or memory" (2: 301). At another point, Charles describes Amy's smile as being like Guy's: "'The little creature was lying by her, and she put her hand on it, and gave one of those smiles that are so terribly like his'" (2: 264). Here, "his," "her" "the little creature," and "it" come together so that all three people—Amy, Guy, and Mary Verena—seem spiritually indistinguishable. Guy's beatific smile on Amy's face, the baptismal resemblance between father and daughter, clarify that family likeness is a spiritual matter.

Further, familial inheritance is not a vertical transaction in which death acts decisively to transfer property from one generation to another but a Christian sharing that transcends this-worldly distinctions of life and death, male and female bodies.[24] Mary Verena and Amy bring Guy back, even painfully so, by resembling him in the spirit: "'I was so glad of her, it was a sort of having him again'" (2: 313). Then Amy and her daughter become Guy's "messengers" in a world badly in need of them (2: 265, 268).

---

24. In general, physical resemblance is cast off in the novel in favor of the ineffable spiritual "something" that makes people look "like" each other. Whereas Guy, afraid of the family curse, thinks he resembles the violent Sir Hugo, when Amy sees the portrait that has long haunted Guy, she sees little resemblance because of the difference in "expression" and "countenance" (2: 350).

To posit that the real "heirs" in the novel are Amy and Mary Verena adopts the longstanding Christian habit of metaphorizing wealth, a habit that would have come naturally to Yonge as to most other Victorians. Later in this study, we will see other contemporary novelists calling into question such problematic metaphors precisely because they were so culturally widespread as to be unnoticeable. We need not argue that readers then or today should value spiritual inheritance over material or surrender matters of economics and politics to religious ways of thinking.

Yet it is meaningful to note that in a world where what sex a person was born made all the difference; where class, too, determined matters no less than life and death, Yonge could envision a world divided by humanity and divinity, organized by humanity's effort to imitate the divine. Metaphor invoked the "better" reality to which believers aspired. The crowning self-sacrifice of a Christ ambiguously gendered offered Yonge an image impossible to hold firmly in the mind, but as promising and sacred as the image of a yet-unknown creature in the mind of its pregnant mother.

CHAPTER 2

Suicide, Sin, and Self-Sacrifice in
A Tale of Two Cities

It is not easy to affirm that Yonge was a Christian novelist whereas Dickens was not.[1] Both *The Heir of Redclyffe* and *A Tale of Two Cities* end in celebration of heroic self-sacrifice, with one man dying so that another may live. "'I am the Resurrection and the Life,'" Sydney Carton repeats in the hours preceding his death, until that memorable first-person speech merges with his own prophecy at the novel's end. A novel that orients itself so thoroughly in the Christian inheritance bears out Owen Chadwick's suggestion that secularization might best be defined in terms of religious continuity: "the relation . . . in which modern European civilization and society stands to the Christian elements of its past and the continuing Christian elements of its present" (*Secular* 264). Carton's substitution and vicarious suffering for Darnay, then his insertion into history, repeat the structure of the Atonement in which the innocent Christ's bloody sacrifice on behalf of a fallen humanity redeems them and becomes the basis of a religion for the ages.

Yet perhaps we can begin to chart the distance between Yonge's High-Church orthodoxy and Dickens' neo-Christian ethics by suggesting that if

---

1. See Emma Mason (2011) on Dickens' Christianity. While twenty-first-century readers have tended to see him as a "benevolent humanist," Dickens' contemporary audience "regarded him as a key defender of a New Testament Christianity under attack from sombre High Church and Low Church evangelising" (318). Schramm offers a helpful recent consideration of the relationship between Dickens' faith, life, and work (140–80).

Sydney Carton is a Christian sacrifice, he is also a Victorian suicide. "Suicide," wrote one of its analysts in 1824, "is generally committed by the sensual dissipated character, who wastes his evening hours in intoxication, and his mornings in sleep and sloth. The man of industry, who rises with the dawn, and refreshes his spirits and renovates his health with the fascinating freshness of the morning, has too much of pleasing and substantial enjoyment to rush madly out of life with disgust" (Piggott 141). Carton the Jackal—"idlest and most unpromising of men" who could be "seen at broad day, going home stealthily and unsteadily to his lodgings, like a dissipated cat" (*TTC* 78)—might be modeled on this passage; indeed, the book abounds with such descriptions of Carton as "self-flung away, wasted, drunken, poor creature of misuse" (138).

In Carton, Dickens merged a spectrum of influential Victorian notions of the suicide only to distinguish Carton from them progressively and categorically by the novel's climax. Suicide is evaded not by a Carlylean industrious reformation or a Millite spiritual conversion, but by heroic self-sacrifice unto death. As readers will remember, Carton becomes less and less "suicidal" the closer he comes to his death (Gates 71). He does not "rush madly out of life with disgust." On the contrary, he assumes responsibility. He acknowledges a wide range of feelings, ennobling and sorrowful and reflective. Affecting memories of his childhood and young manhood stir within him; he reaches out to other weaker human beings. He rises with the dawn but, unlike the "man of industry," he does not seek or find enjoyment. He is reborn not to live, but to die.

Dickens' representation of Carton thus combines in one figure two forms of self-killing—suicide and self-sacrifice—which have required special distinction in Western culture in every era since the Crucifixion. Whereas suicide was considered a sin from Christianity's earliest history, Christ's self-sacrificial death was distinguished as an ethical model, imperative in its demands. Dickens' novel dramatizes a central dilemma for a surrounding culture that took as its founding example Christ's redemptive death and hallowed self-sacrificial virtue, yet often despaired of achieving it.[2] By making Carton a suicidal figure, saved only by another form of voluntary death, the novel asks: what is the difference between suicide and honorable self-sacrifice? In an "age of atonement," as Boyd Hilton has called the years between 1785 and 1865, what was to prevent the best tradition of Victorian selflessness, a noble disregard for self in the service of

2. See Mason: "Dickens's attention to religious questions ultimately suggests that it was not secularization that the Victorians had to confront, but their own inability to put into practice the array of doctrines to which they variously subscribed" (324).

others, from becoming a deformation of that ideal, an inexcusable violence
against the self? Without the sure spiritual heroism of a Sir Guy Morville,
tutored by trusted authorities in the intricacies of sacrificial virtue, deeply
sensible of the continuity between this world and the next, might not maximalist ethical claims kill a person as easily as save him?

By coupling suicide and self-sacrifice in Carton, Dickens' novel threatened the coherence of the self-sacrificial claim that so powerfully organizes
the novel's climax. With his capacity for highly idiosyncratic representation, Dickens might easily have avoided or minimized the cultural mark-
ers of suicide. I argue in this chapter that Carton's suicidal nature allowed
Dickens to introduce and invigorate a religious paradigm of sin and holiness that would not have been available to him had he remained safely
within the descriptive bounds of self-sacrifice. In *A Tale of Two Cities,* the
suicidal personality incarnates sin, yet only such an incarnation provides
the powerfully desired, terribly elusive possibility for its alternative: holiness. For Dickens, such holiness is achieved not as Yonge would have it, by
divine grace, but instead by flawed human beings who struggle to recognize their own necessary interdependence.

As we will see, a vital religious element for Dickens was the idea of
Christ as a substitute, a guiltless one who voluntarily stands in for a guilty
humanity, who pays the ransom of others and redeems them from sin. Critics have noted Dickens' formal attraction to substitution and his Christological characterizations, yet these two elements have only recently begun
to be analyzed in mutual relation and in historical context. Exploring the
possibility that human beings might stand in for each other as Christ himself stood in for humanity, Dickens takes the trope of substitution which
is so central to his novels and to Christian theology, and builds upon it an
aspirational ethics of human interdependence. While the novel confronts
the injustice of vicarious punishment (a major problem for mid-century
Anglican theologians troubled by orthodox versions of the Atonement),
its ending considers the way substitution enables elective and collective
human redemption. Dickensian substitution, which begins tainted by self-
violence, hateful rivalry, and inherited guilt, finds ethical expression by the
end of *A Tale of Two Cities,* mirroring the way that Carton's sinful suicide
is transformed into holy self-sacrifice.

Self-Destroying: Noble or Sinful?

The palpable, shared readerly appreciation for Carton's ending, "the picture of the wasted life saved at last by heroic sacrifice" (Forster 2: 354),

reminds us that the central Victorian struggle "to define correctly the pro-
portions, the means, and the social significance of willful self-martyrdom"
can be described only if we acknowledge the powerful role that the evangelical inheritance played in shaping both middle-class morality and the
period's novels (Kucich *Imperial Masochism* 11). In arguing that Dickens' popular novel resolved suicide into sacrifice by drawing upon a religious paradigm of sin and holiness, I offer a culturally significant exception
to the historical narrative that emphasizes the secularization of attitudes
toward suicide in the mid-nineteenth century. Likewise, I read *A Tale of
Two Cities* seeking to identify precisely where Dickens' Christianity is least
secularized before I turn to his more humanistic resolution of the suicide-
sacrifice problematic.

Both Dickens' representation of suicide and the readerly responses to
the novel are inseparable from a religious history in which suicide had
been held nearly universally as a sin. The "sin" of suicide was the transgression of the biblical prohibition against murder. Augustine had founded
his argument against suicide on the sixth commandment while Aquinas
contended that it violated natural law: God had instilled in human beings
the instinctual desire to preserve their lives and that desire had the force
of law.[3] Locke's influential case against suicide built on Socrates' assertion that people are God's property and consequently have no right to kill
themselves. While defenses of suicide by philosophers such as Voltaire and
Hume had been written, and John Donne had gone so far as to argue that
Christ's passion was the model suicide, the sense of suicide as sinful prevailed well into the nineteenth century.[4] Even in an era of waning faith,
the prohibition against suicide commanded a restraining power; as Carlyle put it in *Sartor Resartus*, for Teufelsdröckh, "'From Suicide a certain
aftershine (*Nachschein*) of Christianity withheld me'" (239–40).

Yet just as early Christians had worried about the line between martyrdom and suicide, Victorians could not always be sure what constituted
suicide. In their cultural history, *Sleepless Souls: Suicide in Early Modern
England* (1987), Michael MacDonald and Terence R. Murphy comment
that "suicide is easier to define than it is to identify" (222). If self-murder
is the voluntary, deliberate destruction of life by a person's own act, nonetheless, "not all self-killing is self-murder" (222). Following the analyses of
early modern writers, MacDonald and Murphy name three categories of
self-killing that were not considered self-murder: martyrs who die rather

---

3. Augustine's argument required him to claim that biblical and early Christian suicides
had been secretly commanded by God.

4. However, some critics say the work, *Biathanatos*, is a parody of scholasticism.
Donne would not allow its publication in his lifetime (MacDonald and Murphy 91).

than recant their faith, soldiers who rush to certain death in battle, and sportsmen killed in dangerous games (222). Nineteenth-century thinkers subscribed to like assessments, often in the imperial context. Samuel Smiles maintained in *Self-Help* (1859) that the "terrible price . . . paid for this great chapter in our [imperial] history . . . may not have been purchased at too great a price" (201–2), if those who follow learn from the courageous and energetic example of their forebears, while John Ruskin would assert in "The Roots of Honour" (1862) that "the man who does not know when to die, does not know how to live" (25). Yet neither Ruskin nor Smiles could guard against the way that "the forms of honourable death" could "elide . . . into outright suicide. Noble acts of sacrifice were not always easy to distinguish from baser kinds of self-destruction" (MacDonald and Murphy 97).[5]

For Victorians, the critical yet elusive distinction between suicide and sacrifice was often represented in the figure of Christ, who served as confirmation or contrast. The frontispiece to Forbes Winslow's influential study *Anatomy of Suicide* (1840), for instance, bore the image of a pious, melancholy Italian shoemaker, Matthew Lovat, who had attempted a self-crucifixion in 1805, affixing a net to his window frame to suspend him visible to the street, nailing himself naked to a cross, and slitting his side.[6] Despite his sense of mission—he was said to have been teaching the lesson, "The pride of man must be mortified; it must expire on the cross"—Lovat garnered no praise from ordinary people or religious figures. Instead, the act was roundly greeted with distress, derision, and a sense of sacrilege moderated only by the subject's evident instability. The image, set as the frontispiece of Winslow's study of suicide, clearly marked Lovat's act as an instance of pathology, not a praiseworthy work of self-sacrifice. Still, at the same time, Lovat raised the question of the problematic role Christ's example played for Victorians. As Ludwig Feuerbach would put it to an English readership thirteen years later: "How should not he who has always the image of the crucified one in his mind, at length contract the desire to crucify either himself or another?" (Feuerbach 62).[7] Was Matthew Lovat not

---

5. Regarding the emphasis on sacrifice in descriptions of imperial conquest and defense, see Kucich, *Imperial Masochism*.

6. Besides Winslow, the other key English primary texts on suicide are W. Wynn Westcott, *Suicide: Its History, Literature, Jurisprudence, Causation and Prevention* (1885), and S. A. K. Strahan, *Suicide and Insanity: A Physiological and Sociological Study* (1893). Enrico Morselli's *Suicide: An Essay on Comparative Moral Statistics* was translated into English in 1881.

7. Linking *TTC* to the Indian Mutiny of 1857, Christopher Herbert argues that the bloodthirsty revolutionaries served the British as a disturbing mirror image. From the time of

the logical conclusion of Christian teaching? Was he not simply a shockingly physicalized manifestation of the self-crucifixions that were recommended to go on in the human heart rather than on the wooden cross?

The intensely mimetic and extreme quality of Lovat's attempt at Christian self-sacrifice in fact eased what Victorians understood as the regular and truly difficult task of "making reliable discriminations between morbidity and authentic virtue" (Herbert *Trollope and Comic Pleasure* 47). Still, if Lovat's case was straightforward, many were not. What made some self-inflicted deaths Christ-like and others not? Near the end of the century, in 1893, Samuel A. K. Strahan answered this question in his lengthy work, *Suicide and Insanity: A Physiological and Sociological Study*. The only "self-destroyers" to whom "any nobility attaches," Strahan argued, were "those who die that others may gain":

> To give up life is the greatest sacrifice a man can make, and when that sacrifice is made without hope of gain or reward, in order that others may escape some terrible calamity which nothing else can avert, then, if the sacrifice be at all justifiable, the act is the grandest and noblest of which fallen man is capable. The most notable of the instances of this form of voluntary death are not to be found among those who directly destroy their own lives, but among those who put themselves in the way of death to save others. To this type of self-sacrifice belongs that of Christ, who died for the world—"gave his life as a ransom for many." (41)

Strahan, a member of the Medico-Psychological Association and a fellow of the Royal Statistical Society, formulates as specific a theoretical recommendation as he can for the method and circumstances under which a man may honorably give up his life. If these terms are met, then the man is nothing short of a modern-day Christ. Yet a moment of doubt here is striking: "if the sacrifice be at all justifiable" seems an unnecessary insertion and even a rhythmic interruption to what is otherwise both a mellifluous and definitive statement. The unasked or answered question troubling Strahan's account is what standard might be applied to determine "justifi-

---

the 1854 publication of Feuerbach, avant-garde intellectuals faced the possibility that the instincts motivating British war crimes were "essential components of religion and civilization themselves" (*War of No Pity* 38): "Nothing is more quintessentially Christian . . . than that special form of demonic possession that expresses itself in a fanatical impulse to slaughter and exterminate those who are not Christians—and that habituates the moral imagination . . . to operating in a mode shot through with phantasmagoric visions of violence" (39). Herbert does not stress Feuerbach's point that Christian violence can take *either* the self or the other as objects. See Feuerbach 247–69.

cation." What might mark circumstances "which nothing else [than voluntary death] can avert"? Everything hangs on that "if," which differentiates
Christlike redemption of those powerless to save themselves from pathological suicide.

Fictional Suicides: Dickens against the Crowd

Victorian fiction played its part in adjudicating cases of voluntary death.
Many Victorian novels responded to the moral uncertainty of voluntary
death with a desire for the strongest possible distinctions between its noble
and base forms. At mid-century, the social scientific category "altruistic
suicide," that Emile Durkheim was to introduce in 1897 in his major work,
Suicide: A Study in Sociology, would have seemed a contradiction in terms
to novelists who worked to oppose the reviled egoism and the vaunted
altruism that might both result in self-inflicted deaths. In *Jane Eyre* (1847),
for instance, St. John Rivers dies a hallowed martyr to his missionary calling in India while Jane's cousin John Reed dies a dissolute bankrupt whose
suicide brings his mother to the grave. Dickens, too, employed a strategy
that paired "moral opposites" in what we might call sacrificial and quasi-
suicidal deaths, such as those of Paul Dombey and Carker or Little Nell
and Quilp (Gates 107).

   As in Strahan's description, the single most important exculpation for
Victorians when they stood to assess voluntary deaths in fiction or real life
was whether *others* stood to benefit (or suffer, for that matter) from the
death. Indeed, Dickens could have excluded all the Christian imagery from
his depiction of Carton's death and still successfully transformed the drama
from suicide to self-sacrifice since Carton dies for the sake of Lucie and
Darnay. As John Kucich points out, "the violent aspect of Carton's "suicide" is redeemed through the preservation of Darnay and his family. Radical self-violence is balanced with meaning derived from its being put to
temporal, conservative use" ("Purity of Violence" 134). Carton's "suicide"
is the rescue of Darnay and the future family he will build with Lucie. The
self-violence of a Lady Dedlock, for example, cannot be described nearly
so neatly or entirely as anyone else's redemption. Carton's death is consequently almost never referred to as "suicide" even in more morally skeptical critical treatments of the novel.[8] When Kucich puts "suicide" in scare

---

   8. The only exceptions that I have come across are Herbert (*War of No Pity* 220);
Schramm (168, 177); Elliot (2009).

quotes, he indicates the success of Dickens' transformation of Carton from a recognizably suicidal figure to a self-sacrificial hero.

With Carton, Dickens separated himself from the more secularized, social scientific project of considering suicide as linked explicitly to Victorian problems of poverty, class identification, sexual morality, and economic virtue. Instead, as we will see, the trope of suicidal despair functioned as an opportunity for the re-inscription of religious values in the novel. At mid-century, understandings of suicide were in transition, as so many religiously rooted concepts were. In fact, we can understand the Victorian representational preoccupation with suicide as at least partly a function of its capacity to be represented in religious, transcendent, and supernatural terms, on one hand, and in increasingly secular, material, and social scientific terms, on the other hand. For Victorians, the "sin" and legal crime of suicide competed with a more modern, secularizing sense of pathology which understood it as a function of insanity or unsound mind. It is not surprising, then, to see fictional etiologies of suicide shaped by both religious and more secular narrative elements. It is notable, though, that at mid-century, it was the minority of suicide stories that followed the lead of Goethe's enormously influential *The Sorrows of Young Werther* (1774) or invoked deaths like Thomas Chatterton's to spin romantic tales of lovelorn or melancholy suicides.[9] The general rule was that English literary suicide bore significant relation to the evils of the world. As novelists drew causal relations between social ills and suicide, depictions of suicide came to function as social critique and as an opportunity for implicit and explicit ethical recommendations. Suicide had entered history and in this manner, at least, it had become a secular concern.

Material and popular considerations contributed to the secularization of suicide. The legal adjudication of suicidal deaths pitted against each other the exculpating verdict, *non compos mentis,* and the criminal finding, *felo de se.* The social and economic consequences for judging suicides to fit the criminal category of *felo de se* were so serious and so contrary to popular feeling, let alone more enlightened, secularized understandings, that it is not surprising that general attitudes toward self-killing had become quite tolerant. The historical evidence from coroners' inquests and jury returns suggests that it was difficult for Victorians to nod to folkloric, religious, and legal practices that desecrated the suicide's body, denied him or her Christian burial rites, allowed the Crown to seize the deceased's

---

9. There were seven English translations of *Werther* between 1779 and 1809 and then none until one in 1854 (Anderson *Suicide* 213).

property as its own, and freed life insurance to withhold payment on a policy. In the 1860s, inquest juries may have returned as few as three per cent of suicide verdicts as *felo do se;* a suicide was judged *felo de se* only if the perpetrator appeared to have very carefully organized or "ingeniously contrived" the death or if he was understood to have been involved in a network of deeds popularly regarded as evil and had plotted his death in order to bring material benefits (Anderson 220–22). Outside of such descriptions, suicides generally went unpunished by juries and by popular opinion. According to Olive Anderson, by 1859, suicide in England was occasionally judged to be "thoroughly wicked," but was more often understood to have been committed in unsound mind, under the burden of difficult circumstances, producing "a sad ending which deserved pity and condonation" (218).

While suicide was reported regularly in a wide range of newspapers in both short notes and more extensive treatments, the novel was a form especially suited to reflect and to shape newly tolerant attitudes towards suicide. The post-Enlightenment revolution in morals had begun to transform "the old crude thrill offered by all violent deaths" into "a new chatty sentimental interest in the lives and endings of other people" (218). In short, suicide was in no way a taboo subject for Victorian novelists who treated it regularly, perhaps seeking to evoke the "horror and compassion so impressively blended" that characterizes Mr. Peggotty when he sees the fallen Martha at the river's edge in *David Copperfield* (*DC* 573). Though suicide often functioned as a plot device in sensation fiction and melodrama of the sixties and seventies, even spawning parodic humor as it became ever more predictable a feature, nonetheless, the social evils which originally sparked mid-century representations of suicide were direct and serious consequences of urbanization and industrialization.[10]

---

10. Anderson's work on suicide offers a wealth of relevant information. On comic treatments of suicide, see *Suicide* 207–213. As the urgency of the "Condition of England" question ran high, literary works joined ballads, plays, paintings, and illustrations in representing the suicide of the poor as part of the larger social problem of poverty. Working-class suicides were strategically depicted by artists but also by Chartists and anti–poor law campaigners as victims whose unbearable plight was considered to be best illustrated by the fact that they elected to give up their own lives rather than endure (202–5). Whereas compassion and forgiveness characterized the readerly (especially the lower-middle-class) relation to "Condition of England" suicides, fallen women and bankrupt men, such as Mr. Merdle in *Little Dorrit* (1857), Melmotte in Trollope's *The Way We Live Now* (1875), and Lopez in *The Prime Minister* (1876), evoked responses from sympathy to satisfaction. Though historical and the literary records part ways over whether sex was so all-determining a divider of suicidal motivation, literary suicides from the 1840s on tended to divide between male and female spheres (147).

Carton departs from the dominant trends in the depiction of suicide and even from Dickens' own participation in those trends.[11] Carton's alienation recalls Carlyle's *Sartor Resartus* which actively engaged the problem of Christianity's weakening hold: "'for man's well-being, Faith is properly the one thing needful . . . with it, Martyrs, otherwise weak, can cheerfully endure the shame and the cross; and without it, Worldlings pule-up their sick existence, by suicide'" (236). For Carlyle, whose *French Revolution* (1837) famously served Dickens as a great inspiration in *A Tale of Two Cities,* the contemporary loss of belief was the loss of everything.[12] Despite the novel's setting in the eighteenth century, the Victorian context marks Carton's "sick existence"—his "irresolute and purposeless" temper (*TTC* 137).

In fact, we can read the suicidal Carton in bleak confrontation with evangelicalism and utilitarianism, the two major philosophies by which Elie Halévy famously characterized the English nineteenth century. Dickens' own antipathy for the inhuman austerity of Mrs. Clennam-like evangelicalism is well known. Likewise, his horror at the Gradgrindian applications of utilitarian political economy remains among his most powerful social commentaries. At base, Dickens rejects vilified versions of both systems because of their tendency to dismiss individual happiness. If for evangelicalism, this-worldly suffering is the coin of the realm, for utilitarianism, the greatest happiness for the greatest number results in suffering that is made more terrible by the fact that under the rules of political economy, it becomes unworthy of note. What sort of happiness is it that pays no heed to keen suffering simply because that suffering belongs to a minority? In his penetrating exploration of the political violence of *A Tale of Two Cities,* John Bowen has shown how the novel dramatizes the confrontation between modes of counting and naming that expose the inescapable tension between irreducible singularity and the calculation of constituencies in democratic modernity. Drawing from Derrida, Bowen notes that the subjects of a democracy must recognize "the radical ethical obligation to the singular claim that the other makes upon me" even as all subjects must be equal and commensurable for the purposes of representation (114).

---

11. However, *A Tale of Two Cities* is of a piece with other representations of heroic self-sacrifice during the Revolution (Glancy 17–18). For other Dickensian suicides, see Ralph Nickleby in *Nicholas Nickleby* (1838), Jonas Chuzzlewit in *Martin Chuzzlewit* (1844), the attempted suicide, Martha, in *David Copperfield* (1850).

12. See Adams on the relation between the novel and Carlylean heroism (*Dandies* 52–60).

While Bowen convincingly demonstrates that this "wound" of irreconcilables structures the novel, his focus is not on Carton. Perhaps the suicidal Carton registers the wound not by reflecting the tension of being caught between opposing claims, but by uniting the claims in a profound emptying-out of self. The radical ethical obligation to the other—which we might link to evangelical selflessness—exerts its claim on Carton; at the same time, the sense of namelessness and replaceability by others—which we can link to utilitarianism—exerts a mutually reinforcing claim. At the nexus of these pressures, selflessness appears nearly inevitable, yet this is selflessness in its worst sense.

That sacrifice becomes Dickens' and Carton's recourse to a sacred rather than empty selflessness makes good sense. As Jonathan Kertzer has noted in a discussion comparing justice to sacrifice, while both systems depend on substitution, "justice is rational; sacrifice is mystical . . . a 'making holy' through unmerited grace" (46). It takes, as Kertzer suggests, a religious sensibility to "reclaim the exactitude obscured by general ideas by acknowledging the precious uniqueness of each soul" (107). For Dickens, who did not see the sacrifices of a self-punishing evangelical faith as affirming the uniqueness of souls and for whom utilitarianism absolutely negated the uniqueness of souls, Carton is a lost man. The novel foregrounds the absence of a vital religious faith that might help heal the difference between selflessness and ethical selfhood, that might sanctify the double consciousness of recognizing the other whose self is to him or her immediate and pressing and, at the same time, privileging the self because one *is* the self.

Sacrifice becomes an entry point to a world of meaning and identity. As Kertzer puts it, "justice satisfies [but] sacrifice blesses" (46). Carton, who works at the law, seeks something beyond justice. In an oft-quoted statement, Carton reflects on the impoverished nature of his life's work when he offers Lucie Manette his pledge: "'For you, and for any dear to you, I would do anything. If my career were of that better kind that there was any opportunity or capacity of sacrifice in it, I would embrace any sacrifice for you and for those dear to you'" (140).

As we explore Carton's path to self-sacrifice, I suggest that when Carton imagines "sacrifice" as a departure from his career, Dickens is using a familiar term in ways that differentiate it from much contemporary usage and re-charge it beyond its moral sense with a sense of the sacred.

If the move toward secularization in Victorian culture might be defined by Charles Taylor's claim that, for educated Victorians, there could no longer be a "naïve acknowledgment of the transcendent, or of goals and claims which go beyond human flourishing," we might see Carton's impulse toward sacrifice as a rejection of a world limited in such ways (21). Perhaps Carton's inclination to self-abnegating substitution and his incapability of exercising his own talents on his own behalf reflect the difficulty of human flourishing for its own sake, particularly in a context where flourishing so often meant "driving and riving and shouldering and pressing, to that restless degree": in short, being a Stryver, like Carton's business associate (*TTC* 81). Carton, whom Dickens describes in simple, rather heartbreaking terms, as a "man of good abilities and good emotions, incapable of their directed exercise, incapable of his own help and his own happiness," refuses to answer Stryver's command to assume "'energy and purpose'" (80). "'Oh, botheration!' returned Sydney, with a lighter and more good-humoured laugh, "'don't you be moral!'" (81).

Paradoxically, Carton's flourishing is inhibited by the sense that no greater purifying principle co-exists with the reigning worldly imperatives of professional life. If sacrifice were to mean something simply moral, Carton's career might indeed offer him opportunities, since, as Jennifer Ruth has argued, the mid-Victorians invested in an idea of the professional life as a form of sacrifice. Yet Carton is not searching for "sacrifice" in that mode of self-effacing service borrowed from contemporary domestic ideology. Neither does he aspire to the mid-century codes of self-discipline that took shape in the ethic of "self-help": the rational, self-improving, pursuit of profit. Carton is more than indifferent to money, position, and advancement, a world made civil and polite through "the orderly exchange of services actuated by mutual interest" (Taylor *Secular Age* 230). We might say that the middle-class moral ethic of self-sacrifice has been tainted for Carton by its reduction to a code of conduct, its domestication, so to speak, from a mode of excess and violence that is inseparable from its inexplicable but assured meaning. Carton's heroics at the novel's end, his "everlasting YEA," suggest Dickens' refusal of a world sufficient onto itself, where human flourishing can take place without the transcendent, without sin and grace. As we will see, alongside sacrifice, it is grace that Dickens redefines, imagining salvation as human, collective, and tragically too late for this world.

Carton's final salvation is routed through the fundamentally religious concept that so seized Dickens' imagination: Christ's role as a substitute, guiltless among the guilty, paying their ransom and redeeming them from sin.[13] Moving away from vilified versions of both evangelicalism and utili-

---

13. Here I contest Levine's claim that Dickens had a "pervasively secular imagination,"

tarianism, Dickens transforms the mechanisms of substitution and interchangeability to fuse a humanist sense of collective ethical responsibility
with a Christian sense of transcendent morality. In this way, he resolves
the anomie productive of suicide and provides an impetus for effective self-
sacrifice, at least in fiction.[14]

Substitution and Its Risks

Though the notion of substitution allowed for the great achievement of
Christian redemption, Dickens and his contemporaries were absorbed
by the ethical risks substitution could pose. As Jan-Melissa Schramm
has explored, the Atonement controversy of the 1850s renewed vigor-
ous discussion about the precise nature of Christ's "substitution" for a
fallen humanity, with Broad Church theologians working to distance
the discourse from a literal understanding of Christ as vicariously expi-
ating others' sins before a God insensitive to the injustice of a debt-payment rendered by one guiltless. For theologians, jurists, and historians, as
well as proponents and critics of utilitarianism and capitalism, questions
of human interchangeability were both daunting and demanding at mid-
century. In *A Tale of Two Cities,* Dickens most clearly dramatizes the costs
to seeing human lives as indistinguishable and interchangeable in the blind
vengeance of the Revolutionaries, the cruel oppression of the pre-Revolu-
tionary aristocracy, and the overt and covert violence of the British legal
and banking systems. Vicarious identification becomes most disturbing in
the novel when it blurs the lines of personal accountability, punishing those
who are innocent of the crimes for which they are accused.

Yet vicarious identification also affords the powerful redemptive ending of the novel: Carton for Darnay, sacrifice for suicide. My focus here
is on the ways that Dickens transformed violent forms of personal interchangeability in service of a new narrative of Christian redemptive substitution. Two forms of violence, rivalry and self-hatred, I suggest, attended
his sense of men as potentially interchangeable. Violent interchangeability could yield to its redemptive form—self-sacrifice on behalf of others—
only when men could balance the tension between their singularity and

though I agree with his sense of the sharp tension in Dickens' novels between a "wished-for
Christian ideal" and the impossibility of its achievement ("Dickens" 17).

14. Dickens thus participates in what Taylor describes as the "nova" effect: "the mul-
tiplication of new options around the polemic between belief and unbelief" (*Secular Age*
391–92).

interchangeability. Dickens takes up this tension when he makes *A Tale of Two Cities* a novel abundant in "others," particularly in others that are "similar . . . though with a subtle difference" (*TTC* 263). It is this subtle difference, as René Girard reminds us, that makes sacrificial substitution possible. The resemblance is close enough to allow one person to stand in for another, yet divergent enough to avoid what Girard calls "the extreme of complete assimilation" in which the sacrificial substitution loses its meaning and effectiveness (*Violence and the Sacred* 11).

Of the many non-identical twinned characters in the novel, Sydney Carton and Charles Darnay play the central roles.[15] But the novel establishes Darnay's father, too, as a twin, the brother of the stone-hearted Marquis, with Darnay rhetorically asking whether it is possible to "separate my father's twin-brother, joint inheritor, and next successor, from himself?" (113). The inset piece that narrates the crime of the Evrémonde brothers, "The Substance of the Shadow," makes it exceptionally difficult to keep track of which brother is responsible for what and which is Charles' father. Yet the narrative contents, the distinctive appellation "elder brother" for one of the twins, and the specification that one is the "worst of the bad race" divide between the two (305). When it comes to Carton and Darnay, the sheer, coincidental physical similarity of the two men allows Carton to save Darnay's life twice. However, that very similarity serves to underscore their enormous differences in outlook and fortune. Dickens' descriptive phrase, "*so like* each other in feature, *so unlike* each other in manner" (70), stresses the force that difference bears when it attends on similarity or repetition. Such oppositions within sameness—where the difference of one word, or as above, even one morpheme, means all the difference in the world—characterize Dickens' prose throughout *A Tale of Two Cities*, as in his opening sentences, beginning with, "It was the best of times, it was the worst of times" (1) or Carton's minimizing response to Darnay's important observation that it is a shame he has not used his talents better, "'may be *so* . . . may be *not*'" (76, emphases mine).

The novel goes back and forth between seeing men as twins—interchangeable, easily capable of substituting for each other—and seeing them as distinct from each other. Carton, described as Darnay's "Double of coarse deportment" (75), bears enough raw physical resemblance to Darnay to save his life twice, yet because of Carton's "reckless" and Darnay's

---

15. The novel also features double identities, for example, Barsad/Solomon Pross, and inter-generational resemblances between Dr. Manette and Lucie, and then between Lucie and her golden-haired children, as well as between Jerry Cruncher and his son in the more comic sections. On familial resemblance and relations, see Miller *Burdens of Perfection* 202–5.

"earnest" manner, the two at times look nothing alike (68). Just as Darnay and Carton's resemblance comes and goes under differing circumstances so that onlookers cannot quite believe they have witnessed its striking power (68), that of the Evrémonde brothers shifts in and out of focus as well (299).[16] Miller aptly describes the phenomenon as follows: "Dickens presents his characters as part of a psychosocial world in which the tension between individualism and the abstracting powers of exchange is intensely felt: even as I can conceive of myself as unique, I also have the pressing sense that others can stand for me" (162).

This double sense—singularity on one hand, interchangeability on the other—quickly takes on moral qualities in Dickens. At the point when Charles is in prison, the novel fosters our recognition that Charles is distinct, the one with whom we are concerned and utterly like all the other unfortunates who remain nameless. The form of the novel plays upon this tension of interchangeability and the audience's complicity in its limits.[17] This moral tension is made explicit when we are told that Lucie prays "the solemn prayer at night for one dear prisoner especially, among the many unhappy souls in prison and the shadow of death" (257) or that "it was so impossible to forget that many as blameless as her husband and as dear to others as he was to her, every day shared the fate from which he had been clutched, that her heart could not be as lightened of its load as she felt it ought to be" (268). Lucie's discomfort at Charles' uniqueness—a uniqueness understandable with respect to his wife—comes from knowing that others are uniquely dear to *their* wives and loved ones.

While Lucie finds empathy and instructive guilt from this work of imaginative substitution in which she is (momentarily) the more fortunate party, readers of Dickens know that, more often, imaginative substitution results in rivalry, as it does in the case of Carton and Darnay.[18] Miriam Bailin has usefully noted the centrality of narratives of rivalry in Victorian literature and argued that they can be explained by the unprecedented social mobility of the period which encouraged an equally unprecedented

---

16. See Ferguson (2005), especially pp. 66–69, for a rich discussion of the "waxing and waning" of similarity and the relation between "indistinctness" and "exceptionalism" in relation to the novel's representation of identity under the reign of terror (61).

17. See Herbert, *War of No Pity* 220; Alexander Welsh, *City of Dickens* 127–28; and Alex Woloch's (2004) book-length account of the privileging of the one over the many.

18. Miller has argued that the technical strategy of substitution represents the way that, for Dickens, "individual experience is routed through others, near and far," so that "one discovers who one is through the recognition of others" (*Burdens* 163). Yet such a formulation suggests mainly a positive interdependence between human beings, while in *TTC*, the recognition of others results at least as frequently in rivalry and self-loathing.

tendency toward comparison of position. This kind of comparison—a flipside of the sympathetic identification described by moral theorists following Adam Smith and prescribed by Victorian writers as the foundation for moral feeling and action—produced intensely unsociable passions such as envy: "While the increasingly democratic society of nineteenth-century Britain may have facilitated identification with others and thus the ability to see another's misfortunes as one's own, it also encouraged the tendency to see another's fortunes as one's due" (Bailin 1022). Carton's competitive relation to Darnay, focused on Lucie's unattainable love and his own unrealized potential, is most memorably and clearly expressed when Carton and Darnay drink together after Darnay's English trial (*TTC* 76). Ironically, what Carton competitively yearns for is the sympathetic identification with which Lucie favors Darnay: "'That's a fair young lady to be pitied by and wept for by! How does it feel? Is it worth being tried for one's life, to be the object of such sympathy and compassion, Mr. D?'" (75). Carton's own wishful identification with Darnay is not only inseparable from fierce rivalry, but leads directly into the hatred for his double that Carton admits to himself: "'Have it out in plain words! You hate the fellow'" (77). But, in a twist that transforms the simple rivalry of the novel, Carton's speech is made facing his own image in the glass. Carton hates Darnay, but he also hates himself: "'Do you particularly like the man? . . . why should you particularly like a man who resembles you? There is nothing in you to like: you know that.'" Then, quickly, the transposition: "'Have it out in plain words! You hate the fellow!'" (76).

The novel's tragic but redemptive ending—Carton's renunciation of his life for Darnay and Lucie—demands interpretation after the antipathy and self-hatred of earlier scenes. Likewise, its model, Christ's redemptive substitution, begs deeper analysis in light of the anti-sociality of some Dickensian substitution. Bailin argues that sentimental plots such as the ending to *A Tale of Two Cities* offered a way to neutralize rivalry, to "transmute . . . the powerful energies of rivalrous vengeance into the powerful energies required to renounce them" (1025). In other words, the rivalry does not go away; it is simply channeled into competitive renunciation.[19] While Darnay gets Lucie in life, Carton can die satisfied that he has bested Darnay in one thing at least: he has out-sacrificed him. And as numerous critics have noted, Carton imagines himself as no less a part of Lucie and Darnay's thoughts than their thoughts of each other. My own understand-

---

19. As Kucich has pointed out in the fullest analysis of the dynamic, "Carton's 'self-sacrifice,' far from transcending structures of rivalry, actually operates within them" (*Excess and Restraint* 132).

ing of the novel does not emphasize the rivalry still present at the novel's end but identifies a heroism that undoes the structures of rivalry without denying them. Dickens' heroism balances the tension between human singularity and interchangeability, a tension with its roots in Christ's singular interchangeability, and replaces rivalry with a notion of the spiritual interdependence of human individuals who do not best each other, but instead complete each other.

The twinnings mentioned above were Dickens' most explicit way of considering the relation between singularity and interchangeability but he also used the trope of "another," or "another man," to address this problem.[20] In *A Tale of Two Cities*, "another" prompts not only the consideration of human interchangeability, but also a common standard of human "goodness," founded by comparison. Dickens announces at the very outset of his novel the difficulties of judging beyond the "superlative degree of comparison" (1). True to its word, the novel ends rendering even Carton's heroism in comparative terms: "It is a far, far better thing . . . it is a far, far better rest" (352), helping us to recognize exactly what a "superlative degree of comparison" might look like beyond the satirical play of paradox. Yet Carton's comparison is with himself: "'It is a far, far better thing that I do, than I have ever done; it is a far, far better rest that I go to than I have ever known.'" We will return to this final statement of Carton's, but we can better understand it if we consider the kinds of discourse that precede it. Carton's self-comparison comes as the apotheosis to the novel's treatment of comparisons *among* men that fail to balance the tension between their singularity and interchangeability.

The novel frequently describes men as interchangeably adequate but undermines that description by revealing them to be singularly good or well-suited for their circumstances. This pattern suggests that singular goodness must be reconstituted against a different model than neutral interchangeability. In the following three examples, "goodness" and "another" are linked in paradoxical ways that suggest that one can evaluate one's goodness—the capacity for bringing good to others—only in being "as good as" or "better" than "another." Singular goodness seems elusive at best. In the first of three examples, Mr. Stryver, claiming credit for Carton's ingenuity at Darnay's English trial, offers, "'I have done

---

20. Rosemarie Bodenheimer addresses Dickens' novelistic and epistolary treatment of doubles and trios of men. She notes Dickens' trope of "another man" and reads those "others" as versions of the self that exceed the limitations of reality (*Knowing Dickens* 125). See Bowen on the place of numbers, great and small, in the novel.

my best for you, Mr. Darnay; and my best is as good as another man's, I believe'" (72). In the course of the conversation that ensues, Mr. Lorry defends himself as a man of business and Carton responds, "'don't be nettled, Mr. Lorry. You are as good as another, I have no doubt: better, I dare say'" (73). In the oddest manifestation of this pattern, much later in the novel, when Lucie inadvertently tells her father that had she never met Charles, she would have been content to remain alone with her father, Dr. Manette replies, "'If it had not been Charles, it would have been another'" (173). And in disclosing his love for Lucie to Manette, Charles expresses an anxiety of comparison: "'I have felt . . . that to bring my love . . . between you, is to touch your history with something not quite so good as itself'" (122). In some unspecifiable way, Manette's history threatens to preclude Charles' suitability as Lucie's next protector.

The passages quoted above at first seem to indicate the fungibility of social life—one man should be able to stand in for another, to do another's good work, easily and effectively, to match one's history with another's— but, in the end, each example fails. Stryver's best, of course, is not as good as another man's, because it *is* another man's. And Carton's quick thinking is second to none. Mr. Lorry cannot be replaced for any other loyal servant (at the very end of the novel, Carton will reverse himself, telling Mr. Lorry that the final escape "'will depend on you and it could depend on no better man'" [321]). And though Charles may in fact be the single person Lucie should not marry, he is also the single person she *must* marry if the novel is to unfold.[21] These passages thus leave the tension between singularity and interchangeability in place; they suggest how compromised the notion of *sheer* interchangeability is, how much it leaves to be worked out in its wake, yet they insist on its value, at the very least as a heuristic.

---

21. The novel has already made entirely explicit that Charles could not be another by setting up both Carton and Stryver as possible but impossible suitors for Lucie. When Darnay asks if there is "any other suitor," and Dr. Manette names both Stryver and Carton, then says, "one of these" and Darnay replies, "Or both," the difference between "either" or "both" simply redraws a kind of Venn diagram of interchangeability, reiterating the problem of Stryver and Carton's interchangeability with each other against their shared interchangeability with Darnay (124). Later on, when the relation between the Evrémonde and the Manette families is revealed, Charles himself says simply, "'It could not be otherwise,'" expressing the prevailing sense of relentless historical inevitability that Dickens interwove with novelistic plot. The possibility of "otherwise" is also negated by Carton, when he dictates his final letter to Lucie and insists three times that nothing would have changed, "'If it had been otherwise'" (329). See Miller *Burdens* 191–218 on the "optative" nature of Dickens' writing in gesturing to lives that might have been led, as well as Bodenheimer *Knowing Dickens* 90–125.

Christ-like Singularity: From Manette to Carton

In one case and, appropriately, one case only, the novel builds a case for human singularity. It is not Carton, whom we might expect to be described as singular given his heroic self-sacrifice, but Dr. Manette whom the novel labors to describe as singular. Yet when Carton assumes the place of hero at the novel's end, saving Darnay when Manette has painfully failed to do so, the novel clearly decouples heroism from singularity. The novel depicts in Carton a singularity limited and constituted by the capacity for interchangeability: Carton becomes the Christ-like hero not because he is unique—though he is—but because he is the one who can stand in for another. Before Carton becomes the hero of the novel, however, Manette stands as the likely possessor of that title. Manette's singularity is signaled most strongly by the refusal of the "as good as another" trope. In a novel, as we have said, concerned with the "superlative degree of comparison" (1), a novel that uses the term "better," ninety times, Manette is simply . . . best. His singularity is a kind of supremacy which brooks no question: "*A more remarkable face* in its quiet, resolute, and guarded struggle with an unseen assailant, *was not to be beheld* in all the wide dominions of sleep, that night" (176, emphases mine). When Manette returns to Paris to rescue Darnay, the narrator again attests to his distinction:

> No *man* better known than he, in Paris at that day; *no man* in a stranger situation. Silent, humane, indispensable in hospital and prison, using his art equally among assassins and victims, *he was a man apart*. In the exercise of his skill, the appearance and the story of the Bastille Captive removed him *from all other men*. He was not suspected or brought in question, any more than if he had indeed been recalled to life some eighteen years before, or were a Spirit moving among mortals. (256, emphases mine)

This short passage notes Manette's distinction from all others four times. Later, Darnay concurs, saying, "'No other man in all this France could have done what he has done for me'" (268). Yet what Manette has done is immediately undone.

What affords Manette his distinction and separates him from all other men seems to be the fact that he has died already. The language of the first passage recalls a struggle with death, the "unseen assailant" of Manette's sleeping calm, and the following passage explicitly imagines him as "a Spirit moving among mortals." The notion that death is what distinguishes between men, even twins, is present elsewhere in the novel as well, when Darnay asks his uncle, the Marquis, "'Can I separate my father's twin-brother, joint inheritor, and next successor, from himself,'" and the Marquis replies, "'Death has done that!'" (113). Likewise, the knowledge that people are distinct and secret from one another is referred to death as well (9). Death divides between the dead and the living even as it renders those dead or dying all alike: we see this with the seamstress and Carton, "these two children of the Universal Mother, else so wide apart and differing, have come together on the dark highway, to repair home together" (350), and we see it in the fear of the peasant woman that the grass will grow over graves, leaving them indecipherable one from the other (107, 116). Manette's extraordinary distinction, then, is not that he has died, but that he has returned to life. Lazarus-like, he has been dead, and come back, and this renders him untouchable and singular in a way that the novel suggests is moral, but also, ontological. Manette's function as a doctor, treating "all degrees of mankind, bond and free, rich and poor, bad and good" (253), "using his art equally among assassins and victims" (256), reminds us, too, of his detachment from the distinctions of this world.

Manette's singularity is signaled as well by repeated narrations of what the passage above calls the "story" of the Bastille Captive. In a novel where no other men have a significant enough history for extended narration—not Carton, not Darnay, not Ernest Defarge, not Mr. Lorry or Jerry Cruncher or Stryver—Manette's past alone merits extended, detailed narrative accounts, not once but three separate times. Twice Mr. Lorry tells Manette's story, first to Lucie, then to Manette himself. In both instances, Mr. Lorry tells Manette's story as if it is the story of someone else, anonymous, yet with defining characteristics. In the first case, the story is of a customer, and in the second case, a very dear friend. Yet the paradoxical effect of telling the story as if it is that of "another man," is that it reinforces the sense that it can be the story of one man only. At the opening of the novel, Mr. Lorry faces the delicate task of conveying to Lucie, who has long understood her father to be dead, the news of her father's having been recalled to life. Mr. Lorry narrates as if telling the story of "one of our customers" (19). The disguise is as thin as Mr. Lorry's claims to all absence of feeling, and Lucie quickly interrupts, "'But this is my father's story, sir'" (19). Mr. Lorry concedes that it is her father's story but when he comes to the painful history of her father's disappearance, he again pretends that he is telling the story of another man: "'Now comes the difference. If your father had not died when he did—Don't be frightened! How you start!'" (20). The series of "if"s go on to describe precisely Manette's history, only to end, "'then the history of your father would have been the history of this unfortunate gentleman, the Doctor of Beauvais'" (21). After Mr. Lorry concedes that Dr. Manette is indeed the very same unfortunate gentleman, Lucie's reaction, before freezing into senselessness, is to say, "'I am going to see his Ghost! It will be his Ghost—not him!'" (21), as if absorbing Mr. Lorry's imagination of a shadow-man, a twin of sorts, to her father's actual self.

The narrative repeatedly "twins" Dr. Manette, for instance, when Darnay tells a legend-like version of the discovery of Manette's imperative, "DIG." At first, its finders take the inscription of the three letters, wrongly construed as "DIC," as its author's initials. But there is no DIC and so, eventually, they re-construe the letters correctly, as a word, rather than as a set of letters indicating a man's name. Again, there is some "other man" besides Manette, here, D.I.C. Yet despite these alienated or doubled versions of Manette, the notable effect is that his identity is intensely consolidated: he is indeed nobody but himself, precisely because of his period of imprisonment, the part of his history that can only be narrated as if it happened to another, the part of his history that renders him a Ghost or a Spirit. It is his death-in-life, or life-in-death, that makes Manette none other than himself and unlike all others.

At what point, then, does Manette lose this singularity, its efficacy, and his claim to being the hero of the novel? Manette's efficacy fails him immediately after Charles is freed from the Bastille, as a result of Manette's great efforts and to his pride. At the moment of greatest relief, a messenger appears to reclaim Charles and to explain the reversal: "'He is denounced—and gravely—by the Citizen and Citizeness Defarge. And by one *other*.' 'What *other*?' 'Do *you* ask, Citizen Doctor?'" (273, first two emphases mine). In tragic fashion, this unidentified "other" is Manette himself. For the first time, he becomes like all those the novel is willing to see in company with "others"; he is like Carton—who is like Darnay who is himself assimilated to his father and uncle; like Jerry Cruncher—who is like his son; like Ernest Defarge—one of a trio of Jacques, and so on. What follows this shift away from singularity is the most important element of Manette's history, the set of events that constitute the novel's all-determining pre-history. In the inset chapter, "The Substance of the Shadow," Manette's story is told in his own voice, but alienated to the court reader who holds the document Manette penned as a prisoner in his cell (354).

Manette loses his efficacious singularity when his story is recounted because it is, in fact, a story of losing oneself in violent identification. The story Manette tells is the story of not one, but two crimes: one committed against him, his unjust incarceration, and one committed against a young girl who is raped and ceaselessly cries, "'My husband, my father, and my brother!'" (300), as she lies dying with brain fever. In Manette's version of the story, he busies himself tending to the girl, unaware that the brother to whom she refers is also present, wounded and dying. Then he is told, "'There is another patient'" (301). "Another" patient then tells his story, a tale of oppression and violence that leaves heightened realism and even intense melodrama behind, to border on the gothic (Koch 354). Here, Manette begins to lose his individuality when the brother as witness and Manette-as-witness coalesce in the re-telling. First, Manette gives voice to the brother's story; the brother's narrating voice takes over where Manette leaves off, then leaves off where Manette resumes. Additionally, multiple times, the novel stresses the circumstantial similarities in Manette's laborious writing from his cell, with an ink made partially of blood, and the unnamed brother's laborious telling from his bloodied deathbed. About the boy, Manette says, "'Nothing human could have held life in the boy but his determination to tell all his wrong. He forced back the gathering shadows of death, as he forced his clenched right hand to remain clenched, and to cover his wound'" (304). Then, in first-person: "'I am weary, weary, weary . . . I cannot read what I have written with this gaunt hand'" (308); "'I am growing more and more unequal to the task I have set myself'" (308).

The merging of narrator and narrated marks Manette's document. The tale the brother tells is of a race of nobles who have cruelly oppressed their tenants, raped his sister, brutalized and tortured her husband to his death, and effectively murdered her father with the knowledge of what has transpired. The brother fights back by drawing a sword against one of the Evrémonde brothers, and forcing upon him the ignobility of defending himself against a peasant. As the brother's narrative and his life come to a close, he curses the Evrémonde race: "'in the days when all these things are to be answered for, I summon you and yours, to the last of your bad race, to answer for them. I mark this cross of blood upon you, as a sign that I do it'" (305). He adds that he summons the brother who is the worst of the race—the rapist himself—"'to answer . . . separately'" and draws another cross in the air to mark the second brother who is not present in the room as he dies. When Manette comes to the end of his narration, that curse becomes his own, for a reason that he makes quite specific: in all the years of his imprisonment, the brothers grant him no "'tidings of my dearest wife . . . whether alive or dead'" (310). Like the dying brother, Manette is outraged by the nobles' scorn for the sanctity of others' marriages and their insensibility to a man's love for his wife. Independent of the dying brother's curse, Manette charges, "'But, now I believe that the mark of the red cross is quite fatal to them, and that they have no part in His mercies. And them and their descendants, to the last of their race, I, Alexandre Manette, unhappy prisoner, do this last night of the year 1767, in my unbearable agony, denounce to the times when all these things shall be answered for. I denounce them to Heaven and to earth'" (310).

Manette's singularity is undone in this story of his becoming a twin to the young man identified solely as "the brother," adopting the curse in the language of the brother. And the dangers of thorough twinning become apparent as those sitting in the courtroom themselves take on a collective consciousness characterized by a thirst for blood. Manette's mimetic relation to the brother leaps its bounds. His desire for vengeance, born of the brother's desire for vengeance and heightened by the twin brothers' depriving him of his wife, breeds the crowd's desire for vengeance. As Girard puts it in his study of the mechanism of the scapegoat, "mimeticism inevitably becomes unanimous," gathering intensity as it goes (Girard 145). As the novel describes it,

> A terrible sound arose when the reading of this document was done. A sound of craving and eagerness that had nothing articulate in it but blood. The narrative called up the most revengeful passions of the time, and *there was not a head* in the nation but must have dropped before it. . . . *The man never trod ground* whose virtues and services would have sustained him in that place that day, against such denunciation. (310–11, emphases mine)

As the crowd ceases to be made of individuals and becomes nothing but wordless, audible desire—the "sound of craving and eagerness"—the logic turns from "another" man and another man and another man, to that of "no man," as in the phrasings, "there was not a head," "the man never trod ground." This time, Manette's human singularity is undone rather than confirmed by this trope. With the mimetic desire for vengeance, Manette ceases to be incomparable in the way that Girard describes the Christ of the Gospels as incomparable:

> One can call him an incomparable victim without any sentimental piety or suspect emotion. He is incomparable in that he never succumbs in any way, at any point, to the perspective of the persecutor—neither in a positive way, by openly agreeing with his executioners, nor in a negative way, by taking a position of vengeance, which is none other than the inverse

reproduction of the original representation of persecution, its mimetic repetition. (*Scapegoat* 126)

Manette's violence cancels out his singularity because his desire merges
with the desire of all others.

And in this bloodthirsty merging of all men, it is not incidental that the
denouncer Manette and the denounced Darnay now become indistinguishable, too, and their fates one (united through their shared object of desire,
Lucie). The chapter ends with Madame Defarge mocking Manette's power-
lessness, "'Save him now, my Doctor, save him!'" though it is Darnay, not
Manette, whom the narrative describes as the "doomed man" (311). Both
are lost in the tableau of vengeance which is mimetic rivalry at its most
basic and most extended manifestation. Neither is guilty: Charles himself is
only a substitute for the Marquis and his father. Saver and saved are both
lost, to violence within and without. Manette's failed singularity yields here
to Carton's doubling heroism. Manette's Christ-like "unbearable agony,"
his testament, his healing touch, and his love for Lucie yield now to Carton's Christ-like end.

For as we have said, Christ himself is nothing but a substitute; at the
same time, He is *the* substitute. His singularity is the effect of his inimitable self-sacrifice in which he exchanges his merit for the guilty debt of
sinners. He willingly takes the punishment in their stead. At the point
when Manette and the brother refuse to identify with the guiltless, suffering Christ and instead elect vengeance and violence; at the point when
Charles Darnay is not free to *elect*, but can only submit to being sacrificed,
Carton elects the identification. It is an identification waiting to be made.
First, Carton's singularity comes, when it comes, from his talent at becoming "another." Early in the novel, when he saves Darnay for the first time,
Carton is described as merely "another person" approaching the group of
main characters who have no idea what a service he has provided (73), and
a little further on, his capacity for anonymity, for self-canceling substitution, is signaled by the term "other" referring first to him, then to those he
serves, with the ironic touch that his sameness over time, his Sydney-ness,
consists in that very other-ness: "'Ah!' returned the *other*, sighing: 'yes! The
same Sydney, with the same luck. Even then, I did exercises for *other* boys,
and seldom did my own'" (80, emphases mine).

Carton finally emerges heroic because of his willingness to be someone other than himself, a willingness resulting as much from rivalry or
antipathy as from sympathy, as we have seen. Kucich effectively reads this
substitutional tendency in Carton to represent a general preoccupation of

Dickens. If for critics such as Bailin and Rosemarie Bodenheimer, Carton desires a different life narrative, Kucich sees in Carton a related, but wider phenomenon: the apotheosis of "a non-specific, primary desire for radical release from limits [that] dominates the very texture of Dickens' novel" ("Purity" 121). When Carton does other boys' exercises, or Stryver's work—or, for that matter, plays Darnay to the death—and refuses credit for it, he rejects the code of self-interest, refuses the banality of economic survival, and uncovers beneath the artificiality of the business world "the profounder reality of death" (122). "Carton's dissipation is presented as the metaphysical crisis over limitations, and not as the vulgarity of the idle bum" (121), says Kucich. But the difficulty with that crisis over limitations is that the pure wish for release becomes tainted when it touches others, when the limitations transgressed are not one's own, but others' (129). Violence is born here, in the desire for release, excess, and change. Carton, then, serves an extraordinarily important function in the novel because he turns inward the violence that elsewhere in the novel is directed outward. And this self-violence, in turn, is transformed by its simultaneously life-sustaining effect. To put it simply, instead of murdering the double who shows him what he might have been, Carton saves him by offering up his own failed self to be murdered. As Kucich notes, the only violence in the novel that the reader can fully affirm is Carton's against himself.

Yet can we fully affirm it? If so, we return here to the deeply problematic resemblance between suicide and self-sacrifice. True, Carton's self-violence might be preferable to the prevailing tendency toward vengeance and vicarious punishment in both the novel's domestic and historical plots, but can the novel suggest nothing better than self-hatred as the basis for self-sacrificial heroism? The troubling notion that Carton's heroism is inseparable from his suicidal drive is reinforced by the fact that the novel makes one of its few explicit references to suicide just as Carton begins to emerge heroic. As Carton lays the groundwork with Mr. Lorry for his rescue of Darnay, he tells Mr. Lorry not to let Lucie know that he will visit Darnay in his cell because "she might think it was contrived, in case of the worst, to convey to him the means of anticipating the sentence" (288). This passage links Carton not only to suicide but to the homicide of his double; and both links are made in the transformative moments of Carton's career. Is self-sacrifice merely sublimated violence against the self or its others?

In the novel's depiction of the heroic, we appear to be left with a choice between two unsatisfying choices. On one hand, we have Carton's suicidal self-hatred. On the other hand, we have Manette and Darnay who suggest a failed Crucifixion. They are two guiltless, wrongly accused men who cannot save others or themselves, but they, unlike Carton, do not suffer from self-hatred. In fact, both men experience some pride that the novel hastens to assure us is "natural and worthy," rather than morally culpable (253). They see themselves as capable of influencing a mad revolution that the novel also states definitively is well beyond the influence of any one man: Manette seeks to save Darnay and Darnay seeks to save Gabelle. As Herbert puts it, Darnay's attempt to save Gabelle reveals "the ludicrous futility of the protagonist's deluded attempt at heroic action" (*War of No Pity* 220). But Gabelle faithlessly turns on Darnay and Manette's own past betrays his present. When it comes to Manette and Darnay, the old Christian model of a sinless Christ dying redemptively for the sins of others does not work since Manette has vowed vengeance on Darnay. What model, then, does the novel put in its place? In Carton, we seem to be left with a modern, self-hating Christ: a man who accurately gauges the evil of the world, sees himself as incapable of any good, and courts his own death. Is that what saves in the mid-nineteenth century? Is it Carton's guilt, rather than guiltlessness, which now effectively atones?

From Suicide to Self-Sacrifice: Sin as the Sacred

Carton's guilt—the opposite of a natural pride and an optimistic trust in the world's goodness—is deeply mysterious and, at the same time, central to the novel's transformation of suicidal despair into noble self-sacrifice. Although the evangelical emphasis on Original Sin yielded in the second half of the century, the sense of the flawed, weak nature of humanity was not an inheritance easily abandoned. As mid-century theologians wrestled with the mechanism of atonement, Victorians who were not able to believe in Christian salvation by grace found themselves worried gravely about the problem of evil in the world and the sufficiency of human resources, resources upon which they now considered themselves and others to depend solely. In Dickens' Carton, we can see the reflection of a man who has convicted himself with no means of expiation.

Carton's guilt is the salient fact about him as the novel gets closer and closer to his transformation. The novel offers us little by way of his personal history. We know nothing of Carton except for his tendency to do his school fellows' work instead of his own (this is the emptying-out of self I described earlier), and his "fam[e] among his competitors as a youth of great promise" (292). He is orphaned early, losing his mother well before his father. But after that, a gap. We expect a story of descent, yet all we get is the depiction of a man who drinks a great deal, which appears to be a symptom of his degraded condition as much as it constitutes the condition. How can we account for a man whom the novel depicts as past redeeming, who is, by his own description, capable of nothing good, when in fact the deeds which supposedly render him so are no where recorded? Consider Scrooge in *A Christmas Carol* (1843) as a contrast: we know exactly what his moral failings are, and miraculously, they are reparable. But *A Tale of Two Cities* is not about moral rehabilitation in the way that *A Christmas Carol* is, not least, because Carton dies before he can fill his life and those of others' with the benefits of his good works.

Carton, however, is not a moral exemplar. I suggest instead that he indicates the profound difference between Victorian moral commitment and the religious sensibility. As Schramm notes, in representing Carton, Dickens faced a major challenge that makes little sense in the context of a rational morality: "he must be good enough to choose self-sacrifice, unanimously upheld as the highest Christian virtue of the period, and yet simultaneously must have no worth independent of that magnanimous gift" (166–67). Carton's simultaneous worthlessness and "goodness" (not a light term for Victorians) make him difficult to draw, since they exceed realist norms of representation and lend themselves more to allegory. Deeply good and thoroughly worthless, Carton is the novel's man of sin and man of holiness. Carton becomes more intelligible when we make recourse to the early twentieth-century theologian Rudolf Otto's distinction between the religious disposition and the moral in *The Idea of the Holy* (1917), his path-breaking phenomenology of the religious experience that comments so aptly on Victorian experience:

> In every highly-developed religion the appreciation of moral obligation and duty, ranking as a claim of the deity upon man, has been developed side by side with the religious feeling itself. None the less a profoundly humble and heartfelt recognition of "the holy" may occur in particular experiences without being always or definitely charged or infused with the sense of moral demands. (51)

The novel's insistent description of Carton's degradation strangely positions him in a fundamentally religious framework in which "moral demands" are, on some level, beside the point. In Carton's critical interview with Lucie, when she suggests reasonably that he might improve, that he might change, he answers, "'It is too late for that. I shall never be better than I am. I shall sink lower, and be worse'" (137). He possesses, the novel tells us, a "fixed despair of himself" (138) and the language of "worth" (melting into "worse") repeats, with Sydney at each juncture insisting that he is not worthy, that he cannot be worthier, that his life is worth less than nothing (139–40). All Lucie's promptings fail to recognize that Carton's self-abasement goes beyond the realm of action to ontology. To her sincere commonplaces, "'I am sure that you might be much, much worthier of yourself,'" Carton can only respond, "'I know better'" (138). "Better" echoes painfully here, as Carton opposes the strength of his presumed self-knowledge with the weakness of its object.

In such statements, Carton reflects the Victorian preoccupation with the force of sin. In a particularly powerful but representative utterance, William Gladstone wrote of his belief "in sin—in the intensity and virulence of sin. No other religion than Xtianity meets the sense of sin, & sin is the great fact in the world to me" (as qtd. in Peterson 451). Three-quarters of a century later, Otto could describe this perception of human sinfulness in phenomenological terms as a profound devaluation of the self:

> It is not based on deliberation, nor does it follow any rule, but breaks, as it were, palpitant from the soul. . . . It does not spring from the consciousness of some committed transgression, but rather is an immediate datum given with the feeling of the numen: it proceeds to "disvalue" together with the self the tribe to which the person belongs, and indeed, together with that, all existence in general. . . . [T]hese outbursts of feeling are not simply, and probably at first not at all, *moral* depreciations, but belong to a quite special category of valuation and appraisement. The feeling is beyond question not that of the transgression of the moral law, however evident it may be that such a transgression, where it has occurred, will involve it as a consequence: it is the feeling of absolute "profaneness."
> (50–51)

Carton possesses that ontological sense of profaneness. It is "a judgment passed, not upon his character, because of individual 'profane' actions of his, but upon his own very existence as creature" (51). The sense of sin is impossible, says Otto, with merely a moral sense of having committed an unlawful act. Sin becomes sin only when the sense of what he calls "numinous unworthiness" or "disvalue" attaches to the act, "And only when the mind feels it as 'sin' does the transgression of law become a matter of such dreadful gravity for the conscience, a catastrophe that leads it to despair of its own power" (52). In "'natural'" emotional terms, Otto says, we can distinguish between an action troubling us, on one hand, and "pollut[ing]" us, on the other; instead of "accus[ing] ourselves," we are "defiled in our own eyes. And the characteristic form of emotional reaction is no longer remorse but *loathing*" (55). Self-accusation and remorse are functions of morality for Otto, while pollution and self-loathing are functions of religion.

The publication of *A Tale of Two Cities* crowned the period of the Victorian theological emphasis on atonement, with theological controversy then turning predominantly to questions of science in the aftermath of the publication of Darwin's *Origin of Species*.[22] Yet through the end of the 1850s, Victorians encountered sermons and devotional hymns that insisted, like Gladstone, on the awful reality of sin and the impossibility of absolution without Christ's sacrifice. In 1856, Charles Spurgeon, preaching on Romans 5:8 ("But God commendeth his love toward us, in that, while we were yet sinners, Christ died for us"), characteristically described the way that

> no *merit* could have deserved the death of Jesus. Though we had been holy as Adam, we could never have deserved a sacrifice like that of Jesus for us. But inasmuch as it says, "He died for sinners," we are thereby taught that God considered our sin, and not our righteousness. When Christ died, he died for men as black, as wicked, as abominable. (Spurgeon 420, emphasis mine)

No matter how black, wicked, abominable sin was, for faithful Christians, there was relief. For Christians across the spectrum of denomination, sin was virtually unintelligible without its counterpart of salvation. In 1850, Thomas Binney had described to his audience of thousands the "fearful agonies that are sometimes endured from the deep sense of unpardoned sin" ("Gethsemane" 164). Binney argued, "Moral means can but feebly arrest [the spread of sin] if at all" (246), yet he could reassure his audience of a "miracle":

> Happy will it be for every one of us, at every return of recollected guilt, to cling to the hope provided for us in the vicarious sufferings of the Christ of God. "The Blood of Christ cleanseth from all sin." Pardon, in the Gospel is promised *for a reason;* that reason is the great redemptive act of the sacrifice of Messiah, which is to be confided in and pleaded by the contrite

---

22. Chadwick notes tellingly, "none of the famous hymns of the passion or hymns for Easter came after 1862," while the most beloved dates from 1848 (VC 2: 469).

man. That reason never failed, and it never will fail, so long as there is a
sinner to believe and a God to hear. (164)

The sinner is not automatically absolved of responsibility via Christ's sacrifice, yet the truly contrite man can plead with hope and confidence that
pardon will come.

In a different lecture published in 1853, Binney noted that the Gospel

> does, in some marvellous manner, so come in between the soul of the sinful
> man (when penitent and believing) and the spiritual consequences of his
> sin to himself, as to save him from fear, soothe his agitation, impart to him
> a calm, deep peace, and encourage him to expect, with the "assurance of
> hope," an immortality of blessedness in a future world. ("Is It Possible"
> 250)

The terrible anxiety of sin, its restlessness and inescapability, could be
answered, but only by the "marvellous," by a "miracle enter[ing] the
world."

Even for those theologians such as F. W. Robertson who refused a literal sense of expiation, a sinful humankind nevertheless required Christ's
atonement. "Sin is the withdrawing into self and egotism," Robertson
preached in a statement that might easily have spoken to unbelieving Victorians as well as the faithful ("Sacrifice of Christ"). But then he added
that this withdrawal took man "out of the vivifying life of God, which
alone is our true life. The moment the man sins he dies. . . . Have we never
felt that our true existence has absolutely in that moment disappeared,
and that *we* are not?" ("Sacrifice of Christ"). For Robertson, Christian
sin was the deathlike cancellation of self and life. "Real human life" could
be restored and enjoyed only so long as human beings were engaged in
"a perpetual completion and repetition of the sacrifice of Christ." They
needed to be "absorbed into the spirit of that sacrifice" in order to return
to the true life that was in Christ ("Sacrifice of Christ"). When, twenty
years later, Thomas Rawson Birks (1810–1883), who succeeded Maurice as Knightsbridge Professor of Moral Philosophy at Cambridge, wrote
extensively on sin as both "a debt, and also a disease," he reflected the
impossibility of imagining absolution without Christ's sacrifice, even for
the most psychologically attuned believers:

> It is a transgression of the divine law, without and above the sinner. It is a
> transgression, also, against the health and life of the spirit within. . . . The

> debt needs a ransom, the disease a cure. If sin were only a disease, there
> would be much room for sympathy, none for substitution. Atonement and
> propitiation would be wholly out of place. (151)

While the "disease of sin" required repentance, "an inward work in the
heart," the debt could "never be done away by repentance alone" (152).

At the center of Atonement theology was the conviction that morality without the religion of Christ could not absolve a person of sin. Yet in
Dickens' world, as in Victorian culture more generally, it was often difficult
work to make divisions between "true" religion and a morality that had
barely distanced itself from its Christian origins. This division was particularly problematic for Dickens who understood the center of Christianity
to be its ethical teachings. It was also problematic as liberal theologians
shifted their emphasis to Christ's Incarnation and focused on his status
as moral exemplar. In spite of these complications, and because of them,
many educated Victorians were sensitive to the borders between morality
and Christian faith, especially as the century wore on.

If for most secularizing mid-Victorians, the demands of morality operated as an all-important bulwark against social disorder, Charles Taylor
has argued that the "narrowing" of religion to moralism was one of the
chief forces to prompt the fin de siècle and post-Victorian rejection of
Victorian ethics as lacking any of the great purpose that gives meaning
to existence. In particular, the ethic of self-discipline came under attack.
Institutionalized in public school, the military, and the government, self-
discipline came to seem empty. Even the "plea for a holy life came to be
reductively seen as a call to centre on morality, and morality in turn as a
matter of conduct" (225).

If we return to Dickens' treatment of Carton, we can see how the novel,
perhaps somewhat presciently, considers the problem of sin and profaneness in terms of mid-Victorian morality, seeking to push just beyond them
to something transcendent:

> Waste forces within him, and a desert all around, this man stood still on
> his way across a silent terrace, and saw for a moment, lying in the wilder-
> ness before him, a mirage of honourable ambition, self-denial, and perse-
> verance. In the fair city of this vision, there were airy galleries from which
> the loves and graces looked upon him, gardens in which the fruits of life
> hung ripening, waters of Hope that sparkled in his sight. A moment, and it
> was gone. Climbing to a high chamber in a well of houses, he threw him-

self down in his clothes on a neglected bed, and his pillow was wet with wasted tears. (82)

"Honourable ambition, self-denial, and perseverance": the watchwords of Victorian morality, stalwart and solid as the realist novel itself, constitute here only a momentary mirage. The passage suggests that these moral qualities simply do not have the power to transform the earthly city of the dissipated, suicidal Carton to the heavenly city of the self-sacrificial man, as described by Revelations 22, replete with fruits of life and sparkling waters.[23] The problem Carton embodies—profaneness—cannot effectively be managed by Victorian middle-class morality, nor can it be wrapped up neatly by a realist narrative. The passage ends by moving from moral to religious registers when it records Carton's "wasted tears." The counterpoint to these "wasted tears" is the "sacred tears" that we find in this novel, as in so many others of the period, and Dickens', in particular (41). Carton's profaneness, his repeated association with waste and the earthly city, is also the novel's opening for the category of sacred value and the heavenly city.

Carton's unfathomably deep sense of unworthiness and waste can thus be read as the novel's most religious phenomenon, one that at times succeeds in scuttling the conventional Victorian moral categories. But Carton is an unfortunate enough man to find himself in a Victorian novel, and in a Dickens novel, no less, where Christian truths are "inescapably there and yet finally elusive" (Welsh *City of Dickens* 141). A fully Christian ending is unavailable to him; an exclusively humanist ending is equally impossible. Cross-pressured by these two sets of claims, Dickens employs a beatific Lucie Manette who serves as the golden thread braiding the claims and promises of Christianity with those of humanism. As Alexander Welsh argued in his early, major study of Dickens, the hearth became the answer to the problem of the earthly city in "an effort to substitute for transcendental beliefs values that could be experienced in this life" (147). As the guardian of the hearth, the angel of the house embodied and simultaneously transmuted those values.[24] If the angel of the house is often an annoy-

---

23. The novel uses the term "mirage" in one other instance, describing Darnay's ill-fated delusion that he might influence the course of the Revolution: the "glorious vision of doing good, which is so often the sanguine mirage of so many good minds, arose before him, and he even saw himself in the illusion with some influence to guide this raging Revolution that was running so fearfully wild" (226). Again, mirage opposes rational morality to a transcendent force, in this case, the sacrificial energy of the Revolution.

24. Welsh's analysis of the angel of the house incorporates but goes beyond the more

ingly blank figure to modern readers, it helps to understand that we are dealing with both less and more than a character. As Welsh puts it, "novelists are hinting at more than just another person in a heroine like Lucie. . . . They are invoking something more nearly divine" (176).

Carton's relation to Lucie—his atonement and redemption through her and for her—comes into clear focus here. As Otto understands it, the sense of creature-consciousness and its deeper level of profaneness comes from the knowledge of one's position before "that which is supreme above all creatures" (51). For Otto, the sense of the holy and the sense of sin, despair, and profaneness are intimately linked. Lucie is Carton's holy object, a "value, precious beyond all conceiving. The object of such praise . . . has . . . the supremest *right* to make the highest claim to service, and receives praise because it is in an absolute sense worthy to be praised" (52). Carton experiences "the feeling that man in his 'profaneness' is not *worthy* to stand in the presence of the holy one, and that his own entire personal unworthiness might even defile holiness itself" (54). It is to Lucie's unquestionable, transcendent worthiness that Carton, unworthy, is drawn. That Lucie as subject speaks in the language of a rational Victorian morality ("is it not a pity to live no better life?"; "why not change it?" [137]), does not limit her role as the novel's transcendent object of worship. It is Lucie that "animate[s Carton] by an intention" (137); as he says to her early on, "'If my career were of that better kind that there was any opportunity or capacity of sacrifice in it, I would embrace any sacrifice for you and for those dear to you'" (140).

In that desire to sacrifice for Lucie and those she loves, Carton describes the need for a form of worship that amounts to religious atonement: "Here, then, comes in the felt necessity and longing for 'atonement,' and all the more strongly when the close presence of the numen, intercourse with it, and enduring possession of it, becomes an object of craving, is even desired as the *summum bonum*" (Otto 54–55).

From Suicide to Self-Sacrifice: The Human Species as the Sacred

Indeed, the novel ends with an achieved atonement that allows Carton to draw close to Lucie, even to possess her, but not in any direct fashion.

---

typical "separate spheres" claim that the hearth was meant to counter the rough-and-tumble of the business world, and refresh and reform returning heroes.

Redemption comes as Carton meets Darnay in the secrecy of a prison cell, dresses in the clothes of his double, answers to his name, dies in his stead, and prophesies a rebirth of cities, peoples, family and self. How does such an ending—specifically, the mechanism of substitution—comment on Carton's deep sense of sin and his craving for atonement, for the holy? How does such an ending help revitalize holy self-sacrifice as something distinct from sinful, suicidal self-loathing? Here, we might turn to the work of the Higher Critics, particularly Ludwig Feuerbach, whose analysis of Christianity was founded on investigating the substitution Christians make in projecting onto God the deepest of human wishes and values. In his stated project of the "awakening of religion to self-consciousness," Feuerbach analyzed the human desire for the holy and worked to understand Christ's hold on the collective imagination (xxi).

Just as *A Tale of Two Cities* depends for its religious apotheosis on "another"—"another man," a brother, a double—*The Essence of Christianity* can envision no religion without "the other," "another than myself," an "alter ego," a "fellow-man," terms that come back in Feuerbach as frequently as they do in Dickens, not least significantly in the quotation with which I began: "How should not he who has always the image of the crucified one in his mind, at length contract the desire to crucify either himself or another?" (Feuerbach 62). Especially striking is the way that these two very different writers and texts link the "other" with the fight against sin. In fact, Feuerbach does have an answer for the question above, a way to avoid contracting the desire to crucify oneself or another. For orthodox Christianity, the "other" functions in the fight against sin in the form of the originary substitution of Christ for a sinful humanity: instead of Christians paying their own just dues, "another" dies for them, thereby redeeming their debt of sin (if not curing their "disease").

For Feuerbach, whose basic assumption was that humanity projects onto God its own nature purified, the atonement was an unnecessarily supernatural response to human sin (14). Sin was only a problem, he held, because of Christianity's unwillingness to recognize the composite of distinct human individuals. Christianity extinguishes the individual in the species; it provides "one and the same means of salvation for all men, it sees one and the same original sin in all" (159). Feuerbach argued that humanism can deal with sin without needing recourse to a supernatural being because it allows *the species* to effect "the redemption, the justification, the reconciliation and cure of the sins and deficiencies of the individual" (159). This idea of the species suggests that one man's sins are *"neutralized by the opposite qualities of other men,"* without which, "my sin is a blot of shame which cries up to heaven; a revolting horror which can be exterminated only by extraordinary, superhuman, miraculous means" (159, emphasis mine). By contrast, the "natural reconciliation" of sin is inherent in the very idea of the species:

> My fellow-man is *per se* the mediator between me and the sacred idea of the species. . . .
> My sin is made to shrink within its limits, is thrust back into its nothingness, by the fact that it is only mine, and not that of my fellows. (159)

Sin is contained by diversity and collectivism: "Hence the lamentation over sin is found only where the human individual regards himself in his individuality as a perfect, complete being, not needing others for the realization of the species, of the perfect man" (157).

Feuerbach's humanism rejects deifying an individualized being, as Christians do when they make Christ that "totality of all perfections" and attribute to him the "freed[om] from all the limits which exist in the consciousness and feeling of the individual" (153). Instead of a deified individual, Feuerbach imagines a multitude of imperfect men uniting to envision and represent an ideal of perfection, the idea of the species. The logic is one of compensation: "in the moral as well as the physical and intellectual elements, men compensate for each other, so that, taken as a whole, they are as they should be, they present the perfect man" (156). But the notion of compensation is itself founded on a profound understanding of the relation between men, one that is not in itself original or unique, but that now finds its way from eighteenth-century moral theory into a nineteenth-century humanist ethics striving to do without the supernatural or divine:

> The other is my *thou* . . . my *alter ego,* man objective to me, the revelation of my own nature, the eye seeing itself. My fellow-man is my objective conscience; he makes my failings a reproach to me; even when he does not expressly mention them, he is my personified feeling of shame. The consciousness of the moral law, of right, of propriety, of truth itself, is indissolubly united with my consciousness of another than myself. (158)

Feuerbach's idea of the other as "the revelation of my own nature" corrects a Christianity that needs to make the revelation of human nature reside unrecognized, mystified, in God. How much more accurate, he says, to recognize oneself in the idea of the species. And that abstract idea of the endlessly multiple and various species first becomes real through a second

person: "my fellow-man is to me the representative of the species, the substitute of the rest" (159).

It is through one's fellow-man that one can see one's own failings, but
recognizing that difference depends on first recognizing similarity: "The
idea of another in general, of one who is essentially different from me,
arises to me first through the idea of one who is essentially like me" (82).
This dialectic between the self and the other—this externalization, objec-
tification, projection process—can be turned upon the self once the lesson
has been learned with a fellow-man: "To ask a question and to answer are
the first acts of thought. Thought originally demands two. It is not until
man has reached an advanced stage of culture that he can double himself,
so as to play the part of another within himself" (83).

Feuerbach rehearses a self-perfecting logic almost identical to that of
the fellow-man-as-objective-conscience, but in relation now to the idea of
the good or the holy:

> The holy is a reproach to my sinfulness; in it I recognize myself as a sin-
> ner; but in so doing, while I blame myself, I acknowledge what I am not,
> but ought to be. . . . But when I acknowledge goodness as my destination,
> as my law, I acknowledge it, whether consciously or unconsciously, as my
> own nature. Another nature than my own, one different in quality, cannot
> touch me. I can perceive sin as sin, only when I perceive it to be a contra-
> diction of myself with myself—that is, of my personality with my funda-
> mental nature. (28)

In this account, sin can be managed by seeing it as a function of and a
demand for what Feuerbach calls, in rather modern terms, "modifications
of my personality" (28). Here, sin is redeemed not by the recognition that
others do not share it, in other words, its limitation and one's "qualitative,
critical difference" from others, but now by the recognition that one does
not share it even with oneself.

Here the lesson, then, is one's difference from oneself: an essentially
good human nature opposed by an imperfect individual personality. But
to get to such an abstract self-understanding, one first must use the other
as both a critical and an affirming mirror. The other is a means to combat both sin and the self-loathing that attends it. With a natural, humanist
understanding of the world, the "revulsion" and "blot of shame" that religion makes of sin, that can be redeemed only through Christ's sacrifice, can
be modified instead by the work of comparison with the other and, subsequently, comparison with an idea of the essential self.

Dickens' novel and its redemptive ending, beloved to its readers, comes into clearer focus when we consider Carton and Darnay as "others" in the Feurbachian sense, two figures who require each other to descend into sin and find holiness; two figures who can make of a despairing suicide, ennobling self-sacrifice. Perhaps we can now hear something new in Carton's famous final words, "'It is a far, far better thing that I do, than I have ever done; it is a far, far better rest that I go to than I have ever known'" (352). Having moved through and beyond Carton's rivalry with Darnay—and here I part ways with critics who emphasize the rivalry as a final condition—the novel now places Carton in positive comparison with *himself*: "better" replaces the novel's despairing refrain of "worse." Meanwhile, the exaggerated superlatives of the novel's opening, "It was the best of times, it was the worst of times," yield to a recognition that against the backdrop of a place where "there is no Time" (351), holiness is a function of dialectic and comparison.

The argument has been made that Carton and *A Tale of Two Cities* ultimately serve an ideology of Victorian liberalism: "Carton can only make the world safe for discrete subjects by temporarily ceasing to be one himself and thereby blocking the plans of a regime bent on abolishing the entire concept of the discrete subject forevermore" (Baldridge 96). Yes, Carton may work against that regime in its worst manifestation but the novel hardly serves as a univocal expression of the liberal ideology of individualism, the work-a-day morality of self-help and discipline.

From rivalry and competition, from the challenges of "another man," Dickens erects an ethic of human interdependence. The novel associates inimitable individuality with Christ's innocence, death, redemption, and resurrection, but ends by finding those ideas bound to violence when they are manifested in "this world," rather than "the other" world (74). I have suggested here that *A Tale of Two Cities* moves toward a notion of redemption based not on innocence, singularity, and rebirth, but on the interdependence of mortal human sinners. Dickensian personhood must face the fundamentally religious challenge of transforming sin and guilt into a consciousness of goodness and holiness: the awful problem is that it takes death to do it.

CHAPTER 3

"Love Yourself
as Your Neighbor"

Guilt and the Ethics of Personal Benefit
in Adam Bede

*n the last chapter we saw that Dickens challenged the ideal of sac-
rifice by comparing it to suicide. Self-sacrifice might be the effect
of nothing greater than a despairing self-hatred, a consuming sense of sin
that can find no absolution. Even as the novel recasts self-sacrifice as a
redemptive substitution of individuals that depends upon and confirms the
powers of collective human identity, its ethic leads the protagonist directly
to his death.

George Eliot's novel of the same year, *Adam Bede*, begins with the
death of a father and has at its center the death of a newborn. Yet the
drama of the novel resides among the living who must absorb such evils
and continue on in a world that offers not only evil, but good, too, in measures that are not fairly or equitably dispersed among people. *Adam Bede*
thus moves forward from *A Tale of Two Cities* to explore an ethics for living. Like the other works in this study, *Adam Bede* reflects the intensity of
an evangelical Christian inheritance that was often understood to insist on
the primacy of the other. Yet, as perhaps no other novelist of her era could
have done as meaningfully, George Eliot, with her philosophical and ethical bona fides, refused too quick an acceptance of a maximalist altruism as
normative ethics.[1] Reaching back toward a tradition of justifiable self-love

---

1. See Dixon on why Eliot did not embrace the Spencerian and Comtean language of
altruism in spite of being enmeshed in religious and scientific writings about altruism from
the 1850s through the 70s (101–13). He contends that Eliot took from Comte not the rec-

most influentially articulated by Bishop Joseph Butler (1692–1752), Eliot
revived a dormant, more balanced notion of social good that allowed for
self-love alongside neighborly love.

In the absence of a unified world view such as Butler's that could harmonize self and other-love in God, Eliot's gospel to "love yourself as your
neighbor" responded to a modern world characterized by abiding self-
interest and inevitable social conflict, where guilty self-sacrifice was useless
to assuage the suffering of others. Never abandoning her ethic of sympathy, Eliot nonetheless rejected unreasonable guilt at good fortune in this
world. She sketched a new moral economy in which the inherited Christian
ideals of brotherhood, poverty, debt and guilt came under critical scrutiny,
while a measured personal pleasure and benefit came to seem justifiable
even in a world of scarcity, where others would continue to suffer. *Adam
Bede* thus constitutes a defining instance of what we might call Eliot's
ethical realism and asks us to continue to refine our notions of a novelist
whom early critics analyzed in relation to Comte's doctrine of altruism and
whom more recent critics have most strikingly described in terms of her
anti-sociality.[2]

Adam Bede focuses on an ethical problem that recurs throughout George Eliot's works and, indeed, throughout Victorian fiction: the
strange, uncomfortable way in which a "past evil that has blighted or
crushed another" is often "made a source of unforeseen good to ourselves"
(*Adam Bede* 573).[3] The novel's plot is simple: a young, narcissistic and
beautiful milkmaid, Hetty Sorrel, the object of Adam Bede's passionate
first love, becomes pregnant to the squire's kind but morally undisciplined
son, Arthur Donnithorne. Hetty bears a child, allows or causes its death,
is brought to trial, has her sentence of death commuted, but is transported
and dies young.

The terrible, almost merciless plotline of Hetty's downfall supports the
path to Adam Bede's finally joyous, fruitful union with the novel's heroine, Dinah Morris, a Methodist preacher, whom he comes to know as she
guides him spiritually through the story's most painful, educative hours.

---

ommendation to selflessness so much as the idea of combining resignation and action (111).

2. For reliable accounts of Comte and Eliot, see Ulrich Knoepflmacher (1968) and
Peter Allan Dale (1990). For a more anti-social Eliot, see Kucich, *Repression*; Nunokawa
(1994) on *Silas Marner*; and Lane. For a conflicted, guilty Eliot, see Neil Hertz's brilliant
reading of Adam Bede (2003). Hertz recounts Eliot's famous description of *Adam Bede* as
the outgrowth of a "seed": a story of infanticide that Eliot had heard. My subject here, the
moral ambiguity in accepting or producing good "harvest" from evil, is encapsulated in
Eliot's description of transforming that story into her novel.

3. All quotations from Gill edition of novel unless otherwise indicated.

Adam's union with Dinah, the narrator tells us, is more powerful and more pleasurable than any with Hetty might have been because of the knowledge through suffering that Adam attains: "what better harvest from that painful seed-time" can there be than this second love? (578). Yet Hetty absorbs all the loss and destruction that enable Adam and Dinah's redemptive future while enjoying no such redemption herself.

While Eliot represents Adam and Dinah's joy as but a remote consequence of Hetty's suffering, with Hetty's suffering perhaps necessary but certainly not sufficient for their joy, the expository labor expended on these distinctions suggests Eliot's discomfort with the ethics of her own plot. Haunting the novel is the worry that Adam and Dinah's happiness feeds on Hetty's suffering and then erases it without a trace. *Adam Bede* thus offers us a new refraction of the maximalist demand of altruism in the moral resistance of the upstanding Adam Bede and the selfless Dinah Morris to accepting a good linked even remotely to another's trouble. It also reflects the difficulties of the novelist George Eliot in an age of maximalist altruism, as she coordinated a plot that she feared might condone the pursuit of self-interested profit.

As Eliot sought to replace maximalist altruism with an ethical realism that balanced the justifiable claims of self and others, she made recourse to some of the most ethically challenging materials of her day: invisible hand economics and utilitarian thought.

Consequentialism and Ethics

As *Adam Bede* traverses time and space from a waning feudal country life to an emerging industrial-capitalist urban economy, Eliot's description of the human relations in which one's loss is subsumed by others' gain evokes a particularly troubling version of the invisible hand economics that divorced the morality of individual intention from the utility of collective effect.[4] In both *The Theory of Moral Sentiments* (1759) and *The Wealth of Nations* (1776), Adam Smith described the way the public good might

---

4. See Courtney Berger (2000) for her excellent discussion of *Adam Bede* as "Eliot's most vigilant attempt to affix the relationship between cause and effect and to attach agents to actions" (310); "Ideally, for Eliot," Berger sums it up, "the causal and the moral would be synonymous" (308). Berger's essay has allowed me to consider how Eliot innovatively responded to her self-created gap between the causal and the moral. I am indebted to her for those terms. I encountered Eleanor Courtemanche's 2011 study of the 'Invisible Hand' after the completion of this manuscript, but refer readers to its highly relevant account of the "fantasy of social holism" in contemporary works of political economy and novels (2–3).

unintentionally be served by individuals pursuing their own self-interest. In the former work, Smith describes rich, unpleasant proprietors who "in their natural selfishness and rapacity," pursue only "their own vain and insatiable desires." They employ thousands of poor workers to produce luxury commodities: yet, "They are led by an invisible hand to make nearly the same distribution of the necessaries of life, which would have been made, had the earth been divided into equal portions among all its inhabitants, and thus without intending it, without knowing it, advance the interest of the society" (184–85). In this scenario, as in the less morally freighted one in *The Wealth of Nations,* self-interest benefits both the self and others.[5]

For Eliot, as for many educated Victorians of her day, invisible hand economics was linked closely to the Benthamite utilitarianism which judged an action "conformable to the principle of utility . . . (meaning with respect to the community at large) when the tendency it has to augment the happiness of the community is greater than any it has to diminish it" (Bentham 18).[6] Utilitarian thought shared with invisible hand economics a focus on end, rather than means, as the criterion by which to judge action. It endorsed happiness, rather than goodness. For Eliot the moralist, utilitarianism seemed dangerously close to the recommendation of a solely selfish pursuit of pleasure (in spite of Bentham's clear designations of a collective basis of utility and, later, J. S. Mill's defense of happiness as virtuous).[7] Eliot commonly reduced Bentham's ideas to the felicific calculus of pain and pleasure and used it to describe her least morally evolved characters. For instance, Hetty's capacity for moral thought, her "vision of consequences," the narrator tells us, is "at no time more than a nar-

---

5. In *Wealth of Nations,* Smith suggests that merchants pursuing their own interests by supporting domestic rather than foreign trade tend to promote the public interest unawares: "By pursuing his own interest, he frequently promotes that of the society more effectually than when he really intends to promote it. I have never known much good done by those who affected to trade for the public good" (32).

6. See Schneewind, *Sidgwick's Ethics and Victorian Moral Philosophy,* for a helpful discussion of Bentham's reception in England and the perception among English intellectuals of utilitarianism. Bentham went largely unread immediately following publication, but by 1838 the climate had shifted and Mill claimed that Bentham and Coleridge were the two great contemporary minds of England while William Whewell began to include lectures on Bentham in his philosophy teaching at Cambridge (130, 148–49).

7. See Schneewind on the pre-1870s trend among Victorians, especially novelists and artists, to reject the utilitarian as "the monster of abstract rationality, basically selfish, denying the importance of friends, family, country, laws, traditions, replacing the Christian virtues of the humble heart by those of the calculating mind, reducing man to a machine for grinding out pleasures" (*Sidgwick's Ethics* 139).

row fantastic calculation of her own probable pleasures and pains" (385).[8] Others' pleasures and pains, and the questions of duty, justice, and goodness never cross Hetty's mind.

If Eliot's representation of utilitarianism was skewed, we can nevertheless understand her reaction to invisible hand economics and utilitarianism as reflecting her anxiety over their common basis in a consequentialist ethics which judged actions by their effects. Consequentialism raised serious problems for novelists committed to anatomizing moral character and fostering moral growth.[9] George Eliot would have agreed wholeheartedly with Samuel Coleridge's assessment that if identical acts were dictated by self-love and Christian principle, there was nevertheless a difference in spite of the sameness of consequence: "'in that, for which all actions have their whole worth and their main value,—in the agents themselves'" (qtd. in Schneewind, *Sidgwick's Ethics* 94).

By contrast with Coleridge's emphasis on the agents, invisible hand economics depended upon ironic paradoxes that, as Emma Rothschild has argued, make best sense from a "distant" point of view associated with scientific systems (142). Such paradoxes may indeed be true, for example, "that selfish individuals can make an altruistic society, that individualism is a basis for social understanding, that saving can be good for the individual but bad for the society at large, that the pursuit of profit can be an ethical failing in an individual but on the social level lead to good" (Gagnier *Insatiability* 22, fn5). Yet, as Rothschild notes, it is precisely such paradoxes that make invisible hand theories "*not notably successful . . . in providing an explanation of ethics*" (142, emphasis mine). When we leave the distant bird's-eye view and adopt instead an embedded, on-the-ground point of view, the paradoxes and ironies can seem merely bids for freedom from personal accountability. Thus, we find Eliot in *The Mill on the Floss*, ironically criticizing those spendthrifts who conveniently condone debt, "in these days of wide commercial views and wide philosophy, according to which everything rights itself without any trouble of ours" (371).

If, as Rothschild says, the obstacles of "consciousness, language, and self-consciousness," pose serious challenges to the weave of ethics with invisible hand economics, Eliot seems to be a case in point, opting for the former over the latter (142). Yet I want to suggest that in *Adam Bede*,

---

8. In *Romola*, the sleek villain Tito Melema likewise justifies his egoism by saying, "What, looked at closely, was the end of all life, but to extract the utmost sum of pleasure?" (167).

9. For a useful compilation of material on consequentialism, see Scheffler's edited volume (1988).

we can see Eliot working toward an ethical consequentialism, one that
departs from but nonetheless is indebted to utilitarian thinking.[10] If Eliot
was quick to reject the Smithian scenario in which one may justifiably act
without considering the risks or costs to others, if she broke from Smith in
punishing her undisciplined, self-interested protagonists with a sure hand,
and if she imagined that self-interest was more frequently socially destructive than constructive, still, she was less certain when it came to the moral
status of collective benefits that came as *unsought* effects of self-interested action. Adam Bede and Dinah Morris' "harvest from that painful
seed-time," their "unforeseen good" brought about by the "past evil that
"crushed another," drove a wedge between Eliot's causal and moral logic,
and pushed her toward a new consequentialism.

   As a novelist unusually gifted at simultaneously sustaining the ironic,
scientific-system, distant point of view (often associated with her narrator) and the embedded point of view (often associated with her characters),
Eliot turned toward the challenge of calculating social benefit precisely at
the point when individual suffering stood to compromise it.[11] *Adam Bede*
thus seeks a livable point of balance between a sufficient recognition of
the individual costs that produce the larger social benefits and the irrefut-
able value of those benefits to those fortunate enough to realize them. If
Eliot expressed serious ethical hesitation about utilitarianism and invisible
hand economics, I suggest further that we can explain her turn to them as
a response to the oppressive maximalist altruism whose effects can be felt
everywhere Adam Bede and Dinah Morris tread in *Adam Bede*.

   While utilitarianism and invisible hand economics problematically
subordinated the value of individual intention and motivation to their

---

   10. See Blake's relevant account of *The Mill on the Floss* in relation to Benthamite
utilitarianism (111–137). Exploring the way that Eliot dramatizes the transition between
a feminine, Christian gift economy and a capitalist economy of investment, Blake claims
that Eliot does not endorse a pre-capitalist economics of gift and sacrifice. Maggie, the
embodiment of such an economy, "does not think like a Utilitarian political economist":
unable to tally up costs and benefits, she sacrifices all in such a way that pain no longer can
be distributed more fairly nor recuperated to serve net utility as it is in capitalist exchange
(129). This point accords with my claim that Eliot seeks to calculate social benefit when it
becomes compromised by individual suffering.
   11. Much more can be said on this balance in Eliot. One useful point of entry can be
found in the innovative recent scholarship on omniscience. See Rae Greiner's treatment
(2009) which features a full bibliography. As far as irony in *Adam Bede,* I see this novel as
among the least ironic in Eliot's oeuvre, with the narrator less distinct from the major characters than in other works. For the opposite claim, see Kreuger who argues that Eliot maintains
an "ironic distance" from Dinah, thus refusing to "align herself with that [preaching] power,
just as she declined direct involvement in the public crusades of her day, particularly feminist
ones" (255).

effects on the collective, they nonetheless offered Eliot the basis for a model of consequences sufficiently divorced from their initial causes and intentions to afford the most conscientious of Victorian moral agents an escape from the exaggerated sense of responsibility represented by the maximalist altruistic demand. Only in a world protected from that demand could Eliot grant Adam and Dinah their innocent marriage which promised the diffusive influence for good in which Eliot believed. Although the novel ends by allowing its deserving protagonists to accept benefits others may not share, guilt and anxiety hover. As we turn to a reading of the novel, it is striking to note that the same Eliot who worried about unjust measures of joy accepted as intuitive wisdom the notion of unjust suffering: "So deeply inherent is it in this life of ours that men have to suffer for each other's sins, so inevitably diffusive is human suffering, that even justice makes its victims, and we can conceive no retribution that does not spread beyond its mark in pulsations of unmerited pain" (*Mill on the Floss* 329). While unearned suffering was a necessary effect of the web of human relations, Eliot was confounded by the inverse injustice of unearned joy, though it was just as much an effect of the web of human lives.

Perhaps the difference was that in Eliot's mid-Victorian imagination, even at the end of a decade of great abundance, the sense of need was inescapable. Unearned personal joy did not seem abundant and diffusive but, like the wealth of material resources, scarce and potentially divisive. We will see that the Christian ethic of suffering and sacrifice shapes the assumptions of *Adam Bede*, even as the forces of nineteenth-century political economy both bolster those assumptions and provide a vital escape.

Scarcity and Competition: Marriage as Deprivation of Others

Eliot's novels repeatedly illustrate the pervasive sense of scarce valuable goods: more mouths than "'scant cakes'" in "'th' hungry country,'" as Lisbeth Bede, the hero's mother, puts it (165). Even when generosity guides human behavior, the rule of resources seems to be that one person's possession requires another's deprivation, as in the narrator's description of "The raw bacon . . . Molly spares from her own scanty store, that she may carry it to her neighbor's child" (82). *Adam Bede*'s exploration of inequality, scarcity, and the exclusivity of enjoyment is not confined, though, to material conditions. Instead, Eliot turns to marriage as an intense, crystallized instance of the competing claims of self and others. In her works, coupling and marriage seem frequently to be acts of robbery or deprivation so violent that they threaten to destroy not only others' material hopes (as in the case of *Daniel Deronda*'s Lydia Glasher), but also to wreck others' selfhood. Love between a man and a woman can mean the responsibility for others' "crushed hearts," as Maggie Tulliver painfully puts it (*Mill on the Floss* 598).

In *Adam Bede*, the stories of the two marriageable young women, the pious, unself-conscious Dinah Morris and the alluring, narcissistic Hetty Sorrel, share a structural element, for all their intended opposition. Hetty's story is built upon two lovers—Adam Bede, the hard-working craftsman, and Arthur Donnithorne, the heir to Hayslope—and two promises of marriage. Dinah's story, too, features two lovers—Adam Bede and Seth, his younger brother—and two proposals. Marriage in the novel requires not simply the acceptance of a lover, but a double action of rejecting one lover and accepting another, emphasizing the way that this brand of possession constitutively requires a second party to experience a serious lack. Marriage is a source of guilt. Hetty's choice of Arthur as her lover determines the dramatic plot of the novel while Adam's suffering in the face of that choice reveals the normative exclusivity of the affective and sexual bond of marriage. Yet we might be tempted to read Adam's outrage at the "robbery" of Hetty as primarily a reflection of marriage as a traffic in women if Eliot had not focused so fully on Dinah's tortured deliberations as well.

Dinah's dilemma asks us to scrutinize marriage as a social and spiritual form. Her choice between two kind and upstanding brothers who are at peace with each other pales in comparison with the far more fundamental decision of choosing to marry at all. What troubles Dinah is simply the idea of confining herself passionately to one human being. From Dinah's first appearance in the novel, she is associated with an ethic of communal spiritual good as well as communal property.[12] The condition of divided human lots that allow one person's evil to bring about another's good is entirely opposed to the Christian vision she articulates.

Sympathy takes its most powerful early expression in the novel in the Christian teaching that Dinah attempts to spread in Hayslope.

"Dear friends," she said at last, "brothers and sisters, whom I love as those for whom my Lord has died, believe me I know what this great bless-

---

12. See Aeron Hunt's (2006) assessment that in the sphere of Dinah's preaching, all value is "transcendent" (554). I suggest that Dinah's religious labor and her anxieties about renouncing it are described as much in terms of communal property as transcendent value.

edness is; and because I know it, I want you to have it too. I am poor, like you: I have to get my living with my hands; but no lord nor lady can be so happy as me, if they haven't got the love of God in their souls. . . . It is not like the riches of this world, so that the more one gets the less the rest can have. God is without end; his love is without end—

Its streams the whole creation reach,
So plenteous is the store;
Enough for all, enough for each,
Enough for evermore." (76)

Dinah is united with her brothers and sisters in Christ who are, like herself, the beneficiaries of Christ's supreme sacrifice. Their fellowship is hallowed from the outset by that founding example of self-forgetful generosity. Dinah wishes to share all she has and repeatedly stresses the similarity between herself and her listeners: "I am poor, like you." She emphasizes the plenteousness of Christ's blessing that does not distinguish between those many that get their living with their hands and that rare lord and lady, appropriately referred to in the singular. We can see the miraculous nature of this blessing in the way that the significations of "it" cascade from blessedness to love of God, to God himself, to his love, to the streams of his love, to a store that is triply enough. Against the single mention of "riches," God's love is abundant in the way that only an immaterial property can be. "Enough for evermore," it offers a temporal surfeit, too.

When Adam proposes marriage to Dinah much later, near the novel's end, her ethic of communal good and communal property—and her sense of herself as a communal possession—are wholly disturbed by the knowledge that if she marries, she will no longer be able to serve a wider community. In response to Adam, she answers,

"I know marriage is a holy state for those who are truly called to it, and have no other drawing; but from my childhood upward I have been led towards another path; all my peace and my joy have come from having no life of my own, no wants, no wishes, for myself, and living only in God and those of his creatures whose sorrows and joys he has given me to know." (552)

Dinah construes adulthood as the spiritual journey from childhood "upward," rather than merely forward in time. The four repetitions of "no" are echoed by Dinah's final "know," so that precious knowledge becomes identical with self-denial. In a fashion typical of the novels Eliot would go on to write, Dinah faces a "great temptation":

> "a great fear is upon me. It seems to me as if you were stretching out your arms to me, and beckoning me to come and take my ease, and live for my own delight, and Jesus, the Man of Sorrows, was standing looking towards me, and pointing to the sinful, and suffering, and afflicted. I have seen that again and again when I have been sitting in stillness and darkness, and a great sorrow had come upon me lest I should become hard, and a lover of self, and no more bear willingly the Redeemer's cross." (553)

Past, present, and future run together here in Dinah's overly developed apparatus of self-checking. The last sentence of the passage reflects Dinah's capacity to project herself into a fully realized future. "And a great sorrow had come upon me," she narrates in the past perfect tense, only to move seamlessly into a future ("lest I should become") as vivid as if it has already come to pass. The great sorrow has come upon Dinah even before she has acted in such a way as to incur its costs. In this novel which so fully associates the capacity and responsibility for foreseeing consequences with moral strength, tense evokes an entire moral universe. Just as Arthur's terrible lack of self-discipline is marked by his refusal to imagine the future, here, Dinah's sympathy is marked by her forbidding projection of the future.

Dinah's vision of marriage suggests a sort of dalliance rather than a consecrated union. In her visual tableau, Dinah, the still and darkened visionary, sits between two male figures. If Dinah sits and Jesus stands, the lack of specification as to Adam's position may indicate that he beckons to her and reaches out his arms from a reclining position, which suggests to the imaginatively guilty Dinah her own "ease" and "delight." But not only does Adam reach out to Dinah from the subjunctive sphere of her own imaginings; he competes with the authority of the Man of Sorrows, whose actions, narrated not in the subjunctive, but in the past progressive accordant with Dinah's own actual sitting, are rooted in the reality of the presence of others, the sinful and suffering.

While Adam occupies one end of the tableau and the Man of Sorrows the other, with Dinah in between, the tableau is more triangular than linear: it opens out onto a whole world of troubled others. In Dinah's intensely guilty vision, the temptation toward ease manifests itself not merely as a choice between serving oneself and serving others, but as a choice between serving oneself and consciously rejecting others. Dinah imagines a scenario of simultaneity where she chooses ease for herself *in the near presence of the afflicted*. Eliot's prose reflects precisely Dinah's fear of narcissism. The insistent repetition of "me" and "my" opens the passage: "a great fear is upon me"; "it seems to me"; "your arms to me"; "take my ease"; "live for my own delight." The repetition of the connective "and" provides the tonal lulling that mirrors Dinah's fear of succumbing to temptation. Although another "and" connects the two opposing images of Adam and Christ, it also signifies the cross at the center of the passage (which ends appropriately with "Redeemer's cross"). The object "me" returns, but only in such a way as to emphasize the monumental divide between the two life-callings. Dinah imagines marriage as narcissistic forgetfulness: "'I fear I should forget to rejoice and weep with others; nay, I fear I should forget the Divine presence, and seek no love but yours'" (552).

It is worth noting that Dinah does not construe marriage as an act of faithful substitution, serving a husband the way she might have served the needy, or as a model for a relation to a wider world. She construes it as seeking love for herself. The narrator of the novel concedes, too, that at least at first, love is forgetfulness; when Dinah admits her love to Adam, "They sat looking at each other in delicious silence,—for the first sense of mutual love excludes other feelings; it will have the soul all to itself" (552). This passage evokes John Kucich's trenchant argument that Victorian intensity of feeling is often rendered private and becomes more valuable when unexpressed or repressed. As he puts it, the styles of nineteenth-century repression were often a "strategy for exalting interiority" in a surprisingly antisocial way (*Repression* 2).[13] Here, Dinah self-consciously fears that particular human love cannot but be narcissistic, so much so that it divides the lover from the very object of his or her love.

Since the rise of feminist criticism, scholars have been troubled by the way in which Dinah's plot is resolved. In such accounts, repression characterizes Dinah's confinement from a public vocation to a domestic role.[14]

---

13. Kucich has been the most subtle critic of the way that in Victorian fiction, "ascetic repression often has the unmistakable force of a desire in its own right" (*Repression* 142). When he established that self-negation held erotic potential for Victorians and required not a surrender of self to external authority but a firm basis of personal autonomy, Kucich challenged scholars to reconsider how we have read many instances of female decision-making in Victorian fiction. My own use of the term repression below refers to the maximalist altruistic demand, a self-denying asceticism. While I do not read Dinah's marriage, then, as an instance of repression, one could argue that she exchanges one form of repression for another.
14. Kreuger argues that Dinah's marriage and subsequent public silence reflects Eliot's refusal of the evangelical female tradition of preaching and writing that allowed woman the spiritual authority to be social critics. Mary Wilson Carpenter (1986), offering a complex reading of the chronology of the novel against the ecclesiastical calendar, argues that the

Certainly the novel itself suggests an ambivalence about this resolution. Yet Eliot's decision to move Dinah from the public to the private sphere asks us to consider Dinah as a devout evangelical practiced in routine self-denial as much as it emphasizes her difficult status as a woman. In Dinah's case, marriage counters the maximalist altruism that would require all her actions actively to seek the good of others. Any private desire for happiness would be obviated by so strict a moral standard. From this point of view, the locus of repression is not marriage and wifely modesty so much as the asceticism Dinah embraces in her single-minded duty as a Christian. This asceticism reflects the "lasting legacy of rigidity concerning public worship, personal morals, and private enjoyments," that J. B. Schneewind tells us persisted beyond eighteenth-century Methodism and Evangelicalism (*Sidgwick's Ethics* 17–18).

If Dinah's struggle, like that of other characters in Eliot's fiction, is "to prevent self-negation from leading only to death or asceticism," marriage to Adam is a move not toward but away from an ethic shaped entirely by asceticism (*Repression* 161).[15] As Dinah's aunt, the voluble Mrs. Poyser, puts it when asked to think about Dinah marrying Adam, "'Nay . . . she'll never marry anybody, if he isn't a Methodist and a cripple'" (555).[16] Mrs. Poyser can imagine marriage for Dinah only hallowed by shared belief— a Methodist—and shaped by self-sacrifice—a cripple. While Mrs. Poyser speaks with her characteristic, untheorized "common sense," she attests

"happy ending" of a wedding is undercut by interleaved biblical readings that insist upon the shared fate of Dinah and Hetty. More recently, Hunt argues that the economic and cultural conditions faced by Hetty and Dinah consign them to the same sacrificial continuum. In a less pessimistic reading of Dinah's marriage, Nancy Paxton (1991) has suggested that Dinah's "surrender" of "sexual innocence," is not represented by Eliot as the Miltonic fall into sin, but rather as a shift from innocence to knowledge (45). James Eli Adams (1991) argues that Dinah's renunciation of preaching "articulates the novel's equivocal view of eloquence" ("Gyp's Tale" 229). If language fails to render the most powerful human experiences, then its status is highly problematic both for a realist novelist and for a preacher. See Blake for a useful summary of feminist approaches to the knot of sacrifice, sympathy, egoism, and capitalist ideology in *Mill on the Floss* (130–31).

15. Dinah's biblical name recalls the daughter of Jacob who is raped by Shechem, then avenged by her brothers, then never heard of again. In light of this intertext, which is surely significant given Dinah's calling as a preacher, Dinah might be seen to embody a transformation from sacrificial object to a desiring subject.

16. Mrs. Poyser's comment evokes Jane Eyre and the humbled, reduced Rochester whom the novel "allows" Jane to marry; Jane's passion (as well as Rochester's) is thus merged in sacrifice. Eliot's comment on the novel in a letter to Charles Bray suggests her impatience with that novel's extremity: "I have read *Jane Eyre*, mon ami, and shall be glad to know what you admire in it. All self-sacrifice is good—but one would like it to be in a somewhat nobler cause than that of a diabolical law which chains a man soul and body to a putrifying carcass" (*Letters* 1: 268).

to the deep tension Dinah experiences between what Charles Taylor has described as "the demands of the total transformation which the faith calls to, and the requirements of ordinary ongoing human life" (44). Caught between "the dominant accepted notions of flourishing and the demands of the gospel," Dinah has yet to find a livable equilibrium between the needs of the self and others (44).[17]

The history of the novel's composition suggests that marriage in the novel indeed does reflect the larger questions of altruism and egoism, in their most polarizing definitions. Marriage—and specifically, marriage to Adam—comes to signify the problem of pursuing one's own desires knowing that others suffer from privation. In the novel's first draft, Dinah was a "widder woman," a widow, rather than the "preacher-woman" described by all subsequent drafts (Martin xci). Eliot records the following in her "History of 'Adam Bede'":

> Dinah's ultimate relation to Adam was suggested by George, when I had read to him the first part of the volume: he was so delighted with the presentation of Dinah and so convinced that the readers' interest would centre in her, that he wanted her to be the principal figure at the last. I accepted the idea at once, and from the end of the third chapter worked with it constantly in view. (Martin xc–xci)

Carol Martin suggests that Eliot may have made Dinah a widow out of convenience, in order to grant her additional moral authority and to allay any readerly concerns as to the propriety of her traveling alone. Yet when Eliot embraced the change to Dinah's status, major thematic changes ensued. As a widow, Dinah confronted none of the "temptations" that provide the tension of her plot as we know it. Perhaps what appealed to Eliot about Lewes' suggestion was the opportunity to illuminate the very risks that had at the first encouraged her to place Dinah outside the marriage plot.

While Eliot had always foreseen Seth's fruitless courting of Dinah, this plot feature would have read entirely differently in the absence of a marriage between Adam and Dinah. Seth's courting would have been either slightly comical, or somewhat melancholy, but ultimately a reinforcement of Dinah's singlemindedness—and that mind entirely distinct from a

---

17. If the "holy renouncer" can follow the example of Christ in making the flourishing of *others* possible, Dinah understands that the person "engaged in ordinary life, married, with children, living from the land or from a trade" is bound to the difficult paradox of living a life of worldly satisfaction without losing herself to it (Taylor 81).

private body and heart. Once Eliot had in mind the change to her plan, she
found it necessary to return to Chapter Three of Book One to re-emphasize
Dinah's early rejection of Seth as a husband, under any conditions. Without such a clarification, Eliot feared that, later, her hero Adam would lose
readerly sympathy since he would appear to be consciously supplanting his
brother in his pursuit of Dinah (xci). Thus from the time Eliot re-conceived
the novel's plot, she contended with the central problems of competition
and the inequality of narrative gifts. The decision to marry off such decisive, self-determining characters—Dinah, firm and steady in her Christian
vocation, and Adam, almost soldierly in his early love and then his compassion for the lost Hetty, and devoted, too, to his brother's happiness—
committed Eliot to treating fully the morality of personal benefit in the face
of others' deprivation.

Eliot's Critique:
"Love yourself as your neighbor"

Among Victorian moralists, the "golden rule of Jesus of Nazareth," as J. S.
Mill described it, was to love one's neighbor as oneself. From Christians
to positivist altruists, this golden rule stood unchallenged and was often
understood to indicate not the equality but the primacy of the other.[18] Yet
in the memorable figure of Mrs. Poyser, Dinah and Hetty's sharp-tongued
aunt, Eliot framed a critique of an extreme version of Christian charity and
offered an inverse lesson: "love yourself as your neighbor."[19]

Mrs. Poyser takes issue with Dinah's austere piety, turning to Scripture
to argue that an alternative to utter self-abnegation lies within the Chris-

---

18. J. S. Mill stated that the rule perfectly reflected the "spirit of the ethics of utility: "As
between his own happiness and that of others, utilitarianism requires him to be as strictly
impartial as a disinterested and benevolent spectator. . . . To do as you would be done by,
and to love your neighbor as yourself, constitute the ideal perfection of utilitarian morality.
As the means of making the nearest approach to this ideal, utility would enjoin, first, that
laws and social arrangements should place the happiness, or the interest, of every individual,
as nearly as possible in harmony with the interest of the whole" and establish in the minds
of individuals an "indissoluble association between his own happiness and the good of the
whole" ("Utilitarianism" 418). Collini argues that Mill indicates just how powerful the
"culture of altruism" was when the spokesperson for Victorian liberalism so frequently
articulated the claims of altruism (74).

19. Mrs. Poyser's analysis comes to seem even more culturally significant when we note
that her sayings were among the most highly praised and quoted elements of the novel upon
its publication. It should come as no surprise that one reviewer labeled her "the veriest
utilitarian" (Carroll 99).

tian system. Dinah's approach cannot be mandated or, at the very least, cannot be the only acceptable form of Christian behavior.

> "But as for Dinah, poor child, she's niver likely to be buxom as long as she'll make her dinner o' cake and water, for the sake o' giving to them as want. She provoked me past bearing sometimes; and, as I told her, she went clean again' the Scriptur, for that says, 'Love your neighbor as yourself'; but I said, 'If you loved your neighbor no better nor you do yourself, Dinah, it's little enough you'd do for him. You'd be thinking he might do well enough on a half-empty stomach.'" (236)

Cannily, Mrs. Poyser suggests that Christian charity cannot really recommend full self-renunciation; if it did, the system would implode upon itself, making it impossible for human life to be sustained.[20] The Bible's command to love one's neighbor as oneself *must* presume self-love in order for it to be meaningful. As she sees it, a good Christian loves him or herself, clothes and feeds him or herself, and then learns from that self-regarding love how to treat others. Self-regard, then, not self-abnegation, is the root of piety and loving-kindness. If one doesn't love oneself, there is no effective standard for how to treat others.

Mrs. Poyser's notion—that self-love might foster loving others—was deeply unintuitive to many nineteenth-century thinkers who were not only unconvinced that self-love could foster loving others but, on the contrary, imagined the former as likely to preclude the latter. Yet less than a half century earlier, Bishop Joseph Butler had sought to harmonize self-love and benevolence, arguing that they were no more contradictory than self-love and the pursuit of any particular source of happiness. Butler's work, particularly his *Analogy of Religion* (1736), was widely studied at the Scottish universities in the late eighteenth century and at Oxford and Cambridge by the beginning of the nineteenth century, and significantly influenced thinkers such as David Hume and Thomas Reid.[21] In 1859, Eliot's close associate, Sara Hennell, had written a long essay on Butler,

---

20. By 1880, Herbert Spencer would make this ethical argument on the basis of evolutionary biology: "Ethics has to recognize the truth, recognized in unethical thought, that egoism comes before altruism. . . . Unless each duly cares for himself, his care for all others is ended by death; and if each thus dies, there remain no others to be cared for" (*Principles of Ethics* 1: 217).

21. For a helpful account of Butler's philosophy, see Schneewind, *The Invention of Autonomy*, especially 344–50. For Taylor's reading of Butler as an apologist who begins to reduce religion to morality in response to the "long march" of the economic notion of mutual interest, see 225–26.

noting his doctrinally surprising "reverence" for "Human Nature" (44) and arguing that he had not been convinced by his own defense of religion and thus should be esteemed a "legitimate precursor" to the positivists as represented by Auguste Comte (55). Butler's centrality required even his natural detractors to address his philosophical position.

In clear terms, Butler argued that self-love was both natural and Christian: "religion, from whence arises our strongest obligation to benevolence, is so far from disowning the principle of self-love, that it often addresses itself to that very principle" (480). In his *Fifteen Sermons Preached at the Rolls Chapel* (1726), Butler devoted Sermons XI and XII to the "Love of Our Neighbor" (467), responding to the verse in Romans 13:9, "And if there be any other commandment, it is briefly comprehended in this saying, namely, Thou shalt love thy neighbor as thyself." In Sermon XI, Butler contended that self-love was no more opposed to benevolence than any other particular affection was. His contention was based on the distinction between a man's self-interest—his "general desire of his own happiness"—and the actual passions, affections or appetites that provide him such happiness. Both love of our neighbor and all particular affections providing happiness take objects external to the self, thus love of our neighbor is no more opposed to self-love than any other external object which gratifies the self.

Yet even as Butler argued for harmony between self-love and benevolence, he recognized that the challenge was to determine the correct proportion between these interests, since there was no absolute measure of love due another (238). The due proportion between self-love and benevolence reflected nothing less than a person's moral character. In Sermon XII, Butler focused upon the ambiguous ending of the commandment to love one's neighbor, "as thyself." What does it mean, he asked, to love another as one loves oneself? His answer came in three parts. First, he taught that the precept of loving one's neighbor "as thyself" required that "we have the same *kind* of affection to our fellow-creatures, as to ourselves"; that as we avoid our own misery and consult our own happiness, so we should cultivate this "kind of regard" for our neighbor (231, emphasis mine). Second, he argued that on the important matter of proportion, men needed to determine quite practically "what is a competent care and provision for ourselves" (238). By reasoning that "persons do not neglect what they really owe to themselves," Butler then concluded that after self-care, "the more of their care and thought, and of their fortune they employ in doing good to their fellow-creatures, the nearer they come to the law of perfection, Thou shalt love thy neighbor as thyself" (239). Third, Butler claimed that even if we were to understand "as thyself" to mean in equal measure with oneself, our priority would still be to ourselves for the following reason. Beyond self-love, each individual pursues particular passions and affections that take an external object conducive to his or her happiness; logically, human beings are unlikely to pursue the particular passions and affections that conduce to others' happiness, and so, even assuming an equality of affection for self and other, nonetheless, one will naturally attend more to one's own happiness.

Strikingly, Butler's acknowledgment of the necessary, natural priority of the self is not only tolerant but positive. Though he notes that "moral obligations can extend no further than to natural possibilities," he also approves this situation: "from moral considerations it ought to be so, supposing still the equality of affection commanded: *because we are in a peculiar manner, as I may speak, entrusted with ourselves*" (241, emphasis mine). If Butler's abstract notions seem a world apart from Mrs. Poyser's homely epigrams, nonetheless, his non-sacrificial ethic accords with her demand for a benevolence that coincides with and draws from a natural, moral, and Christian self-love. Likewise, his foundational assumption that "persons do not neglect what they really owe to themselves," is the source of Mrs. Poyser's indignation at Dinah's behavior. Attempting to teach Dinah to join the ranks of humankind who do not neglect what they really owe to themselves, Mrs. Poyser would have Dinah substitute self-love for self-abnegation as the basis of her love for others.

Seeking to defend Dinah against herself, Mrs. Poyser attempts to reclaim a scriptural, Christian religion that is reasonable, commonsensical, and "good for yourself."

> "You may say what you like, but I don't believe *that's* religion: for what's the Sermon on the Mount about, as you're so fond o' reading to the boys, but doing what other folks'us have you do? But if it was anything unreasonable they wanted you to do, like taking your cloak off and giving it to 'em, or letting 'em slap you i' the face, I dare say you'd be ready enough: it's only when one 'ud have you do what's plain common-sense and good for yourself, as you're obstinate th' other way." (518)

Mrs. Poyser elides a simple act of Christian charity—taking off a cloak and giving it to another—with masochistic trial and suffering—Dinah allowing someone to slap her in the face. Such suffering would, of course, also require the willingness to let another become cruel enough to inflict it. This elision is meaningful when we consider that both John Stuart Mill and Herbert Spencer would later argue that one social extreme tends to produce the opposite extreme.[22] Mrs. Poyser's rationale wards off such extremes and instead recommends a basic evenness and similarity among "folks." She reasons that other folks want of Dinah, as they want of all people, the sort of reasonable behavior that includes keeping one's own cloak or standing up for one's own physical well-being.

In Mrs. Poyser's model, just as extremity is avoided, so is non-reciprocity more generally. Everyone takes care of him or herself, so there is little charity that remains to be given or received.[23] By imagining that all people want each other to take care of themselves, Mrs. Poyser turns self-regard into a double phenomenon which is also socially generous because it protects others' autonomy and independence. Perhaps folks want Dinah to keep her own coat precisely so that none of them will later need to supply her with one when she has given her own away. If this appears to be an ethics built on "how we should leave each other alone," the individualistic edge of Mrs. Poyser's argument is softened by its cause: Mrs. Poyser cares for Dinah and seeks to protect her, too (Held 15). Dinah must be reminded of what others, from ordinary folk to the Hetty Sorrels of the world, intuitively know: self-regard.

More than one hundred years later, late-twentieth and early-twenty-first century theologians have likewise sought to reclaim Christian ethics from what Radical Orthodox theologian John Milbank has called a "modern purism" about non-reciprocal giving that emphasizes

> one theological strand in thinking about *agape* which has sought to be over-rigorous in a self-defeating fashion. This rigour takes the form of dissociating *agape* . . . from the giver's own happiness or well-being. . . . The trouble with such rigour, unbiblical for all that it seeks to be super-biblical,

---

22. See Mill, *On the Subjection of Women*, where he argues that equality between the sexes would simultaneously make women less self-abnegating and men more unselfish (166); Spencer writes about this phenomenon more generally, as a social-biological rule, though he also addresses "indiscriminate charity" specifically: "in the mendicant there is . . . a genesis of the expectation that others shall minister to his needs" (226).

23. For further examples in *Adam Bede*, see the scenes with Lisbeth Bede, Adam and Seth's mother, who is "at once . . . renouncing and exacting," and precariously balances self- and other-regard in the wonderful scene in which she succeeds in bringing about Adam and Dinah's marriage (87). See also Lisbeth's lecture to her Methodist son, Seth, "'Thee 't gi' away all thy earnins, an niver be unaisy as thee 'st nothin' laid up again' a rainy day. If Adam had been as aisy as thee, he'd niver ha' had no money to pay for thee. Take no thought for the morrow—take no thought—that's what thee 't allays sayin'; an' what comes on't? Why, as Adam has to take thought for thee'" (90).

is that extreme "distinterest" in one's activity, though it can only be exercised by a subject, tends also to a suicidally sacrificial will against oneself. That is to say, it tends ineradicably to depersonalize or devolve into a will to be a fully usable object. (Milbank 132)[24]

Milbank's theological argument is a more elegant version of Mrs. Poyser's critique of Dinah's selflessness, with the additional caveat that total selflessness can also result in a dangerous emptiness.[25] Suicide and self-sacrifice collapse back into each other here, recalling Dickens' concerns in *A Tale of Two Cities*.

Duty Is More Than Enough: Abandoning Sainthood

Milbank's critique and Mrs. Poyser's appealing reversals get at a truly difficult moral problem for mid-nineteenth-century thinkers: supererogation, or the status of virtue beyond duty. Eliot's novels, I suggest, dramatized the surprising moral that duty itself can be enough and that self-abdicating heroism may not be desirable; may at times be a positive evil. Eliot's position thus questioned the sort of distinctions made by Adam Smith in his *Theory of Moral Sentiments:*

in the common degree of the moral, there is no virtue. Virtue is excellence, something uncommonly great and beautiful. . . . There is, in this respect, a considerable difference between virtue and mere propriety; between those

---

24. See also Stephen G. Post (1990). In the last approximately twenty years, revisionist Christian theologians have provided alternative analyses of agapeic love and the reciprocity of Christian giving. For the classic account of eros and agape, see Anders Nygren (1969).

25. Milbank's theological argument finds some echoes in the philosopher Susan Wolf's 1982 "commonsense" attack on sainthood, where she argues that altruistic ideas "are not ideals to which it is particularly reasonable or healthy or desirable for human beings to aspire" (433): "Thus, when one reflects, for example, on the Loving Saint easily and gladly giving up his fishing trip or his stereo or his hot fudge sundae at the drop of the moral hat, one is apt to wonder not at how much he loves morality, but at how little he loves these other things . . . the ideal of a life of moral sainthood disturbs not simply because it is an ideal of a life in which morality unduly dominates. The normal person's direct and specific desires for objects, activities, and events that conflict with the attainment of moral perfection are not simply sacrificed but removed, suppressed, or subsumed. The way in which morality, unlike other possible goals, is apt to dominate is particularly disturbing, for it seems to require either the lack or the denial of the existence of an identifiable, personal self" (424). While Wolf makes a good argument for what we might consider mental and emotional balance, it is hard to imagine Eliot sympathizing with her vocabulary.

qualities and actions which deserve to be admired and celebrated, and
those which simply deserve to be approved of. (25)

If Smith saw virtue as uncommon and deserving of admiration, and propriety as common and merely worthy of approval, Eliot confounded
those categories in ways that exceeded even John Stuart Mill's objections
to Comtean altruism which appeared a few years after the publication of
Adam Bede. Mill, sounding a note very different than Smith's praise for
virtue, distinguished between "obligatory" and "meritorious" behavior,
and between faithful "believers" and those who are "saints": "There is
a standard of altruism to which all should be required to come up, and
a degree beyond it which is not obligatory, but meritorious" ("Auguste
Comte" 337). Behavior exceeding that standard (to "restrain the pursuit
of his personal objects within the limits consistent with the essential interests of others") deserved praise and gratitude, Mill said, but could not and
should not be expected more commonly (337).[26]

By contrast with Mill, Eliot set aside distinctions between "believers" and "saints," articulating later, in the Preface of *Middlemarch*, the
impossibility of sainthood in a modern world inhospitable to single transformative acts of moral heroism. Instead, she turned her fiction to the
dramatic imperatives of duty. Though to modern ears, the category of
duty can often sound like a minimal standard for moral behavior, as one
contemporary philosopher puts it, "we should not forget how hard the
way of duty may be, and that doing one's duty can at times deserve to be
called heroic or saintly" (Dombrowski 57). We might consider the scene
in *Middlemarch* where Mrs. Bulstrode is quietly loyal to her husband

---

26. Mill defends utilitarianism, arguing that self-sacrifice itself reveals happiness as the
absolute end. At the same time, he distinguishes between asceticism when it is for the sake
of no identifiable human benefit, and noble self-sacrifice on behalf of others: "It is noble to
be capable of resigning entirely one's own portion of happiness, or chances of it: but, after
all, this self-sacrifice must be for some end; it is not its own end; and if we are told that its
end is not happiness, but virtue, which is better than happiness, I ask, would the sacrifice
be made if the hero or martyr did not believe that it would earn for others immunity from
similar sacrifices? Would it be made if he thought that his renunciation of happiness for
himself would produce no fruit for any of his fellow creatures, but to make their lot like his,
and place them also in the condition of persons who have renounced happiness? All honor
to those who can abnegate for themselves the personal enjoyment of life, when by such renunciation they contribute worthily to increase the amount of happiness in the world; but he
who does it, or professes to do it, for any other purpose, is no more deserving of admiration
from the ascetic mounted on his pillar. He may be an inspiriting proof of what men *can* do,
but assuredly not an example of what they *should*" ("Utilitarianism" 417). In a more evolved
world, each individual's happiness will increase as the general sum of happiness increases
because self and other interest will accord more and more fully.

in his guilt or the scene in which Rosamund visits Dorothea to disclose to her that Will Ladislaw has no romantic interest in her, in spite of appearances. These acts are mere duty in the sense that marriage demands commitment in good and bad times; Rosamund, too, is merely telling the truth rather than allowing a mistaken perception to stand, hardly what we would consider moral excellence. Yet, as the novel makes perfectly clear, these acts are nonetheless extremely difficult, even if they are only what we would expect of good people.[27] The elevation of duty did not efface the heroic as a distinct ideal. Yet its performance also deserved record, especially because it occurred among ordinary mortals—not Lord Nelsons or Dukes of Wellington—who appeared for the moment to be transcending themselves.

In *Adam Bede*, Eliot hallows duty but not by educating morally evolving characters towards its high, everyday standards. Instead we witness in *Adam Bede* a kind of backwards trajectory toward duty. In Dinah Morris' plot, the heroine goes from sainthood to what we might call good-womanhood. What should look like moral devolution is arguably now an evolution, making Dinah truly an unusual figure both in Victorian fiction and in Eliot's works: the genuinely ethical subject whom the narrator respectfully but clearly reforms toward self-interest.

Percentages of Egoism

What would good womanhood—or good personhood—look like? Eliot moves from the mode of Mrs. Poyser's argumentation to dramatize a social reality balanced by altruism and egoism. In the scene where Hetty has run after her lover Arthur and finds herself exhausted and penniless, seeking help in an unfamiliar town, Eliot explores the coincidence of self-interest and concern for others. The scene does not bear the heightened rhetoric of Dinah's sermon, but is instead situated in an inn, a location that emphasizes the meeting of marketplace and domestic values, of strangers and family. When Hetty faints upon discovering that Arthur is not at Windsor, an unnamed but "goodnatured" landlady and her husband take her in, offering her food and drink, and ministering to her needs as she sleeps the

27. Eliot thus distinguished herself from Yonge, for example, who established Sir Guy Morville in idealized terms as a Christian, chivalric hero, exceeding all others in humble but clear shows of supererogatory virtue. In spite of Yonge's cautions about sacrificial zeal, *The Heir of Redclyffe* enshrined super virtue, perhaps moving a generation of readers precisely because of its romance elements.

night in their "comfortable bed" (421, 424). In the morning, Hetty produces a beloved locket and earrings, gifts from Arthur, and tells her bene-
factors that she wishes to sell them. The landlady suggests that instead of
selling the items at a loss, her husband can advance Hetty some money on
the items. If Hetty wants to redeem them, she should contact them within
two months; if not, the items will revert to their possession. The narrator
comments as follows:

> I will not say that in this accommodating proposition the landlady had
> no regard whatever to the possible reward of her good-nature in the ulti-
> mate possession of the locket and earrings: indeed, the effect they would
> have in that case on the mind of the grocer's wife had presented itself
> with remarkable vividness to her rapid imagination. The landlord took up
> the ornaments and pushed out his lip in a meditative manner. He wished
> Hetty well, doubtless; but pray, how many of your well-wishers would
> decline to make a little gain out of you? Your landlady is sincerely affected
> at parting with you, respects you highly, and will rejoice if anyone else is
> generous to you; but at the same time she hands you a bill by which she
> gains as high a per-centage as possible. (428)

This passage poses an interpretive challenge with regard to the novel's attitude toward self-interest. On one hand, we might read the passage ironically, as an exposé of self-aggrandizing hypocrisy. On the other hand, we
might read it as a reasonably even-handed evaluation of human motivation that recognizes both the generosity of its impulses and the self-
regard.[28]

The novel asks us to consider seriously whether sincerity, respect, and
sympathy (the entrance into another's happiness or suffering) can co-exist
with a division between the self and another that does not hesitate to gain
from the other's loss. Eliot's narrator proceeds with irony, opening in the
double negative, "I will not say that . . . the landlady had *no* regard,"
and moving within the space of the sentence to a contrary assertion of the
landlady's "remarkabl[y] vivid" vision of reward. And both the landlady
and her husband entertain the hope that Hetty will not return to claim the
ornaments, with the couple itself divided by private interests ("The husband thought, if the ornaments were not redeemed, he could make a good
thing of it by taking them to London and selling them: the wife thought

---

28. For a like example of commercial and sympathetic relations merged, see *Mill on
the Floss* where Mr. Stelling "foresaw a probable money loss for himself, but this had no
appreciable share in his feeling while he looked with grave pity at the brother and sister"
(269).

she would coax the good man into letting her keep them" [429]). None-theless, such projections are functions of "imagination," a term which in Eliot's lexicon evokes the capacity to sympathize with others and the capacity to predict probable consequences which is both a moral and an economic function.[29] Finally, the couple refuse in the end to take anything from Hetty for room, board, and tending in illness: "And they were accommodating Hetty, poor thing!—a pretty, respectable-looking young woman, apparently in a sad case. They declined to take anything for her food and bed; she was quite welcome" (429). Eliot's free indirect discourse allows for the possibility of irony; the reader may consider the landlord and lady as self-interested and self-deceived do-gooders. Yet, alternatively, I suggest, the free indirect discourse may indicate the dynamic mix of impulses, the weave of self and other-interest.

In this scene of negotiation, we encounter a nuance in moral-economic thought that we have not yet seen in the Dinah-Mrs. Poyser divide and helps the novel resolve the contest between the self and others. The problem all along has been the moral rectitude of benefiting from another's loss. Self-sacrificial logic tends to emphasize the economic efficacy of sacrifice: the renunciation of personal benefit was often imagined to prevent or seriously limit the other's loss, as in Mill's description. But in reality, as Eliot knew, this is not always the case. In the scenario of the landlord and lady, a new possibility is raised. Perhaps the other's loss is *inevitable* no matter how one behaves or what one renounces. In the case of the small, regular, and illustrative drama of dealing with a landlady, the narrator's assumption seems to be that the great majority of people will operate with some self-interest: "how many of your well-wishers would decline to make a little gain out of you?" In fact, many people will operate with greater self-interest. The landlord and lady will likely make some profit from their offer to Hetty, but if Hetty sells the jewelry to the jeweler, "'Lord bless you, they wouldn't give you a quarter o' what the things are worth'" (427). Perhaps it is even hubristic to imagine that one could operate unlike all others, in the absence of all self-interest. As Bartle Massey, Adam Bede's former schoolteacher, asks him, "Do you mean to go turning up your nose at every opportunity, because it's got a bit of a smell about it that nobody finds out but yourself?" (291).

In a world where self-interest must be assumed, the moral question becomes one of percentages, of balances. The landlady must consider

---

29. Both Hardy and Berger take up the issue of Adam's imagination. While Hardy emphasizes imagination as necessary to Adam's slow growth of sympathy, Berger focuses on Adam's insistence on liability for action and thus his distaste for imaginative "'speculation'" (311).

whether she is seeking to gain from others "a little" or "as high a percentage as possible." Eliot's irony at a less than absolute moral standard sits side by side here with an empiricist neutrality that anticipates shifting ideas about the effects of too thorough-going an altruism. The narrator introduces the landlord by telling us that he "was a man whose abundant feeding served to keep his good-nature, as well as his person, in high condition" (421). It is the money the landlord takes in from his guests that allows him to eat well and it is his eating well that allows him to turn more generously toward Hetty. A quotient of self-interest proves to be the very source of his generosity. In the 1880s, Spencer would assert this in scientific terms: "The adequately egoistic individual retains those powers which make altruistic activities possible. The individual who is inadequately egoistic, loses more or less of his ability to be altruistic" (*Principles* 194).[30] Adequate egoism does not cancel out altruism, but allows it.

Still, this position on egoism, for all its innovation in 1859, was limited. Eliot endorsed a measured self-interest when it came at small cost to others and she challenged the desirability of selfless sainthood as an ideal for people already highly self-disciplined and concerned for others. With Dinah and Adam Bede, Eliot was willing to draw characters who painfully, equivocally find a middle ground—not entirely self-renouncing, certainly not entirely self-seeking.[31] That the narrator betrays great uncertainty about the ethics of such a middle ground emphasizes for us just how powerful was the dominant maximalist understanding of altruism at mid-century. Against our theories of the rise of individualism, Eliot's novel prompts us to acknowledge the intense communal counter-strain Victorians encountered in their day-to-day experience and to recognize how gradually it was that "duty" moved away from its maximalist interpretation. Moving saints "backward" to good personhood was not the fashion.

Thriving on Another's Trouble: Guilt, Amends, and Homicidal Knowledge

It is not surprising that a novel that values both self-renouncing sympathy and a measured egoism will find itself enmeshed in the problem of guilt,

---

30. Such formulations have prevailed into our own time not only in economic contexts but in ethical ones as well. See Jane Mansbridge (1990).

31. Eliot treats true egoists with little sympathy in other works and, in *Adam Bede* itself, Arthur Donnithorne meets a strong nemesis while Hetty suffers for her sins in ways that can seem needlessly cruel on the author's part.

both actual guilt for sin and felt guilt at one's own good fortune in the face of others' suffering.[32] The first half of *Adam Bede* makes us privy to an unrelenting series of self-interested events that culminate dramatically in Hetty's burial and abandonment of her infant. However, the second half of the novel moves toward a social redemption dependent on the earlier failures. Personal suffering and the experience of closely witnessing the suffering of others offer a by-product that Eliot's narrator explicitly defines as sympathy, an organ of knowledge infused with feeling; out of the "baptism" of Adam's pain and sorrow, sympathy emerges (471). But as Suzanne Graver has noted, Eliot's well-developed "aesthetic of sympathy and ideology of community" does not always succeed in moving from the province of narratorial pronouncement to dramatic action (282). *Adam Bede* reflects such complication when unredeemed and unredeemable evils yield other parties unforeseen personal benefits that cannot be justified strictly as sympathetic knowledge.

The possibility of subsequent good in some way revising the meaning of Hetty's infanticide motivates Adam Bede's and the novel's epistemological difficulty for its second half. In other terms, Eliot takes up the problem of consequentialist ethics: can ends justify dubious means? The third volume of the novel is devoted to clarifying the true relation between Hetty's suffering and Adam's joy, his entrance into a profoundly satisfying and edifying life with Dinah, a life which would never have come about if not for Hetty's trouble. Yet the narrator insists that Adam's marriage to Dinah is but a remote consequence of Hetty's circumstances. The distinction—and often, the confusion—between painful cause and pleasurable effect concerns the novel from its earliest pages. Dinah Morris first enters the Bede household on the occasion of the tragedy of Seth and Adam's father's death. The narrator tells us:

> Seth was so happy now Dinah was in the house that he could not help thinking her presence was worth purchasing with a life in which grief incessantly followed upon grief; but the next moment he reproached himself—it was almost as if he were rejoicing in his father's sad death. Nevertheless,

---

32. The ethical value of guilt in Eliot's work needs more attention. Rachel Ablow has claimed that in *The Mill on the Floss*, Eliot uses guilt to distinguish morally unproductive sympathy from its positive counterpart. It is guilt that allows a character to combat a sympathy that would collapse human beings into each other falsely, or equally troublesome, that would set up their pain in a potentially dangerous measure where one's own suffering would outweigh or challenge the claims of the other's. On the history of liberal guilt (as opposed to religious), see Daniel Born (1995). Welsh's 1985 account of blackmail is also relevant.

the joy of being with Dinah *would* triumph; it was like the influence of climate, which no resistance can overcome. . . . (156)

At first, the passage seems to suggest a model of fair exchange in which Seth "purchases" joy with grief. The reproach comes in the phrase, his "father's sad death," which underlines not only Seth's lack of filial affection but also the larger implication: that the death is not primarily Seth's to barter. The true subject of the death is his father for whom the cost of death cannot be redeemed by any purchase. Yet this moral certitude yields to a remarkable doubling back characteristic of Eliot's narration of moral vacillation. "Nevertheless," like the powerful influence of climate, joy that leaves the dead behind prevails over any stricter moral-rational teaching. In what could be an epigram for the novel as a whole, Lisbeth Bede reprimands Seth by saying, "'thee may'st well talk o' trouble bein' a good thing, Seth, for thee thriv'st on it'" (156).

Thias Bede's death produces good for those who survive him (it serves to introduce Dinah into the life of the Bedes), just as Hetty's evil prompts the thriving of others. For years before Hetty's exposure, Adam has held rigidly to the idea that she is a woman of feeling. Meanwhile the narrator has told us explicitly that Hetty feels for others only through her pride (435). When Adam discovers the truth of Hetty's liaison with Arthur, her pregnancy and murder, he reasons as follows: "'if he'd never come near her, and I'd married her, and been loving to her, and took care of her, she might never ha' done anything bad'" (504). While Barbara Hardy reads Adam's assertion as reliable, arguing that "the social waste is underlined by the tragedy of Hetty, which 'might never have happened' if Adam's circumstances had been different," the novel offers us a competing understanding (35). During the period of Hetty's trial, Adam is confronted by his former schoolmaster, Bartle Massey. Massey gently suggests to the grief-stricken Adam that Hetty's hard, closed, and deceptive nature, disclosed so fully by her downfall, might have led to a very different sort of marital life than Adam had ever imagined. The implication here is that Adam is better off without Hetty. To use Hardy's terms, Bartle suggests that had the marriage taken place, the "social waste" might have been primarily at Adam's cost, rather than Hetty's. Bartle's wisdom precedes that of the narrator of *Middlemarch* who illustrates the dissipation of the idealized imaginings of a marriage partner in the harsh light of day. Adam's Hetty resembles Lydgate's Rosamund and Dorothea's Casaubon, as his pain resembles theirs when his loving, idealized vision is bruised.

Certainly, Adam's attempt to exonerate Hetty and to blame Arthur arises from that pain, yet his response also reflects his unwillingness to construe an evil as *any* form of a good, however limited. Adam rails against a morality that would evaluate an action—Arthur's seduction—solely by the sum of its social ramifications. In a passage that boils down the problem to its essence, Adam responds passionately to Bartle Massey:

> "Good come out of it! . . . That doesn't alter th' evil; her ruin can't be undone. I hate that talk o' people, as if there was a way o' making amends for everything. They'd more need be brought to see as the wrong they do can never be altered. When a man's spoiled his fellow-creatur's life, he's no right to comfort himself with thinking good may come out of it: somebody else's good doesn't alter her shame and misery." (504)

Adam perceives Massey's idea as part and parcel of the transactions Adam likes least: making amends, trying to undo ruin. Adam considers this attempt to be made of empty words ("that talk o' people") that cannot alter the reality of deeds and consequences. Theories such as invisible-hand thinking only obscure relations of personal responsibility which are so central to Adam. The *Oxford English Dictionary* tells us that "amends" are "moneys paid or things given to make reparation for any injury or offence." The phrase "make amends" came to mean the offering of "reparation, retribution, restitution, compensation, satisfaction" both inside and outside a legal system. The term asserts a continued relationship between one action and another: precisely the connection that Adam Bede finds so offensive. Reparation and compensation represent the second half of a transaction in which one party has incurred an unjust loss and the responsible party attempts to repair it and re-establish a neutral basis of exchange from which to move forward.

In cleaning the slate and rendering the parties even again, compensation can be seen just as Adam sees it, as an amoral and even immoral mode of behavior that works against the individuality of persons and the uniqueness of events. Compensation suggests that for all values, a commensurate value can be found. Not only that, but the commensurate value can be revisited upon the human site where the original value was lost, as if in the time elapsed, that site has undergone no change.

By contrast, *Adam Bede* is remarkable for Eliot's rather shocking insistence on the disappearances and "deaths" of living people: after Adam has learned of Hetty's situation, the narrator tells us that he appears as "the spectre of the Adam Bede who entered the Grove on that August evening eight months ago" (509). "This pale hard-looking culprit," that Adam sees when he encounters Hetty evokes for him the earlier woman: the culprit "was that Hetty's corpse" (477). And Adam's remembrance for "that Arthur Donnithorne whom he had believed in . . . was affection for the dead: *that* Arthur existed no longer" (510). In a moral logic consonant with Eliot's chilling metaphors of defunct versions of the self, Adam argues that there are those wrongs which simply can never be made good because there is no longer any address at which to come knocking.

The irrevocable nature of sin and wrongdoing was a deep preoccupation for Victorians. As we have seen, the power of sin manifested itself in Dickens' portrait of the suicidal Carton who cannot imagine redeeming himself in spite of Lucie's indications that the future need not repeat the past. And, of course, Yonge's portrait of Sir Guy Morville describes not only his battle against personal sin but his conviction that the sins of his fathers limit his own spiritual future. As Alexander Welsh has written, "Victorians of all persuasions were genuinely hard pressed to explain what could be done about sins once they were committed" (*City of Dickens* 112–113) and novel readers of various levels of education came to novels with minds prepared by sermons, religious novels, essays, and philosophy to consider sin and its difficult expiation chief dramas of human experience.[33] The field of examples is thick. Among the Victorian "sages," Ruskin insisted in the preface to *Sesame and Lilies* (1871) that "the very definition of evil is in this irremediableness" (17), and in *Ethics of the Dust,* he addressed the subject of repentance by saying, "You have no business at all to do wrong" (qtd. in Welsh *City of Dickens* 112–113). Meanwhile, in *Social Statics,* Spencer stated, "whether it is possible to develop scientifically a . . . Moral Therapeutics seems very doubtful," thus distinguishing between the answerable question of what the "right principles of human conduct" are, on one hand, and the more difficult problem of what might be done when "those principles have been broken through" (58).

For believing Christians, sin was a frightening reality. John Henry Newman, who famously left the Anglican Church for Roman Catholicism where sacraments and confession addressed the horror of sin, described the "Moral Consequences of Single Sins" in terms that afforded little comfort to faithful listeners and readers:

---

33. I am indebted to Welsh's discussion of the "morality of strict consequences" (*City of Dickens* 107–17). He sketches this morality as an effect of "a confluence of Puritanism, economic theory, historicism, and science," but in light of advances made in all these subfields of Victorian studies, the subject of sin and evil needs new, extended critical treatment.

It is an undeniable fact still, that penitents, however truly such, are not secured from the present consequences of their past offences, whether outward or inward, in mind, body, or estate. . . . Great, then, as are our privileges under the Gospel, they in no degree supersede the force and the serious warning of the words in the text. Still it is true, and in many frightful ways, nay more so even than before Christ died, that our sin finds us out, and brings punishment after it, in due course; just as a stone falls to the earth, or as fire burns, or as poison kills, as if by the necessary bond of cause and effect. (756–57)

The law of consequences, of causes and effects, explored in science and political economy could be seen now to operate in the realm of the spirit.

Other Victorian preachers conveyed the magnitude of sin by emphasizing the singular and miraculous efficacy of Christ's vicarious debt-payment on the Cross. In his Good Friday sermon of 1839, Thomas Arnold described Christ's great, single sacrifice that atoned for humanity and warned that "for those who despise this there remains no more offering for sin, but their sin abideth with them for ever" (260–61). In the 1850s, as debate came to focus on the nature of Christ's "payment" for humanity's sin, sacrifice was still understood as necessary for redemption from sin, though often in less literal terms. F. D. Maurice, whose 1854 work *The Doctrine of Sacrifice Deduced from the Scriptures* was critical to the Atonement debates, described Christ's sacrifice as that which alone "purges the conscience from dead, selfish works, to serve the living God" (180). Explicating the Epistle to the Hebrews, F. D. Maurice distinguished sin from the simple transgression of law—"Sin has been brought before us in its inward radical significance; sin as the disease of the will; sin as conscious separation from a pure and holy will" (179)—and demonstrated that just as the blood of animals had atoned for transgressions in Jewish law, for Christians,

The blood of the son of God . . . becomes that remission of sins, that purification of the spirit from the guilt or guile which is the essence of sin, that assurance of divine forgiveness for the acts which have flowed from it, that token of restoration . . . which nothing else in heaven or earth could be. (180)

Only Christ's sacrifice and no human work alone could reach the conscience, the "seat of sin" (183).

If human beings could painstakingly repair their relation to God through repentance and Christ's sacrifice, and sacrament, for Catholics, Victorians nonetheless struggled with forgiveness on "the human scale," as *Adam Bede* dramatizes so vividly (Welsh, *City of Dickens* 111–12). Forgiveness posed a theological difficulty because believers understood that only God could forgive sins in the sense of altering their consequences, while human beings who forgave were merely emulating God, but unable to assume his prerogative. Humans could forgive those who had sinned against them, but justice and its abridgement was God's domain and as such, human forgiveness was not understood to have any immediate bearing on the *consequences* of sin. Thus when we turn back to *Adam Bede,* we can newly appreciate Adam's insistence on the wrong that can "never be altered"; the "ruin that can't be undone" (504). It comes as little surprise that in July 1859, Anne Mozley, writing for *Bentley's Quarterly Review,* maintained that the chief moral of the novel was "that the past cannot be blotted out, that evil cannot be undone" (*Critical Heritage* 88). Theological differences aside, Victorians could well identify this teaching in the works of their major novelists.[34]

In Eliot's novel, the single word "amends," used eleven times, encapsulates her belief in the irrevocability of evil but also challenges the ethics that would be shaped by so strict a conviction. As we have begun to see, it is mainly Adam Bede who represents a sense of irrevocability (good cannot come of evil), while it is Arthur Donnithorne who embodies the countertrend of "amends." Nearly every usage of the term underscores the impossibility or poverty of making amends: "That was an ugly fault in Arthur's life, that affair last summer, but the future should make amends" (486). Arthur's logic, rendered in damning free indirect discourse, is self-forgiving to a fault. Where Adam evinces a faith in stalwart reliability, trustworthiness, and the strict relation between actions and their consequences, Arthur holds an equally firm if unstated belief in changeability, conversion, and the harmless, redeemable possibilities of play (Hardy 38). The narrator lets us know that Arthur has relied upon compensation from his youth:

> Arthur's, as you know, was a loving nature. Deeds of kindness were as easy to him as a bad habit: they were the common issue of his weaknesses and good qualities, of his egoism and his sympathy. . . . When he was a lad of seven, he one day kicked down an old gardener's pitcher of broth, from no motive but a kicking impulse, not reflecting that it was the old man's

---

34. As Joanne Wilkes notes, Mozley, a believer herself, did not seem to realize that the "hard-won experience from which the novel had emerged had entailed a severance from the Christian belief system . . . in its theological aspects" (107).

dinner; but on learning that sad fact, he took his favourite pencil-case and a silver-hafted knife out of his pocket and offered them as compensation. He had been the same Arthur ever since, trying to make all offences forgotten in benefits. (356–57)

Arthur's unfortunate victim here is a gardener, a man whose work depends on a deep recognition of natural processes of development that unfold, as Eliot's metaphors regularly insist, much like her doctrine of consequences. Gardening might be the very opposite of functioning by the logic of the abstract exchange of values. Arthur's warm-hearted attempt to balance the scales with objects that cannot be eaten by a hungry gardener at mid-day do not help because the objects are not commensurate and lost time cannot be reclaimed. "He had been the same Arthur ever since, trying to make all offences forgotten in benefits" (357). The passage concludes on an ironical note, since Arthur's very sameness, his unchanging nature, reflects his tendency to assert sameness where there is difference: to exchange incommensurate objects as if they are commensurate and to trade on the present as if it were the lost time itself. The silver-hafted knife and pencil-case, luxury objects associated with marking and inscription, work tellingly against Arthur here.

Adam Bede finds the notion of compensation offensive and associates it with class difference: the easy act of a rich man who has wronged a poor man. With Arthur, the narrator tells us, "[Adam] had the wakeful suspicious pride of a poor man in the presence of a rich man" (511). When Arthur and Adam confront each other after Adam has learned the truth, a pained and penitent Arthur offers Adam, "'there is no sacrifice I would not make, to prevent further injury to others through my—through what has happened'" (511). Adam mishears the tone of Arthur's words and thinks he perceives in them "that notion of compensation for irretrievable wrong, that self-soothing attempt to make evil bear the same fruits as good" (511). Sounding a good deal like Ruskin on repentance ("You have no business at all to do wrong"), Adam responds by insisting, "'The time's past for that, sir. A man should make sacrifices to keep clear of doing a wrong; sacrifices won't undo it when it's done'" (511–12). A post-facto sacrifice, Adam indicates, is by definition not a sacrifice, but a guilt-offering, a debt-payment. Arthur's reliance on compensation also illuminates the way that if one knows from the outset that compensation is an available form of recourse, one need have no sense of responsibility.

Adam's rejection of Arthur's regret, spoken as if the future might be responsive to it, reflects his distaste for "that talk o' people, as if there was a way o' making amends for everything." Adam does not recognize the link between repentance and attempted compensation. He cannot encompass any idea of a future shaped by the past's lessons. Yet, much earlier in the novel, Adam intuits that true moral lessons can only be learned through "irretrievable wrongs." After the death of his father, Adam regrets his own harshness, his inability to treat his father's weaknesses—drink, the evasion of work—with a kind word or an eye that would occasionally overlook such faults. Sitting in church, Adam muses to himself,

> "It seems to me now, if I was to find father at home to-night, I should behave different; but there's no knowing—perhaps nothing 'ud be a lesson to us if it didn't come too late. It's well we should feel as life's a reckoning we can't make twice over; there's no real making amends in this world, any more nor you can mend a wrong subtraction by doing your addition right." (247)

Adam makes an interesting if painful suggestion. True remorse may come only from recognizing that the wrong one has done is irrevocable. And it is true remorse that effects a real lesson, Adam suggests. Yet it is hard to imagine the workman Adam (or the novelist Eliot) understanding a lesson, moral or otherwise, as an abstract, unapplied and inapplicable increase in knowledge. If the knowledge is really to be a "lesson to us," doesn't it have to have some applicability for later in life? Can it really be considered entirely "too late" if it is known at all? As Eliot's colleague and friend Charles Bray would put it a few years later in revision of his 1841 work, *The Philosophy of Necessity*, "the past is past and cannot be altered at all," *yet*, "experience, or knowledge of the consequences of the past, ought to guide our conduct for the future" (24). In fact, argued Bray, "all true responsibility for the past must have reference for the future, never as is commonly supposed to the past" (23).

Adam's reflection which seems but to re-state his conviction of irreparability in fact cracks open the possibility of morally useful mistakes. His logic undoes itself because the sort of knowledge he endorses, even in coming "too late," does become useful: "it's *well* we should feel. . . ." The country phrase—"well"—means nothing other than good, productive. What precisely, though, is the use of such knowledge? The paradox of moral theory and epistemology in which what is most worth knowing can only be known too late has been described by George Levine as the "suicidal narrative of knowledge" that characterizes Victorian culture and writing (*Dying to Know* 5):

Part of the paradox of dying to know is, of course, that one cannot know anything when one is dead. The phrase implies, then, a kind of liminal position, at the end of nonbeing, and it implies a persistent tragedy: only in death can one understand what it has meant to be alive. The continuing aspiration to get it straight, to understand what it means, to transcend the limits imposed by the limiting self, depends on the elimination of the self. The world out there that it chooses to know is only knowable when it is too late. (2)

This paradox may strike our ears as tragic in two senses: first, it suggests a kind of hopeless surrender to a lack of knowledge, to incorrect or merely partial knowledge, and second, it insists on self-abnegation and self-sacrifice in remarkably unmodern ways, as if coming to know depends upon achieving a similitude to death by emptying the aspirant of all traces of selfhood. Yet, as Levine remarks, for George Eliot, among other Victorian intellectuals, these last virtues were the "conditions, as she understood it, for her own intellectual successes" (6).

In *Adam Bede,* too, the knowledge that follows upon the heels of death or the life-altering sin is rarefied and most valuable, yet the particular manifestation of the "dying to know" paradigm does not solve but recapitulates the novel's central problem in which one party's benefit—his invaluable new knowledge—results from a terrible and irreparable imbalance of gifts and opportunities. When Adam suggests that regret is the fundamental mechanism of moral action, he establishes a firm division between the subject and object of the wrong where the irreparable cost affects primarily *the victim* of the wrong. Adam thus seems actually to agree with Arthur's approach in which "sacrifice" or morally appropriate behavior succeeds rather than precedes error: repentance becomes the offending party's return to life. The unchanging and unchangeable reality that the novel insists upon is, then, not as universal as it might seem. In one party's case, sin is succeeded by moral growth while in the other party's case, sin is succeeded by moral or physical death.

The novel's investigation of the paradox of "dying to know" departs from Levine's model in this important detail: as a central character afforded interiority, Adam's "death" in the novel is metaphorical and followed by rebirth. Yet the novel's victims (albeit victims to varying degrees of personal guilt) die actually and permanently: Thias Bede does not come back to life to give Adam another chance at patient kindness; Hetty Sorrel does not return from her sentence of transportation to allow Arthur to ease the remainder of her life; the unnamed infant never resurfaces to allow its parents their opportunities of responsibility. Thus just as Levine describes George Eliot seeing the paradigm of "dying to know" as the heuristic that fostered her intellectual successes, the novel, too, excises its actually dead characters to make a helpful metaphor of the ideas that true knowledge comes "too late," and that obsolescence or death is precisely the condition of knowledge. In the case of the novel's two major developing characters, Adam and Arthur, personal knowledge comes as a consequence of mistreating others, deluding them, hastening their deaths, and other forms of regrettable behavior (for example, Adam's physical attack upon Arthur in the Grove). We might say, then, that *Adam Bede* offers not exclusively a suicidal narrative of knowledge but perhaps a homicidal one and certainly one that is intimately linked with guilt.

Unblending Human Lots: Joy in the Face of Sorrow

The final domestic scene of Adam and Dinah's family, including Uncle Seth, the Poysers, and a child named for Adam's mother, Lisbeth, underscores the exclusion of both Hetty and Arthur. The family system embraced by the novel seems again to approve a consequentialist ethic where the general sum of happiness matters more than the individual sorrows undergirding it. Hetty and Arthur start out with expansive privileges of focalization and dramatization in the first half of the novel but lose these privileges entirely by the novel's end where reports of the two replace dramatic scenes.[35] Alex Woloch has recently demonstrated that the nineteenth-century realist novel is built upon what he calls an "asymmetric structure of characterization" (30) in which many characters are represented but only a privileged protagonist is "defined through his or her interior consciousness" (31). Woloch argues that the exclusion of minor characters shapes the realist novel—and subsequently our understandings of modern individualism—in a far more fundamental way than we have previously thought. In the nineteenth-century novel, the process of delineating the minor and the major is both mimetic and productive of social hierarchy: "minor characters are the proletariat of the novel; and the realist novel—with its intense class-consciousness and attention toward social inequality—makes much use of such formal processes" (27). Hetty and Arthur are the moral proletariat,

---

35. Blackwood, the novel's publisher, commented that the final scene between Adam and Arthur should have been "shown" rather than described: "I should have liked to see the meeting between Adam and Arthur, but I daresay you were wisest only to indicate it'" (Martin xliv).

we might say, of *Adam Bede* and no one is more aware of this than the novel's eponymous hero who continues to focus the narrator's own anxiety at the moral class-structure and the inequality of lots that he portrays.

The prolonged redemptive ending of Adam and Dinah's novel is marked by a pervasive sense of trouble that the narrator acknowledges, then attempts to funnel into a moral lesson. In the final Book Six of the novel and in the chapters preceding it, the narrator repeatedly analyzes and justifies the "transformation of pain into sympathy" and the transformation of sympathy into the "sweetness" of love (531, 547, 555). By the novel's end, the narrator can assert that Adam's love for Dinah has fed on the roots of his earlier affection and its tragedy: "Tender and deep as his love for Hetty had been . . . his love for Dinah was better and more precious to him; for it was the outgrowth of that fuller life which had come to him from his acquaintance with deep sorrow" (574). It tells us something important about Eliot's aim in the novel that the above passage comes a full one hundred pages after her delineation of Adam's "baptism" by suffering on the morning of the trial: his "regeneration, the initiation into a new state . . . and we may come out from that baptism of fire with a soul full of new awe and new pity" (471–72). The narrative pace of the transformation of sorrow into sympathy and then love is admirably slow and unrushed, suggesting that this psychic process is not secondary but primary to the novel's concerns.

Yet this psychic process is one that the omniscient narrator cannot leave alone, indicating that it teems with contradiction and mystery. The following passage (which requires quotation at nearly its full length) is Eliot's most concentrated attempt to disentangle the knot of ethical confusion and guilt at the heart of the novel's representation of the inequality of lots. As Adam returns to Snowfield to find Dinah in a meeting which will result in their engagement, he remembers his first journey there, seeking the runaway Hetty. The narrator accompanies him:

> What keen memories went along the road with him! . . . but no story is the same to us after a lapse of time; or rather, we who read it are no longer the same interpreters; and Adam this morning brought with him new thoughts . . . which gave an altered significance to its story of the past. That is a base and selfish, even a blasphemous spirit, which rejoices and is thankful over the past evil that has blighted or crushed another, because it has been made a source of unforeseen good to ourselves: Adam could never cease to mourn over that mystery of human sorrows which had been brought so close to him: he could never thank God for another's misery.

And if I were capable of that narrow-sighted joy in Adam's behalf, I should
still know he was not the man to feel it for himself: he would have shaken
his head at such a sentiment, and said, "Evil's evil, and sorrow's sorrow,
and you can't alter its nature by wrapping it up in other words. Other
folks were not created for my sake, that I should think all square when
things turn out well for me."

But it is not ignoble to feel that the fuller life which a sad experience
has brought us is worth our own personal share of pain: surely it is not
possible to feel otherwise, any more than it would be possible for a man
with a cataract to regret the painful process by which his dim blurred sight
of men as trees walking had been exchanged for clear outline and effulgent
day. (574)

A powerful fear of egoism motivates this passage. Here, as throughout the
novel, Eliot struggles to preserve egoism as a negative ethical category but,
at the same time, to limit its definition so that an ascetic altruism does not
remain the only viable ethic. Eliot first takes pains to distinguish Adam
from the "base and selfish . . . spirit" that would be "thankful over the
past evil that has . . . crushed another, because it has been made a source of
unforeseen good to ourselves." Yet in Eliot's narrator's disallowed hypo-
thetical—"And if I were capable of that narrow-sighted joy in Adam's
behalf. . . . "—we can recognize the decisive question of the novel: is there
a way to embrace private good without merely denying the individual
costs that have helped to produce it? Can we as observers and readers distinguish the narrow, egoistic joy at the benefits that come to us upon the
fall of others from the sympathetic knowledge that is the precondition for
a fuller, more socially inclusive joy?

The passage's double conclusion, its presentation of two distinct ideas,
suggests serious irresolution for Eliot. First, the narrator goes back to the
notion that Adam has fully paid for his pleasure: "But it is not ignoble
to feel that the fuller life which a sad experience has brought us is worth
our own personal share of pain." Adam, the again-impersonal narrator
asserts, has bought his fuller life with his *own* pain, not with Hetty's or
anyone else's. This more comfortable conclusion is one ascribed to by a
critical reading such as U. C. Knoepflmacher's. Hetty's pain and her actions
and punishments can thus be separated now from the path that is Adam's.
Adam himself must become convinced of the non-ignobility, the accept-
ability, of having fairly earned or bought his life's joy. This idea of perfect justice finds expression earlier in the novel, when Dinah seeks to leave

Hayslope, not knowing of Adam's love, and utters a prayer for those she leaves behind: "Make them glad according to the days wherein thou hast afflicted them, and the years wherein they have seen evil" (539). When a divine hand dispenses suffering and gladness, then personal benefit accords precisely with the sum of accrued affliction. There is no risk here of oppression, theft, unpaid debts, or unearned benefits. Days of gladness should and can fairly repay days of evil.

Yet Dinah's prayer, mirroring Adam's moral standard for himself, features a slight, but significant change from the original verse in Psalms 90:15, which states, "Make *us* glad according to the days wherein thou hast afflicted *us*, and the years wherein *we* have seen evil." Dinah does not include herself in a prayer that expresses a desire for parity between the days of suffering and joy, as if such a human desire—not to suffer more than one's fair share—is meant for others, but not for her. That the Psalm is associated with Moses ("A prayer of Moses, the man of God" [90:1]), who leads his also-sinful people to the Promised Land but cannot enter it with them, suggests at first a standard stricter and more exacting than common justice—a standard like Dinah's—for those close to God. Yet in the scriptural case, it is God's decree, not his own, that Moses not enter the Promised Land, and it is a decree that Moses himself most humanly appeals; even the man of God can be, at times, a man. In Dinah's stricter-than-Scripture universe, suffering beyond justice does not come down from above but is self-imposed. Denial, as have seen above with Adam, is self-denial.

Yet if such stringent self-denial comes under critique, as I have suggested above, it is not obvious what the alternative might be. Can Eliot suggest anything beyond the fair-and-square happiness which "is not ignoble," but not exactly noble either? If we return one last time to the final sentence of that passage, haunted as it is by its double negatives, we are left with significant questions about social costs that nobody can be expected to pay and thus remain unpaid, unredeemed: "Surely it is not possible to feel otherwise, any more than it would be possible for a man with a cataract to regret the painful process by which his dim blurred sight of men as trees walking had been exchanged for clear outline and effulgent day." Here, Eliot abbreviates and desacralizes the narrative of divine healing related in the Gospel of Mark:

And He came to Bethsaida. And they brought a blind man to Him and begged Him to touch him. And He took the blind man by the hand and led him out of the town. And when He had spat on his eyes and had put His hands on him, He asked Him if he saw anything. And he looked up and said, I see men as trees, walking. And after that He put His hands again on his eyes and made him look up. And he was restored and saw all clearly. (Mark 8:22–25)

Eliot changes the scriptural basis by insisting on the pain of the process, which is central to her exculpation of Adam's pleasure. But she also scales back on the goodness of the miracle described. For Eliot, the process of embracing a fuller life and assuming clear sight can only be described as "impossible to regret." In this absence of a full affirmation, we can trace not only Adam Bede's but Eliot's own hesitations in the face of the difference between Adam and Hetty. Perhaps Adam's sight has been sharpened and restored but the trees walking—the odd hybrid of natural and supernatural which Eliot above calls "that mystery of human sorrows"—simply fall out of sight.

Who are these "men as trees walking" in Eliot's naturalized narrative? In Chapter Twelve, "In the Wood," when Hetty and Arthur meet for the first time, "Arthur's shadow flitted rather faster among the sturdy oaks of the Chase than might have been expected from the shadow of a tired man" (174). He enters Fir-tree Grove, "just the sort of wood most haunted by the nymphs: you see their white sunlit limbs gleaming athwart the boughs, or peeping from behind the smooth-sweeping outline of a tall lime; you hear their soft liquid laughter—but . . . they vanish . . . they make you believe their voice was only a running brooklet" (175). When Hetty appears "first, a bright patch of colour . . . then a tripping figure," she is "borne along by warm zephyrs . . . she was no more conscious of her limbs than if her childish soul had passed into a water-lily, resting on a liquid bed, and warmed by the midsummer sunbeams" (175–76). Much later, immediately before Adam's life-altering vision of Arthur and Hetty kissing in the Grove, Adam stops to appreciate the beeches: "Adam delighted in a fine tree of all things; as the fisherman's sight is keenest on the sea, so Adam's perceptions were more at home with trees than with other objects" (341). He pauses at a particular beech to "convince himself it was not two trees wedded together, but only one," and it is at that moment that he confronts the image of Arthur and Hetty kissing and separating to walk in two different directions (281).[36]

---

36. I quote here from the Oxford edition which takes its text from the corrected eighth edition. In earlier editions, the phrase had been "welded together," which Eliot subsequently emended to "wedded."

Disavowals and myth-making visions prevail here in the Grove. The "men as trees walking" in this novel are Hetty and Arthur who disappear, not only in Eliot's description of the trees walking turning to "clear outline and effulgent day" but in the scope of the novel's dramatization as well. Eliot's metaphor darkens because the trees do not turn into the faces and bodies of human beings; at the moment that Adam's vision grows acute enough to begin to see Hetty and Arthur, they are nearly destroyed figures. The capacity of the seeing man to recognize human bodies and faces in living action, which should be the very aim of healed sympathetic sight, is left in question. How is such a resolution distinct from the previously disavowed "narrow-sighted joy"? Does Adam's clear, simple idea—"Evil's evil, and sorrow's sorrow, and you can't alter its nature by wrapping it up in other words"—solve the problem of social cost?

Eliot seems to be suggesting something different than Adam's objective formulation. One person's evil or sorrow is only limitedly the evil of another who has had no hand in creating it. The definitions of these experiences must be more complex because they originate with different subjects who see from distinct points of view. In saying at the outset of the passage that thought and interpretation as they occur across time alter our meanings, the narrator indicates also that it matters *who* is interpreting. Hetty's evil and sorrow cannot be to Adam what they are to Hetty. Eliot draws lines here between individuals precisely in order to allow Adam the freedom to accept the good that has ultimately come from Hetty's evil but cannot, from Eliot's point of view, be considered its direct effect. The separation of human lots then must suffice to explain or justify the inequality of the lots to those who benefit perhaps guiltily, but not undeservingly. Adam's challenge here is not to determine, as Mr. Irwine puts it, "how far a man is to be held responsible for the unforeseen consequences of his own deed" (468), but at what point a man can *un*"blend" (469) himself from others' deeds.

Eliot's moral lesson in this novel is the inverse of what we often remember her novels teaching: that human lots are a web, that individual lives cannot be separated. The two trees that are one may be another mystery of human sorrows: they may be not only Arthur and Hetty, two trees who by rights should be a wedded one, but Adam and Hetty, two distinct trees whom Adam has wedded as one. Rather than affirming a consequentialist ethic or a systemic theory of an invisible hand, Eliot instead crafts a moral individualism. Perhaps Eliot could articulate an individualist ethic in *Adam Bede* because this novel featured characters whose moral work lay as much in recognizing human separation as connection, who needed a moral vision less extreme than saintly self-abdication. That her novels went back to feature protagonists who still needed to be shown the candle and mirror of egoism, and that Eliot's narrators so often preached interdependence and connection, suggest the bind constraining Victorian moralists as they struggled to define and re-define the terms altruism and egoism.

CHAPTER 4

"Unnatural Self-Sacrifice"

Trollope's Ethic of Mutual Benefit

hronicling the day-to-day dramas of his imagined county, Barsetshire, Anthony Trollope challenged the mid-century sacrificial ideal
in a series devoted to exploring church politics. While the Barsetshire
series is known for treating the Church more as a social and economic
institution than as a religious body, I will suggest in this chapter that Trollope's forceful challenge to sacrifice did not appear coincidentally in a
context that emphasized the Christian and classical origins of the ideal.
Trollope's rejection of an ascetic ideal was not only an expression of his
attitude toward church politics, but also toward the tenets of an inherited Christian morality made unnaturally demanding and self-punishing at
mid-century.

"The novelist, if he have a conscience, must preach his sermons with
the same purpose as the clergyman, and must have his own system of
ethics," wrote Trollope in his *Autobiography* (222). Trollope's ethics,
as developed in the series' opening and concluding novels, *The Warden*
(1855) and *The Last Chronicle of Barset* (1866–1867), sought to transcend the isolation and individualism he associated with asceticism and
to imagine a world beyond sacrifice where a deep mutuality of existence
would bring about collective economic and spiritual plenitude. Where the
sacrificial ethic enforced a division of experience in which one party voluntarily suffered so that another party need not suffer, Trollope's ethic
depended upon Adam Smith's insight about sympathy: joy entered into by

another is multiplied, while suffering entered into is divided or minimized (*TMS* 14–15). For Trollope, sacrifice was nothing but a misperception of those who insufficiently understood the mutuality of truly generous, loving, and self-forgetful relations in which loss for one was automatically loss for the other, and gain for one, gain for the other.[1]

Trollope offered the most powerful critique we have yet seen of maximalist altruism, the purist notion that true generosity must afford its agent no reward. Instead, true generosity, for Trollope, *necessarily* offered its agent a reward because of the identity of interests between profoundly connected individuals. Trollope thus took a step beyond Eliot in offering the possibility of a guilt-free form of personal benefit, ethically justifiable because it emerged out of shared, rather than divided, experience. For Trollope, two parties benefiting as one was a nearly utopian form of social life. Ethical behavior was no longer a matter of self-killing heroism. Instead, it arose among ordinary people living together in generous and committed relations. Normative rather than exemplary, this ethical life was paradoxically hardly worthy of remark and thus, for Trollope, deeply worthy of esteem.

Theft and Sacrifice

It remains a curiously unnoted fact that both *The Warden* and *The Last Chronicle of Barset* tell the stories of upstanding clergymen accused of theft; both men suffer acutely under the accusations, both are unsure of the veracity of the claims made against them, and both finally sacrifice their livings in response. Likewise, in both novels, the daughters of the clergymen unsuccessfully seek to sacrifice their lovers in response to the suffering of their fathers. These two novels differ in so many things—length, tone, dedication to psychological realism, the character and social circumstances of the clergymen in question—that these important similarities have gone undiscussed. Narratives of theft and sacrifice in the vocational and domestic spheres delimit the chronicles of Barset.

Like the terms debt, credit, and trade, both sacrifice and theft belonged to an economic-moral vocabulary whose weave characterized Victorian fiction by inheritance from Christian theology and classical learning. Bearing obvious connotations to Victorian readers, sacrifice and theft often

---

1. My argument seeks to bring an economic dimension to Christopher Herbert's generic analysis of Trollope's novels as "serious modern comedy" that depict "the neurotic estrangement from pleasure as a hallmark of modern life" (*Trollope and Comic Pleasure* 47).

functioned as straightforward metaphors for the social relations of altruism and egoism. In George Eliot's work, for instance, thieves were defined fundamentally by their egoism: "Brother Jacob" steals from his all-generous mother's small store to finance his self-serving ambitions, while Silas Marner is framed for theft by his self-righteous rival and then shorn of his beloved gold coins by a malevolent spendthrift. By contrast with Eliot and other contemporaries, Trollope reflected on commonalities between sacrifice and theft. The two were both forms of exchange with "the advantage lying completely on one side and the burden falling completely on the other" (Simmel 290). For Trollope, theft and sacrifice were not opposites, but two linked forms of unilateral, non-reciprocal demand upon others. In spite of sacrifice operating, in theory, as the denial of the self in favor of others, in practice, it tended to result in the magnification of the self at the expense of others.

Trollope thus responded to the self-sacrificial impulse not with praise, but with effective irony. His self-sacrificing protagonists were often among his least appealing characters (morally speaking), prone to narcissistic self-dramatizing and the callous abdication of responsibility to others.[2] In *The Eustace Diamonds* (1873), it is the thief Lizzie Eustace who wishes that she had a grand ideal for which she might sacrifice all. In *The Small House at Allington* (1864), the traitorous Adolphus Crosbie fears that his marriage to Lily Dale will make him "a victim caught for the sacrifice," bound for the altar (92). And in *The Last Chronicle of Barset*, as we will see, the self-involved Maria Dobbs-Broughton imagines herself an Isaac piling the faggots for his own immolation. In all three of these cases, those who imagine their own self-sacrifice wind up making others sacrificial victims, while the plot changes from ironic shading to something nearer tragedy. It is the rare Trollopian moment in which a serious sacrifice is made, and made estimable, as in *Can You Forgive Her?* (1864), when Plantagenet Palliser gives up his long-coveted appointment as Chancellor of the Exchequer in order to establish his marriage to Glencora on a firm foundation.

For Trollope, sacrifice was morally empty because it had become identical for Victorians with its most extreme sense: pure giving without any return, a relation he saw as both unrealistic and undesirable. Rejecting a purist standard for sacrifice, Trollope did away with the attempt to retain a sphere of sacrifice beyond a capitalistic, surplus-producing circuit of exchange. Instead, Trollope allowed morally desirable acts to reap reward

---

2. For an invaluable analysis of Trollope's aesthetic and moral disparagement of romance in favor of realism, see Walter M. Kendrick (1980) 62–82.

for their agents; in economic terms, to generate various forms of surplus that could then be fed back into a circuit of sympathetic human relations. Trollope thus followed the lead of the scriptural tradition that relied heavily on merging moral and economic vocabularies. Yet he transformed this tradition to imagine a non-sacrificial vision of harmony and shared plenty that might provide rich dividends without cost.

Further, he emphasized the material as much as the metaphorical: his consideration of the established Anglican Church was inseparable from the consideration of its moneys and their disbursement. While his contemporaries faulted him for what they termed this "vulgarity," Trollope's interest in economics was unapologetic.[3] In her study of the historical relationship between the genres of economic and literary writing, Mary Poovey has described the way that Trollope's treatment of economic matters in *The Last Chronicle* offered a "picture of the credit economy" that differed from the picture offered by contemporary economic theorists: "that the two could coexist in the late 1860s reminds us that economic theorists had not yet succeeded in making their account of 'the economy' the only plausible way of understanding the complex dynamics of credit and debt" (*Genres* 385). We might add that the pictures of the moral economy offered by fiction writers coexisted with the pictures offered by religious and philosophical writers (to be sure, sometimes those figures doubled as political economists). Trollope's fictions thus entered an arena in which notions of credit and debt, and theft and sacrifice, were contested from multiple directions and where novelists were in a strong position to help shape popular conceptions of moral economy.

Sweet Harmony vs. Interests at Variance

The economic drama of *The Warden* turns on the accrual, possession, and circulation of surplus funds. The title describes the post of Reverend Septimus Harding at Hiram's charitable hospital. Mr. Harding is a gentle, beloved figure in Barchester whose peaceful death years later coincides with the end of the chronicles of Barset; such is his quiet centrality

---

3. See the early reviews in Donald Smalley, ed., *Trollope: The Critical Heritage*. Many reviewers faulted Trollope for his treatment of "vulgar" subjects, though some asserted that he was able to treat such subjects without himself descending into vulgarity. Trollope's entrepreneurial relation to his writing long marred his reputation. Kendrick's 1980 study offered a vision of Trollope the professional writer and a more nuanced consideration of Trollope's famous work ethic and prolixity. On Victorian vulgarity, see Elsie Michie (2011).

to Trollope's imagined universe. The events narrated in *The Warden* are set into motion when the avid reformer John Bold suggests that the trust of Hiram's Hospital is being unfairly divided between the warden and the wards—that, according to the stipulations of Hiram's will of 1434, the old men's pay should have increased as the value of the property and its rents increased over its four centuries as a charitable trust. Trollope here provides an ironic corrective to Thomas Carlyle's classic *Past and Present* (1843), which he lampoons later in the novel. The ancient monastery is hardly a modern workhouse: the wool-carders for whom the trust was originally set are "no longer," since wool carding itself is no longer (3). The twelve spots are given to any old, needy men, regardless of profession. Wool has become sheer metaphor: the reverend as shepherd; the wards as sheep. In the centuries that have occasioned these changes, however, the salary of the hospital's poor has remained almost entirely stable while the wardenship has benefited from the land's improvement. Bold contends, boldly, that the warden is robbing the old men of their due. The bedesmen are brought to believe this as well: the parson, they say, is trying to "rob [them] all" (48).

Bold's understanding, and the understanding he transmits to the bedesmen, is based on the economic conviction that one man's benefit must mean another man's loss. Bold sees the interests of the old men and of Reverend Harding as being "at variance" (77, 273). Yet Trollope demonstrates how incorrect a perception this is and how mistaken John Bold is in assuming, first, that happiness can be measured monetarily, and second, that the circumstances before him should be understood in terms of competition for scarce resources.[4] On the contrary, the hospital is characterized as a place of mutual benefit. The circulation of such unquantifiable goods as pleasure, comfort, and concord marks the economy of the hospital, while reciprocity of intention characterizes the relationship between warden and wards. Reverend Harding, a musician by avocation, is described as creating "sweet harmony" (31). The old men for whom Reverend Harding cares listen to the warden play his violoncello with "eager listening faces." The narrator adds: "I will not say that they all appreciated the music which they heard, but they were intent on appearing to do so. Pleased at being

---

4. See Blake for an argument that focuses on the dynamics of church reform, a process she suggests is less open to resolutions of mutual benefit. Situating the novel's dramatization of reform within Benthamite utilitarian thought, Blake argues that Trollope creates in Mr. Harding an acceptance of a new work-ethic that combines much pleasure with some pain. Her claim that the novel clearly endorses the warden's resignation focuses more on the warden than on the wards (100–108).

where they were, they were determined, as far as in them lay, to give plea-sure in return; and they were not unsuccessful" (28). This description of reciprocity does not assume identity between parties; neither does it insinu-ate hypocrisy. The wards seek to please the warden because he seeks to please them. The violoncello gives the warden pleasure, which he wishes to share with the wards; they offer him back a genuine response of apprecia-tion. When John Bold sows the seeds of discord in what the novel calls an "Elysium," he is disrupting a peaceful, mutually satisfying order (8). It is a very stratified order, but it is harmonious.

The narrator is committed to the idea that the interests of the warden and his wards are shared and he states from the outset that the bedesmen will not profit from Bold's lawsuit:

> *Poor old men!* Whoever may be righted or wronged by this inquiry, they at any rate will assuredly be only injured: to them it can only be an unmixed evil. *How can* their lot be improved? all their wants are supplied; every comfort is administered; they have . . . above all, that treasure so inesti-mable in declining years, a true and kind friend. . . . (43, emphases mine)

True to his promise, the narrator brings about a series of events that makes of the lawsuit and the warden's resignation an "unmixed evil" for the old men. Echoing the early premonition, the narrator concludes in perfect parallel:

> *Poor old men! how could* they be cordial with their sore consciences and shamed faces? *how could* they bid God bless him . . . , knowing, as they did, that their vile cabal had driven him from his happy home, and sent him in his old age to seek shelter under a strange roof-tree? (274–75, emphases mine)

Here the narrator quietly points to the likeness between the situations of the bedesmen and the reverend: all are old men in their "declining years." The novel ends with the reverend deprived of his "happy home," a home that was happy for both parties and is now happy for neither. In imagining that their "interests were at variance," the bedesmen have made them so (273; 77). In fact, their interests were in perfect consonance, had they only been able to see it.

The unnecessarily variant interests that spring up between warden and wards are quickly replicated in the romantic plotline of the novel. When John Bold is not busy reforming, he is the lover of Eleanor Harding. By taking up a lawsuit against his beloved's father, whom Bold has known cordially since childhood, the young reformer sets an extraordinary stumbling block in the way of his desired and otherwise easily obtained marriage. Bold's self-division is quickly replicated in Eleanor Harding, who finds herself forced to choose between two loves: father and suitor. Eleanor is as devoted a daughter as can be; her father's primary companion since her mother's death and older sister's marriage, she has effectively served him as both daughter and wife. In this Edenic harmony, which John Bold so unceremoniously interrupts, the force of adult sexuality has been all but absent. While we have seen that Victorian novelistic sexuality is rife with limitations (the satisfaction of one man necessitates the deprivation of another man), in the garden of shared interests Eleanor has been able to belong to her father and contemplate a lover without a conflict of interests. Theft is as unthinkable as it was before Eve took the apple.

Yet when the conflicts of the lawsuit and love-suit come, and Eleanor's father expresses an inclination to resign his post and give up its contested benefits, the daughter plights her troth to him:

> " . . . if there be such cause for sorrow, let us be sorrowful together; we are all in all to each other now. Dear, dear papa, do speak to me."
>
> Mr. Harding could not well speak now, for the warm tears were running down his cheeks like rain in May, but he held his child close to his heart, and squeezed her hand as a lover might, and she kissed his forehead and his wet cheeks, and lay upon his bosom, and comforted him as a woman only can do. (133–34)

The reciprocity of feeling, activity, and speech in the passages describing Eleanor and her father is remarkable. The repetition ("sorrow," "sorrowful"; "all in all"; "dear, dear"; "speak . . . speak"), rhythm, and syntax all indicate perfect agreement, one gesture eliciting another in continuous fashion ("he held . . . and she kissed"), the wordless agreement of lover and woman, father and child. Yet the confusion here of wife and daughter suggests that John Bold and his lawsuit, his introduction of "interests at variance," and the competition for scarce resources, have all forced the father–daughter relationship into an exclusivity Trollope judges as unnatural to it.[5] Here, we see a significant variation on the pattern Allison Giffen has described as central to nineteenth-century popular literature, where the

---

5. For a wide-ranging study of fathers and daughters, see Lynda Boose (1989). Gayle Rubin's 1975 essay, "The Traffic in Women," is the foundational critique of the patriarchal assumptions of a Lévi-Straussian model of female exchange.

daughter's place is one of "loving service . . . the highest aim for a daughter is to live for her father. Model daughters practice self-abnegation and
service, internalizing these codes and deriving fulfillment from ministering
to paternal need" (256). Typically, Giffen argues, such narratives all but
efface "the other side of the emotional equation: paternal desire for the
daughter" (256). A good daughter then chooses her father over a suitor
and finds this choice desirable (262).

By contrast, as we will see, Trollope's eroticized representation of Eleanor and her father seeks to re-describe not only the father–daughter relation but the good marriage, too. For Trollope, both relations depend on
a rejection of the code of self-abnegation (as it applies both to men and
women) and an embrace of mutual satisfaction. The novel, as we will
see, may hold to the patriarchal ideal that a young woman is best served
by marrying, yet it does not fit easily into a Lévi-Straussian framework
in which the daughter is a gift from father to husband, cementing social
bonds, nor is it uncritical of an inappropriately incestuous relation between
father and daughter. The critical satire that follows the passage quoted
above, as the novel heads into a serious rejection of self-sacrificial logic,
suggests that equally critical satire may also attend what precedes it: the
self-giving between daughter and father rendered in amorous terms above.

Sacrifice without Reward

In response to her father's circumstances, Eleanor comes up with a plan
whose analogies are central to the novel's critique of sacrifice:

> When Eleanor laid her head on her pillow that night, her mind was anx-
> iously intent on some plan by which she might extricate her father from
> his misery; and, in her warm-hearted enthusiasm, self-sacrifice was decided
> on as the means to be adopted. Was not so good an Agamemnon worthy
> of an Iphigenia? (138)

Iphigenia, the daughter of Agamemnon, appears in many episodes of Greek
tragedy. In Euripides' play *Iphigenia at Aulis*, Iphigenia believes that she is
to be married to Achilles, only to discover that the marriage is a ruse of her
father's and that he has pledged to sacrifice her to Artemis. Upon hearing
this, Iphigenia voluntarily sacrifices herself.[6]

---

6. While early Greece and Phoenicia turned to human sacrifice before war and at other
times of danger, Euripides' fifth-century B.C.E. plays describe Iphigenia's sacrifice in more

In Trollope's plot, Eleanor, imagining herself a tragic heroine, decides to convince John Bold to abandon the lawsuit. While the reasonable minds around her—her sister, Bold's sister—think the easiest, most natural path is for Eleanor to tell Bold that she loves him, to beg him to desist, and then to marry him, Eleanor rejects this plan outright. The narrator tells us:

> She would herself personally implore John Bold to desist from his undertaking; she would explain to him her father's sorrows, the cruel misery of his position; . . . she would appeal to his old friendship, to his generosity, to his manliness, to his mercy; if need were, she would kneel to him for the favour she would ask; but before she did this, the idea of love must be banished. There must be no bargain in the matter. To his mercy, to his generosity, she could appeal; but as a pure maiden . . . she could not appeal to his love. . . . Of course, when so provoked he would declare his passion; that was to be expected; . . . but it was equally certain that he must be rejected. She could not be understood as saying, Make my father free and I am the reward. There would be no sacrifice in that—not so had Jephthah's daughter saved her father—not so could she show to that kindest, dearest of parents how much she was able to bear for his good. (138–39)

Eleanor will beg Bold to drop his suit, but she vows not to reap any personal benefits from her supplication. Like Iphigenia, Jephthah's daughter redeems her father in Judges with a true sacrifice. Before going out to war, Jephthah vows that if he is victorious, he will offer in sacrifice the first person who comes out to greet him. When he returns home, it is his daughter who welcomes him, only to find herself the object of the pledged sacrifice. Indeed, after a reprieve of two months to bewail her maidenhood among her friends, the daughter returns as a voluntary sacrifice. With such a model of self-abnegation, Eleanor can hardly boast a marriage as the payoff of her "sacrifice." Sacrifice is no sacrifice when it comes with a reward.

Sacrificial Value

It is a mark of the particular purism of Victorian ideas of sacrifice that it was considered problematic as soon as it reaped any form of reward for its agents. Yet, perhaps unbeknownst to Eleanor, from ancient Christianity onward, the concept of sacrifice had always borne a balancing force of

---

ambiguous terms. In *Iphigenia in Tauris* the girl is taken by Artemis to serve her, and in *Iphigenia at Aulis* she is replaced by an animal at the moment of sacrifice.

profit or gain. If sacrifice may be defined, as the *Oxford English Diction-ary* does, as "the destruction or surrender of something valued or desired for the sake of something having, or regarded as having, a higher or more pressing claim," we can see that two almost equally powerful values or desires compete, with the result that the lesser is lost and the greater is gained. We might call that positive difference sacrificial value. While sacri-fice requires loss, it bears an ontologically prior promise of value that moti-vates and underwrites the entire project of sacrifice. From the etymology of the word, *sacrificio*, Georges Bataille tells us that sacrifice is "nothing other than the production of *sacred* things. From the very first, it appears that sacred things are constituted by an operation of loss" (119). Loss makes value.

Christian sacrifice itself functioned as a spectacularly productive nar-rative, one that the Higher Critics were quick to recognize. Christ's self-less death upon the Cross redeemed his people in an act that stood forever after as the unapproachable sacred ideal at the center of the religion: a tor-tuous loss matched by its creative rewards. The humanist narrative offered by Ludwig Feuerbach set sacrifice as the motor for the human work of "creating" God in humankind's image: "whatever religion consciously denies—always supposing that what is denied by it is something essential, true, and consequently incapable of being ultimately denied—it uncon-sciously restores in God" (27).

Across the Channel and in later decades, thinkers across disciplines would similarly reclaim the idea of sacrifice and provide it with a stock of new associations and meanings that would separate it from its maximal-ist sense. For early-twentieth-century social scientists such as Emile Dur-kheim, Marcel Mauss and Henri Hubert, "the social [was] defined by what is given up in order to reproduce it" (Mizruchi 23).[7] And for Georg Sim-mel, who positioned sacrifice centrally in *The Philosophy of Money* (1900), his wide-ranging study on the economics and psychology of exchange, sac-rifice was a process that necessarily created value. In his words, "the value that a subject sacrifices can never be greater, in the particular circumstances of the moment, than the value that he receives in return" (87). During a famine, someone might sacrifice a jewel for a piece of bread. In effect, says Simmel, the sacrifice has brought a profit, since the bread is far more valu-

---

7. Mizruchi sees these social scientists as having been attracted to the concept of sac-rifice because it could sustain both a commitment to scientific rationality and a loyalty to inherited religious values (6); sociology was, then, a "vehicle of secular recuperation, associ-ated with spiritual loss" (26). For other accounts of proto-sociology and anthropology, see George W. Stocking, Jr. (1987) and Herbert (1991).

able to the person than the gem is; if it were not, then the person would never have made the trade.[8] Simmel went further to call sacrifice

> not only the condition of specific values, but the condition of value as such. . . . To recognize value as the result of a sacrifice discloses the infinite wealth that our life derives from this basic form. Our painful experience of sacrifice and our effort to diminish it leads us to believe that its total elimination would raise life to perfection. But here we overlook that sacrifice is by no means always an external obstacle, but is the inner condition of the goal itself and the road by which it may be reached. (84–85)

Simmel understood sacrifice to constitute desire and to allow its realization. There could be no true sacrifice without its promised reward, and no reward without sacrifice.

Among contemporary English Christians, there were those who sought to accept and sanctify a closely defined sense of reward for sacrifice. Against John Stuart Mill's chagrin that Christianity operated "mainly through the feelings of self-interest" ("the habit of expecting to be rewarded in another life for our conduct in this, makes even virtue itself no longer an exercise of the unselfish feelings" ["Utility of Religion" 423]), the Congregationalist preacher Thomas Binney noted as a simple truth that Christianity was based on such an economics. "We are well aware that there is a great dread among some people of any approach to such a word as 'reward,'" he preached in 1853 ("Is It Possible" 197). However, Binney went on, the idea of reward "pervades the New Testament. . . . It is of no use shutting our eyes to this fact" (198). Scripture represents Christian beneficence as "productive, to those who exercise it, of many and varied beneficial results . . . beneficent acts are followed by reward" (197).

Unlike Eleanor, convinced that her sacrifice must be pure, Binney claimed that the structure of reward need not be a degradation of service. While salvation was a gift, rather than a payment in kind, there were still works which "constitute the obedience of a Christian man. These, though

---

8. Simmel claims that the value of the product created by sacrifice is defined by "an elaborate complex of feelings which are always in a process of flux, adjustment and change": "Quite independent of this is the question as to where the object received derives its value; whether it is perhaps the result of the sacrifice offered, so that the balance between gain and cost is established *a posteriori* by the sacrifice. . . . Once the value has been established—no matter how—there is a psychological necessity to regard it as being of equal value with the sacrifice" (87).

See Gagnier on the shift around 1871 from paradigms of value as a function of labor to value as an effect of consumer psychology (*Insatiability* 19–60).

always imperfect, and never entitled to a reward of merit, are yet represented as being followed by what may be called a reward of congruity" (201). Congruity, a concept Binney explored at length, allowed him to argue that "properly understood," such reward could not be "productive of anything like selfish and sordid calculations" of the sort that Mill feared (201).

For the faithful Christian, "the desire for the reward becomes one and the same with love for the service" (201). While it was common for Victorian preachers and theologians to revert to the teaching, "He who would lose his life shall save it," Binney sounded a less common note as he entered into the subjectivity of sacrifice and analyzed the "actual personal satisfaction" that might be got by sacrifice, rather than that which "could be secured without it," particularly for a Christian inclined to it:

> From the state of their minds, it would be the worst sort of suicide for martyrs to act otherwise than they do—the suicide of their moral and spiritual nature. "He who would lose his life shall save it." . . . [T]hey have internal resources of adequate *compensation*, not only in the hope of future reward, but in the luxury of their present experience,—"for as their sufferings abound, so do their consolations also abound in the Christ." (112)

Binney could not see the internal experience of a faithful life as one bereft of comfort and even luxury. And yet, for him, this did not disqualify acts of sacrifice as ethical ones.

Shared Interests and the Impossibility of Sacrifice

When we turn back to Trollope's Eleanor, we can see that *The Warden* shares with Binney's "'ethics of common life'" and the findings of later social scientists the sense that sacrifice generates value ("Is It Possible" 236). Yet whereas Binney saw this gain as the sanctification of sacrifice, Trollope adopted the prevailing maximalist standard and disqualified such acts as sacrifices. And when the sacrificial agent denied the gain she realized, then all the more so.

Eleanor is our case in point. Dreading her sacrifice, Eleanor at the same time desires it with all the romantic powers of her imagination. Trollope emphasizes the imaginative recompense by narrating in free indirect discourse the pleasure that Eleanor takes as she envisions the entire scene in advance, as we have seen: "She would herself personally implore John Bold . . . but as a pure maiden . . . she could not appeal to his love. . . . Of course, when so provoked he would declare his passion; that was to be expected . . ." (*The Warden* 138). Trollope's irony here marks his critique of Eleanor's brand of sacrifice, the delusively purist sort that wants only to give up, not to gain, and, equally important, refuses to acknowledge the pleasure brought about by loss. (Left unsaid also is the fact that Eleanor will take pleasure not only in self-denial, but in denying the other, too: John will be deprived of what he wants after he has so callously risked both her love and her father's well-being.)

But mainly what Eleanor stands to gain from her sacrifice is her father's gratitude and love: this is why she takes it on in the first place. While Trollope comically criticizes the impurity of Eleanor's aims and her impaired self-understanding, the novel far more seriously suggests that pure sacrifice is a potentially unresolvable paradox. Eleanor will never be able to succeed in her sacrifice because the person to whom she offers it wants nothing less. Eleanor anticipates the great pleasure of "show[ing] to that kindest, dearest of parents how much she was able to bear for his good." Yet the narrator relates Mr. Harding's vow at the outset: "her young heart should not be torn asunder to please either priest or prelate, dean or archdeacon. No, not if all Oxford were to convocate together, and agree as to the necessity of the sacrifice!" (137). Certainly, the father dreads the sacrifice because he wants his daughter's happiness. But it is also true that the refusal is for his own sake as well, since her happiness makes his. This is precisely the meaning of shared interests.

Eleanor and her father are too closely identified with each other and their interests are too fully united for Eleanor to be able to sacrifice her own happiness for her father's pleasure. As Trollope so beautifully shows, in relations of deep mutual devotion, acts of self-interest and altruism become increasingly difficult to separate. If one seeks the other's good, then when that good comes, both parties feel its benefit. By the same token, if one denies oneself, it is also a denial of the other. In a sacrificial system that defines sacrifice as *pure* giving (that is, giving with no smidgen of personal return), intimates can never effectively sacrifice themselves for each other.[9] The sense in *The Warden* is that there is no need to. What is of most value, "that treasure so inestimable," human sympathy, is already present (43).

---

9. Colin Grant (2001) reapplies the term "hedonic paradox" to describe this problem: "any pleasure we experience is our own pleasure" (77).

Sacrifice and the Church

Trollope's critique of sacrifice is not only personal, however. By cleverly lit-
eralizing the metaphor of self-sacrifice, Trollope suggests that such a sacrifice is not sanctioned by the Anglican Church. Eleanor explicitly compares
herself to Iphigenia and to Jephthah's daughter, two archetypal images of
female sacrifice.[10] Of course, the irony of Eleanor's comparison comes partially from her glossing over the central distinction we have just noted: her
sacrifice has *not* been sought, pledged, or even unhappily approved by her
father, as in the classical and scriptural patterns. But in the language of
his vow—"her young heart should not be torn asunder to please either
priest or prelate, dean or archdeacon. No, not if all Oxford were to convocate together" (137)—the warden raises the stakes. He imports the idea of
human sacrifice, the "tearing asunder" of Eleanor's heart, into the Christian Protestant world of Oxford.

Trollope's comparison here between selfless Christian sacrifice and
involuntary pagan human sacrifice is hardly a compliment to his portrait
of the Anglican Church. As Debora Shuger has demonstrated, Christian
thinkers from the sixteenth century on categorized societies as archaic or
modern based on their relation to personal sacrifice: the mark of the modern society, she says, became its rejection of human sacrifice: "Substitution
and suicide—assertions of one's *dominium* over the body—mark the break
between archaic and modern cultures" (72). In the nineteenth century, the
idea of human expiation coupled with unjust substitution appalled such
higher-biblical critics as David Friedrich Strauss, author of *The Life of
Jesus* (1835):

> It can scarcely need to be pointed out that a perfect jumble of the crudest
> conceptions is comprised in this one of an atoning death, of a propitiation
> by proxy. To punish some one for another's transgression, to accept even
> the voluntary suffering of the innocent and let the guilty escape scathless
> in consequence, this, everybody admits now, is a barbarous action. (31)

And, as we have seen, the Atonement controversies of the 1850s responded
to the move of Broad Church thinkers toward a like critique of vicarious

---

10. The literature on the Jephthah and Iphigenia stories is extensive. For a history of the
Iphigenia tradition in early modern English theater and the work of Christian theologians
seeking to distinguish Christian and pagan notions of sacrifice, see Debora Shuger (1994).
On the Jephthah story and its readings throughout Christian history, see John L. Thompson
(2001) 100–178.

expiation. In Trollope's novel, Eleanor finds objectionable precisely this confusion of guilt and victim in Bold's persecution of her father for the larger purposes of ecclesiastical reform: "'It is [Mr. Harding] that has to bear the punishment; it is he that suffers,' said Eleanor; 'and what for? what has he done wrong? how has he deserved this persecution? he that never had an unkind thought in his life, he that never said an unkind word!'" (148–49). Yet Eleanor proposes to solve this unjust substitution with a voluntary one of her own, and she glories in her analogy to the daughter of Jephthah or Iphigenia.

While Jephthah's daughter was commonly understood by Christian readers as a typological exemplar, Eleanor's reference to her alongside not a Christian virginal martyr, but the pagan Iphigenia, suggests that Eleanor is probably not thinking of the story in typological terms, but literal. For Trollope, this is where Eleanor goes astray and betrays an overenthusiasm for the sacrificial ideal. Victorian Christian thinkers were deeply invested in the idea that Christian sacrifice was a refinement of Jewish sacrifice as we saw with F. D. Maurice in the last chapter.[11] This idea was not confined to clerics and found its way into other prose works as well. John Ruskin, for instance, stood on the distinctions in manner of sacrifice from Old Testament to New, from Jewish ritualism to Christian spiritualism:

> [I]t was necessary that, in order to the understanding by man of the scheme of Redemption, that scheme should be foreshown from the beginning by the type of bloody sacrifice. But God had no more pleasure in such sacrifice in the time of Moses than He has now; He never accepted, as propitiation for sin, any sacrifice but the single one in prospective. . . . God was a spirit, and could be worshipped only in spirit and in truth, as singly and exclusively when every day brought its claim of typical and material service or offering, as now when He asks for none but that of the heart. (*Seven Lamps of Architecture* 32–33)

As Trollope describes it, the "heart" that Eleanor offers and that her father wishes to defend is not exactly Ruskin's "heart": Eleanor imagines herself sacrificed like the daughters of Agamemnon and Jephthah—smoke on the altar. It is ironic that the Christian critique that Eleanor has not absorbed is redoubled in the scriptural reference to Jephthah, where much of the

---

11. Strauss attacked this claim and argued that the idea of the sacrifice of Christ's fleshly self marked not a refinement but a regression from animal sacrifices back to human (29).

horror of the story is meant to come from the knowledge that Jephthah's vow obligates him to the sort of human sacrifice common among the Canaanite nations but forbidden to the Israelite people. This terrible confusion of acceptable and unacceptable forms of worship inspired the rabbinic and later the Christian tradition that suggested, against the plain meaning of the text, that Jephthah never sacrificed his daughter but instead anointed her as a servant of God's sanctuary.[12] Trollope's passage benefits from layers of scriptural and exegetical tradition which subvert any sacrificial demands of "all Oxford." The end result is to suggest instead that there is no good Christian basis for a sacrifice on Eleanor's part. Such a demand, no matter what its dismissal should cost the Church, would be unwarranted, excessive, and barbaric.

Quickly enough, Eleanor fails her resolve not to benefit materially from a transaction meant to aid her father alone. Not only does she get kissed by Bold, but she is prevailed upon to forgo her vows of chaste sacrificial maidenhood and to accept her lover as a future husband. The narrator comically describes this turnabout as a triumph and a loss in one:

> . . . and so at last, all her defences demolished, all her maiden barriers swept away, she capitulated, or rather marched out with the honours of war, vanquished evidently, palpably vanquished, but still not reduced to the necessity of confessing it.
>
> And so the altar on the shore of the modern Aulis reeked with no sacrifice. (155)

Trollope reemphasizes the contrast between Euripides' drama (set in Aulis) and Eleanor's modern predicament. In light of the comparison, the value of the transaction between Bold and Eleanor is dubious: has she been vanquished, in a defeat of her sacrificial aims, or has she won the honors of war? Eleanor's loss is comically realized in the necessity of personal gratification. She has had to give up her sacrifice.

---

12. Readings of Jephthah's daughter can be divided into the "survivalist" interpretations, which argue that the daughter's life was preserved, and the "sacrificialist," which argue that her life was lost. The survivalist version I mention above was first suggested in the early thirteenth century. The story of Jephthah's daughter has generated much feminist criticism in the last thirty years. Tikva Frymer-Kensky (2002) provides a good introduction to the biblical and historical context (102–17); Phyllis Trible (1984) offers a reading that has been foundational for feminist critics (93–116).

From Sacrifice to Mutual Reward

Yet there is a real loss here. In an irony that is not lost on Eleanor, marriage replaces maidenly self-sacrifice. The moment that Eleanor's marriage is assured, the dramatic instance that she envisioned of simultaneous self-realization and negation disappears, and with it, her right to herself. If, as Trollope explores elsewhere (notably in *The Eustace Diamonds*), the freedom to alienate is a proof of ownership, then the freedom to give oneself is a decisive proof of self-possession. This model is possibly at work in the story in Judges, and it is surely at work in Trollope's other intertext, *Iphigenia at Aulis*. Classicist Helene P. Foley points out that in this drama Euripides "emphasizes the homologies between marriage and sacrificial rites": "Iphigenia's sacrifice is first disguised as marriage, then unmasked and actually transformed into a real marriage, only to be undertaken finally as a combined marriage/self-sacrifice" (68). But the voluntary nature of Iphigenia's final sacrifice is vital here, because the decision to offer herself as sacrifice against the wishes of her family and *polis* makes her finally a model of self-determination in Euripides: "What I have to say is meant to please no one / But myself"; "Look. I give my body away. / . . . / I give it willingly" (67 [1416–17]; 72 [1552–55]).

Likewise, Eleanor's sacrifice bears meaning for the entire body politic, just as, in the story in Judges, Jephthah's victory has political ramifications. The fact that in *The Warden* Trollope does not have Eleanor explicitly imagine herself as any sort of female Christian martyr suggests women's limited agency in the Church he depicts. It is Eleanor's father, not Eleanor herself, who absurdly imagines her heart on an altar in Oxford. In Eleanor's vision, her heart is on the altar at Aulis because there is no place for it at Oxford.

In Eleanor's case, neither marriage nor daughterhood allows her self-determination. When we next see her, in *Barchester Towers* (1857), she is a widow with a child, supported emotionally by Bold's sister, Mary. The contiguity of Mary and the absence of a husband suggest that if Eleanor can be analogized to any heroic figure, it is finally and appropriately the mother Mary. This is a significant alteration from the empowering analogy that she imagines for herself in *The Warden*. While Jephthah's daughter was of course female, one line of Christian interpretation had understood her typologically as Christ's mortal or fleshly self. In the third century, Origen understood Jephthah's daughter to stand for the Christian martyrs of his own day, and in the fourth century, when the persecution of Christians and their martyrdom waned, she became recognizable among Christian readers

and hearers as a figure of selfless chastity and asceticism and was used rhetorically to commend consecrated ecclesiastical virginity (Thompson 172).
These allegorical readings lay the groundwork for the consideration of the
daughter as a type of Christ.

Yet Trollope was certainly not the first to transfer what might be called
the sacrificial credit away from a young woman to a man. The association of Jephthah's daughter with Christ was contested most notably by
Augustine, who fully reconfigured the typological schema. In the Augustin-
ian reading of Judges, it is not the daughter but Jephthah who prefigures
Christ: this is not the fleshly mortal Christ, but the Christ who sacrifices
the kingdom that is the Church to God the Father (1 Cor. 15:24). Accordingly, Jephthah's daughter prefigures the Church, which at times is called
the spouse or wife of Christ but, at other times, is called the chaste, virginal
daughter. When Eleanor compares herself to Jephthah's daughter, the analogy thus draws on a beautifully complex hermeneutical tradition: Eleanor
is at once a type of Christ himself and the object of Christ's sacrifice, his
figurative wife and/or daughter. Eleanor volunteers herself selflessly but is
volunteered choicelessly by another.

In this typological image, we can see the conflict embedded in the sacrificial ideal as Trollope imagines it in a fallen world: *the sacrifice of oneself is usually replicated by the sacrifice of others.* For Eleanor to sacrifice
herself is also, therefore, to cut her father. It is not surprising, then, that
for Trollope the only sacrifices that are productive are those that have as
their aim the unity of two parties, usually marital. Thus in *Can You Forgive Her?*, the necessary professional sacrifice of Plantagenet Palliser for
the sake of his tottering marriage is later rewarded not only with marital
stability but also with the renewal of the professional offer that Palliser
nobly chose to forgo. Palliser's private duty is "made compatible with [his]
public service"—suggesting that sacrifice becomes valuable when it brings
about mutual satisfaction in marriage and in the larger social world (2:
198).

This ideal of mutual satisfaction explains why the narrator's satirical treatment of Eleanor yields to sympathy. Eleanor, too, has merged her
own imagined happiness in her father's and, as such, is admirable for her
generosity and deserving of appreciation—ours and her father's. When
Mr. Harding greets her news of the abandonment of the lawsuit without
a sense of relief or real appreciation, and when Eleanor learns that her
romantic sacrifice has been politically and morally inefficacious, the narrator tells us:

> Poor Eleanor! This was hard upon her. Was it for this she had made her
> great resolve! For this that she had laid aside her quiet demeanour, and
> taken upon her the rants of a tragedy heroine! One may work and not for
> thanks, but yet feel hurt at not receiving them; and so it was with Eleanor:
> one may feel disinterested in one's good actions, and yet feel discontented
> that they are not recognised. Charity may be given with the left hand so
> privily that the right hand does not know it, and yet the left hand may
> regret to feel that it has no immediate reward. Eleanor had had no wish
> to burden her father with a weight of obligation, and yet she had looked
> forward to much delight from the knowledge that she had freed him from
> his sorrows. (173)

Eleanor must come to terms with her failure, as she sees that she has not
helped her father materially. As her father tells her, Bold's decision can neither recall the scathing newspaper descriptions of Mr. Harding nor satisfy
him as to the rights of the case. Thus Eleanor's delight at the change in
events cannot be merged in the delight of her father.

Yet the narrator does not criticize her for this failure very harshly. On
the contrary, his reference to Matthew 6:1–4 poses a serious ideological
challenge to the ideal of selfless, secret charity that the writer of the Gospel
demands:

> Take heed that ye do not your alms before men, to be seen of them: other-
> wise ye have no reward of your Father which is in heaven. Therefore when
> thou doest *thine* alms, do not sound a trumpet before thee, as the hypo-
> crites do in the synagogues and in the streets, that they may have glory of
> men. . . . But when thou doest alms, let not thy left hand know what thy
> right hand doeth: That thine alms may be in secret: and thy Father which
> seeth in secret himself shall reward thee openly. (Matt. 6:1–4)

Having failed to keep her sacrifice pure, Eleanor has also failed to understand that sacrifices are not gifts. She has attempted to offer her father the
sacrifice not in secret, or for the deferred gratification of heavenly reward,
but for a this-worldly, human recompense of feeling. Trollope here writes
his own coda to the verses in Matthew, changing their sense dramatically:
"one may feel disinterested in one's good actions, and yet feel discontented
that they are not recognised. Charity may be given with the left hand so
privily that the right hand does not know it, and yet the left hand may
regret to feel that it has no immediate reward." Trollope revises Matthew

in order to suggest an ethic that departs from the unilateral transactions of self-sacrifice, and he adopts instead the circular returns of gift giving and its attendant sense of plenitude. The left hand and the right hand, after all, belong to one person; the father and the daughter belong to one family; and all of England, ideally, belongs to one Church or at least one set of values. For Trollope, Eleanor's gift is not charity that must be given secretly, then recompensed by God because it was required all along. Instead, it is the natural outgrowth of a relationship that has been characterized from its outset by the joyous giving which the passage calls "much delight."

The delight of giving both prompts the giving and answers it, in a non-sacrificial structure that theologian Stephen H. Webb has described as combining elements of excess and exchange: "both extravagant and reciprocal," this generosity is always responding to an earlier, foundational generosity but not in order to repay it (9). Instead, this generosity aims at inspiring and sustaining a "community of mutual givers" (9).

Reconsidering Resignation

With respect to Eleanor's romance, Trollope rejects the solution of a painful sacrifice on behalf of others from whom one is divided. Yet if the analogy that Trollope imagines for Eleanor is in the end critical of an unnecessary romantic sacrifice on her part, then the same analogy implicitly raises the problem of Mr. Harding's vocational sacrifice, precipitated by the accusations of his theft. While Mr. Harding discourages Eleanor's renunciation, he faces a vocational conundrum parallel to Eleanor's romantic one: should he resign his beloved and comfortable position? Is renunciation mandated, or may he rightfully go on enjoying the pleasures of his post?

In his excellent study of the comic ethos in Trollope's novels, Christopher Herbert asserts that "[Trollope's] stories turn endlessly on this paradox—that is, on the extreme difficulty of making reliable discriminations between morbidity and authentic virtue" (*Trollope and Comic Pleasure* 47). What Herbert calls "morbidity" and "estrangement from pleasure," I have been calling the self-sacrificial impulse (47). Yet as Herbert reminds us, there would be no paradox, no moral dilemma, if it were not true that self-sacrifice is sometimes the right thing to do:

> This pathological syndrome [the estrangement from pleasure] takes its deep significance for Trollope in being intimately linked to many of what he sees as the worthiest elements of his culture: its moral idealism, its cult

of altruism, its romantic and chivalrous concept of love, among other things. (47)

In other words, the questions stand: should the warden resign? Is Mr. Harding benefiting from stolen goods, or is he simply a man earning a generous salary while providing an invaluable service?

It is noteworthy that contemporary reviewers of *The Warden*, even those who found much to praise in the novel, were made uncomfortable by the ambiguity surrounding Mr. Harding's income, his renunciation, and, more generally, the moral of the story.[13] In a notice in *The Athenaeum* for 27 January 1855, an anonymous reviewer reported:

> "The Warden" is a clever, spirited, sketchy story, upon the difficulties which surround that vexed question, the administration of the charitable trusts in England. . . . The whole story is well and smartly told, but with too much indifference as to the rights of the case. The conclusion is inconclusive enough, inasmuch as it is left for the reader to infer that nobody has any right to the charity. (107)

Likewise, a reviewer for the *Eclectic Review* wrote in the March 1855 issue:

> There is . . . one defect in the volume, which, in our judgment, mars the whole. A *moral* is wanting. To say nothing of the fact—in itself significant—that the views of the author on the subject of ecclesiastical revenue are not apparent, there is no fitting end attained by all which is done. . . . Everything is left in disorder and ruin. (360)

The Victorian zeal for a moral is not misplaced: after all, Trollope leaves the question of theft and the fate of the money troublingly unresolved, as he does the large ideological question of renunciation. We might say that in all circumstances that pose the possibility of sacrifice, the fear

---

13. Our own critical treatments of *The Warden* have been less troubled by the omission of a clear moral, perhaps because we have had reference to Trollope's posthumous aesthetic apology for the novel. In his *Autobiography,* Trollope describes himself caught between two "opposite" evils: a deep concern over the diversion to idle clerics of Church funds designated for charity, and a hatred for the journalistic irresponsibility that savaged the reputation of those who, like Mr. Harding, were not "the chief sinners in the matter" (94). Most recent critics have seen Trollope's inability to come down firmly on one side as a sign that he truly was, as he called himself, "an advanced conservative Liberal," aware of the need for reform but nostalgic for stability (*Autobiography* 294).

of theft cannot be far away. For sacrifice, much as it indicates an action beyond the measure of the law, also paradoxically assumes moral obligation—and obligation assumes debt. For Victorians caught in the extreme moral polarity that I described at the outset, omission becomes commission. Not to repay debt, not to restore what does not belong to you, is tantamount to theft. And Mr. Harding, the novel tells us explicitly, is a debtor. Early on in the story, we learn that despite Mr. Harding's comfortable income, he "is never quite at ease in money matters" (9). His debt is assimilated to his generosity—to his daughter and the old men—but the vellum and gilding of church music he has published "cost more than anyone knows" (9). This debt, as elevated as may be its source, couples with the warden's fear that people will say of him that he is a robber: "Should it ever be said that he had robbed those old men, whom he so truly and so tenderly loved in his heart of hearts?" (71).

These overtly economic descriptors of the warden, particularly the matter of his debt, suggest a fissure in Trollope's confident and conservative approach to the subject of the distribution of wealth. The notion that the bedesmen should merit a fraction of Mr. Harding's income is never taken seriously; the narrator suggests adamantly that the poor old men should have been grateful for the extra twopence Mr. Harding was generous enough to give them, and the novel's ending is a kind of punitive rebuke to them. Yet just as the terms of "debt" and "robbery" open up the space for a critique of Trollope's economics, so do they open space for a critique of the ethics of renunciation.

Trollope, I suggest, questions whether the warden's renunciation of his post might not be the true selfishness, the true theft. While this question asks us to sidestep the sort of class-based critique just noted, in so doing, we leave a clear-cut ideological critique for a realm where Trollope's position is far more difficult to ascertain. That the question of Harding's character has rarely registered in criticism may be an effect of post-Victorian readers coming to know Mr. Harding as a cumulative effect of the entire Barsetshire series. By the series' end, he is clearly a heroic figure, in Trollope's favored quiet, modest key. But when we read sequentially and consider the independent evidence offered to us by *The Warden* (which is how Victorians first encountered it), Mr. Harding's heroism is less certain. While readers such as Sherman Hawkins and Hugh Hennedy have understood *The Warden* to celebrate the warden's resignation of his post as a perfect self-sacrifice, the novel, on the contrary, may just as well signal what Paul Lyons calls the mixture of "old-testament willingness to sacrifice with moral indiscriminateness."[14] Mr. Harding may not be willing to sacrifice his daughter but, in the end, his resignation leaves the bedesmen largely to fend for themselves. The position is left open, to be resolved only in *Barchester Towers,* where the busy Mr. Quiverful eventually takes over with only a quotient of the attention and care that characterized Mr. Harding's tenure.

While this decision hardly makes the former warden a moral monster, Mr. Harding's decision nonetheless emphasizes the way that sacrifice marks social division in Trollope's novels and, rather than healing it, perpetuates it:

> And how fared the hospital. . . . Badly indeed. Six have died, with no kind friend to solace their last moments. . . . Mr. Harding, indeed, did not desert them; from him they had such consolation as a dying man may receive from his Christian pastor; but it was the occasional kindness of a stranger which ministered to them, and not the constant presence of a master, a neighbour, and a friend. (280)

In an odd sense, then, despite Mr. Harding's privileged position in the Barsetshire chronicles, the resolution of Eleanor's plot is more in line with Trollope's vision than is Mr. Harding's resignation. That Trollope seems mainly to cast blame for the final situation on the old men and Bold does not mitigate Mr. Harding's own responsibility, especially since the end of the novel details a materially comfortable arrangement for him near his best friend, the bishop, while the old men incur a net loss of twopence a day and their dear friend.

The novel's references to Iphigenia and Jephthah's daughter beg at least a brief consideration of Mr. Harding as Agamemnon or Jephthah, questionable figures both. Clearly, the warden does not wish to sacrifice his daughter, but perhaps the sacrificial dilemma has been transposed here. Just as Eleanor's comic dilemma regards *self*-sacrifice, her father's more nearly tragic dilemma does as well. Perhaps the warden's paternal generosity occludes the moral ambiguity of his response to his own vocational problem. After all, if the point of Eleanor's story is to sacrifice the sacrifice and to accept the pleasure of her suitor, then it seems equally plausible that Mr. Harding's mission may be similarly oriented.

---

14. James R. Kincaid (1977) argues somewhat more neutrally that Trollope makes a moral example of Mr. Harding's resignation (92–113).

If we are willing to consider Trollope as critical of Mr. Harding's self-sacrifice, then the reference to the story of Jephthah comes into clearer focus. As the biblical scholar Tikva Frymer-Kensky reminds us: "The book of Judges [and Jephthah's story] takes place in the real world, historical time, in a world in which God will no longer intervene to save individuals . . . the world of the book of Judges is more like the world of the readers, past and present" (116). As in the world of Judges, the founding problem in *The Warden* is a human world that must operate on the mandate of absent founders. Hiram's Hospital is the product of his last will and testament, a text left behind in the fifteenth century by a speaker who cannot elucidate or implement it. As Hawkins has noted, both the church and Hiram's Hospital "were established in the remote past by 'godly' men whose enigmatic intentions can be interpreted only through their written testaments and their own 'godlike work.' . . . Both institutions . . . must now interpret the literal terms of the 'testament' to fit new social conditions, while remaining true to the original 'will' of the founder" (215). Reverend Harding's sacrifice or resignation is quintessentially a modern problem, then. The consideration of doing something beyond the call of duty arises here precisely because it is no longer clear exactly what one's duty is.

The exegetical history of the story of Jephthah and his daughter encourages us to read *The Warden*—and the warden himself—with a hermeneutic of suspicion. For Christian exegetes from at least the early fourth century onward, troubling moral questions were raised first by Jephthah's overeager vow to sacrifice whatever came from his door upon his return from battle, and then by his subsequent adherence to the vow, which might have been redeemed in other ways. While the story in Judges was read in typological terms beginning with Augustine, an intervening typology was equally important to its interpretation. This story of child sacrifice was read against the narrative of Isaac and Abraham, a less troubling narrative because, despite the transformation of the story into a sacrificial example, Isaac is bound but not sacrificed in Genesis. When the two stories of child sacrifice were set side by side, the other signal distinction for centuries of commentators was that Abraham's sacrifice had been mandated by God, but Jephthah's had not. Augustine, in particular, was terribly troubled by this distinction upon which the religious meaning of Jephthah's character hinged. In the end, Augustine concluded that Jephthah was mistaken to think that God could be pleased by human sacrifice: for him the story of Isaac, where such a sacrifice was commanded by God, is an exceptional one. According to John L. Thompson, Augustine reads the story of Isaac as a reminder to Christians "that God opposed not just human sacrifices but all animal sacrifices"; to Augustine, "the sacrifices enjoined in the Old Testament were tolerated only because 'they were signifiers and shadows, so to speak, of things to come'" (128).

While these exegetical details may seem far afield of *The Warden*, the debate and dismay evinced by commentators from ancient times underscores the way that sacrifice balances a line between sacrilege and piety. Augustine's firm resolution of Jephthah's status and his distinction of Abraham and Jephthah clarify the stakes of the moral problem in a post-prophetic world. In the end, Mr. Harding's renunciation is as ambiguous as Jephthah's vow and sacrifice.

Renunciation Not a Right

I would like to turn now to *The Last Chronicle of Barset*. A longer, more fully realized narrative than the fable-like *Warden*, *The Last Chronicle* circles back to the first novel of the series in its repeating plot of a clergyman accused of a theft and a daughter ready to sacrifice her lover. Offering a more pointed critique of "unnatural self-sacrifice" than *The Warden*, *The Last Chronicle* clarified Trollope's anti-ascetic position in both the vocational and domestic sphere (*Autobiography* 105).[15]

The Last Chronicle begins, like *The Warden*, with vocational trouble, money, and the Church. When the impoverished, indebted, but highly educated and upstanding curate Reverend Crawley attempts to use another man's check of twenty pounds, whose origins he cannot account for, a scandal arises. For chapters, the full slate of Trollope's characters debate whether Mr. Crawley can have stolen the check, how it can be that he does not recall where the check originally came to him, whether he

---

15. In one of the few critical discussions of wealth and exchange in the Barsetshire novels, Michie (2001) has noted that the composition of *The Last Chronicle* is roughly contemporaneous with a paradigm shift in British political economy associated primarily with W. Stanley Jevons' *The Theory of Political Economy* (1871). Considerations of production in the writings of the classical economists yielded to discussions of consumption just as the commercial ethic of saving was shifting to one of spending. Michie argues that in *The Last Chronicle*, Trollope "explore[s] a set of ascetic values that were ceasing to be tenable in a culture where social interactions were depending more and more on the credit nexus" (79). While Michie assigns Trollope's own paradigm shift toward an acceptance of the "'mercenary tendencies'" to this last novel of the series, we have seen that as early as *The Warden*, Trollope had begun to articulate an anti-ascetic philosophy (86). For a full treatment of the paradigm shift, see Gagnier, who notes that even in times when one paradigm dominates, competing social and economic visions demand historical accounting (5).

suffered temporary insanity brought on by the sufferings of poverty and shame that made him unaware of receiving or taking the check, and so on. In Mr. Crawley—tormented, morose, pious, yet terribly proud—Trollope offers us as good a psychological portrait as any his novels have to offer. The character is so vastly different than Mr. Harding's (especially the Mr. Harding who has materialized over the full Barsetshire series) that the parallel between the stories has received no attention, yet the entire drama of the mysterious check and possible theft funnels into the very question Mr. Harding faces as well: whether he can, by rights, retain his position and his home.

Deep into the novel, as Mr. Crawley's civil trial approaches, he learns that the bishop has set up a commission of clergymen to determine his position in the diocese should the jury find him guilty. In the face of that information, Crawley examines his own conduct as closely as he can and concludes that though he is not a thief, only a "terrible incapacity" can have rendered him so unable to manage his affairs (580). Thus Mr. Crawley decides to give up his position preemptively and independently, before he has been judged and before the commission has come to any recommendation. Quickly, he becomes obstinately, eagerly willing to give up his position: "The name and fame of a parish clergyman should be unstained," he argues (586). Crawley becomes convinced that giving up the parish is his positive "duty as a clergyman" (588).

Yet against the ethically loaded term, "duty," and the seeming self-renunciation it appears to demand, the novel piles up its incriminating evidence. The direct spokesperson against Crawley's inclination is Dr. Tempest, the head of the clerical investigation committee, who sees the situation unambiguously and energetically responds to Crawley: "'Man . . . if you do this thing, you will then at least be very wicked. . . . And you will turn your wife into the poorhouse for an idea!'" (587). The next day, Dr. Tempest reiterates his view even more sharply and logically in a note to Crawley:

> I tell you with absolute confidence, that it is not your duty in your present position to give up your living. . . .
>
> And you must remember that if it is not your duty as a clergyman to give up your living, you can have no right, seeing that you have a wife and family, to throw it away as an indulgence to your pride. (672)

Now, not only is renunciation not Crawley's duty, but it is not even his right. As we have seen George Eliot testing whether sainthood is best, here,

Trollope argues that what may look like supererogation—the taking on of responsibility beyond duty—is in fact masking a contravention of duty: an inability to live up to duty, not its transcendence.

Trollope goes to pains to clarify that Crawley has no justification to resign. First, there has been no doubt, not to Crawley himself nor even his detractors, that his ministrations in his parish have been good. He has been diligent among his people who have held him in high respect and his sincerity has "won its way even with the rough" among whom he has toiled (581–82). As in Mr. Harding's case, who will be the caretaker of the forgotten friendless to whom the clergyman has ministered?

But Reverend Crawley's resignation is primarily wrong because it invites utter ruin for his family. Here, a comparison to *The Warden* is helpful. Unlike Reverend Harding and his daughter, Mr. Crawley and his family are mired in poverty that the novel takes great pains to dramatize: from the problem of tattered, unwearable clothing to firewood to food to transportation to a dearth of readable volumes in a highly literate family. Small sums make great differences to the Crawleys and the yearly parish living of £130 only barely sustains the family. By contrast, although the warden's resignation in the former novel is, as we have seen, ambiguous, it can hardly be said to be fatal for his family, since it leaves him with £150 a year, and it might well be the justified redress of a wrong. Mr. Harding, in fact, tempers his desire to resign with careful consideration of whether the resignation is practicable for himself and his daughter. His mind runs to life insurance, to maintaining his own independence without burdening others: "He knew he had not thought sufficiently of this; that he had been carried away by enthusiasm, and had hitherto not brought home to himself the full reality of his position" (221). Only after serious thought does the warden judge his freedom to resign. Finally, the difference in sum—Mr. Crawley's questionable £20 versus Mr. Harding's yearly £800—may also suggest the disproportionate nature of Mr. Crawley's response.

More clearly than in the similar circumstances in *The Warden*, the theft that Mr. Crawley has been accused of is a plot device. In his *Autobiography*, Trollope himself said of *The Last Chronicle*: "I was never quite satisfied with the development of the plot, which consisted in the loss of a cheque, of a charge made against a clergyman for stealing it, and of absolute uncertainty on the part of the clergyman himself as to the manner in which the cheque had found its way into his hands. I cannot quite make myself believe that even such a man as Mr. Crawley could have forgotten how he got it" (274). While Poovey has argued that Mr. Crawley's uncertainty and his dissociation from himself marks Trollope's desire to shift readers' attention from a simple identification with character to an appreciation of the artistry of the novel, I suggest that in this novel, as in *The Warden,* the ambiguity surrounding the accused theft allowed Trollope to explore its shadow relation, sacrifice.[16] And again, it is sacrifice, not theft, which threatens to leave debts unpaid.

Pride and Sacrifice

Crawley's resignation is posed as a moral conflict between attending to the needs of his family and satisfying his own need. His own need is the painful but publicly and privately vindicating self-satisfaction of sacrifice. Over and over, Crawley divides between himself and his family in ways that recall the unnecessary and problematic "interests at variance" we have seen in *The Warden.* When he imagines trying to help his family, it is by suffering for them so that they may suffer less or, alternatively, by severing himself from them. In either case, it is by dividing his fate from theirs. And when Crawley nurses his own need, they recede from his consideration and he takes steps toward doing something for himself that will actively harm them:

> [H]e pitied himself with a tenderness of commiseration which knew no bounds. As for those belonging to them, his wife and children, his pity for them was of a different kind. He would have suffered any increase of suffering, could he by such agony have released them. Dearly as he loved them, he would have severed himself from them, had it been possible. . . . But the commiseration which he felt for himself had been different from this, and had mostly visited him at times when that other pity was for the moment in abeyance. (581)

Crawley does not feel with his family.[17] This point is brought home ever

---

16. See Poovey's detailed account of how Trollope used this element of plot to develop a new mode of characterization. The check serves an "aesthetic function" for Trollope (*Genres* 391): "Trollope uses Crawley's inability to believe what he knows . . . to generate plot, instead of using plot to generate character" (395). She argues that the novel opposes gift and credit relations along the lines of gender in order to ground moral value in "the natural hierarchy of gender" (404).

17. Michie argues that even as Trollope moves toward an embrace of the "'mercenary tendencies,'" he "cordon[s] off an idea of honor" by associating "women with economics and men with asceticism" ("Buying Brains" 86). Crawley's poverty and asceticism may have

more vividly by the sustained contrast with his wife. Heroically long-suffering and self-effacing on behalf of her husband and children, Mrs. Crawley cannot imagine her fate distinct from that of the family, especially her exacting and egoistic husband.

And so, Trollope's narrator concludes, Mr. Crawley's commiseration with himself is "sickly in spite of its truth" (582):

> He pitied himself with a commiseration that was sickly in spite of its truth. . . . He could do a great thing or two. . . . He could tell the truth though truth should ruin him. He could sacrifice all that he had to duty. . . . But he could not forget to pay a tribute to himself for the greatness of his own actions. (582)

Trollope's repeating structure here, "He could, he could, he could," followed by, "But he could not" suggests that all that Crawley can do is canceled out by what he cannot do. What Mr. Crawley seeks, alongside justice, is moral recognition. Justice does not demand that he resign his position, but pride does.

Clarifying the Crawley plot is an elaborate sub-plot in which another marriage founders and a life is lost when a self-sacrificial imagination occludes a young wife's interest in her husband. The recently married Maria Dobbs-Broughton plays at falling in love with the painter Conway Dalrymple and then entertains herself by imagining her sacrificial virtue in "submitting to her husband," and renouncing Dalrymple so that he will be able to marry for money:

> [S]he herself would, with suicidal hands, destroy the love of her own life, since an overbearing, brutal husband demanded that it should be destroyed. She would sacrifice her own feelings, and do all in her power to bring Conway Dalrymple and Clara Van Siever together. If, after that, some poet did not immortalise her friendship in Byronic verse, she certainly would not get her due. Perhaps Conway Dalrymple would himself become a poet in order that this might be done properly. (LC 469–70)

While Maria has a "good time" imagining herself a conscious Isaac, "piling the faggots for her own pyre," her husband navigates dire financial and

---

made him noble in the eyes of Victorian readers seeking an ethics uncontaminated by market relations, but Trollope is so unsparing in his description of Crawley's pride and its effects on his wife that readers would have had to set aside much in order to admire him.

emotional straits alone (481). Maria's reversible games and indulgent self-imaginings come into relief when Broughton, with no advance warning or fanfare, commits suicide, an event of magnified significance in a novel of almost no decisive or dramatic action. While the novel's few other major events are also deaths (those of Mr. Harding and Mrs. Proudie), Broughton's death stands out as self-induced and genuinely rather than falsely sacrificial. His death is tragic, yet not at all heroic as in the Dickensian transformation of suicide to self-sacrifice. Though Maria is not held responsible for Broughton's suicide, Trollope nonetheless suggests that self-sacrificial dramas tend at their most serious to deadly ends.

Just as Crawley offers a "higher" version of Broughton's vocational dilemma, Crawley's daughter, Grace, allows Trollope to explore the self-imagining we have seen in Maria now embedded in a more significant moral character. In a romantic plotline that intersects with her father's, Grace, a girl of high intelligence and strong loyalty to her family, responds to a moral dilemma with sacrificial pride that Trollope corrects. Major Grantly, son of the worldly though fundamentally decent Archdeacon Grantly, has proposed to Grace despite the cloud over her father. In response to Major Grantly's noble loyalty, Grace refuses his proposal so as not to injure her suitor's standing nor come between him and his family while her own father's name is still besmirched by the accusation of theft. Grace's friend, Lily Dale, herself the "old maid" of the series, lectures Grace with good, practical sense that resonates because of Lily's own intimacy with morbid self-denial: "'Because this major of yours does a generous thing, which is for the good of you both,—the infinite good of both of you,—you are to emulate his generosity by doing a thing which will be for the good of neither of you'" (295). Grace resists Lily's advice, saying: "'Do you think that I will let him sacrifice himself?'" (294). But Lily resists, too, disputing Grace's terms: "'There will be no sacrifice. He will be asking for that which he wishes to get; and you will be bound to give it to him.'" Grace closes the possibility with the following reasoning: "'If it be as you say, he will have shown himself noble, and his nobility will have consisted in this, that he has been willing to take that which he does not want, in order that he may succour one whom he loves. I also will succour one whom I love, as best I know how'" (294). If Major Grantly is making a sacrifice in offering marriage to Grace, then Grace is obligated not to allow him to do so. If he is not making a sacrifice, then Grace is doubly obligated to return his love by protecting him from himself. But, of course, in both these scenarios, Grace and the major remain apart.

For Trollope it is always pride, or even the more neutral "reputa-tion" or "name," that motivates such questionable sacrifices. The narrator describes Grace's instinct as follows: "[Major Grantly] had been gener-ous, and her self-pride was satisfied. But her other pride was touched, and she also would be generous" (300). Here Trollope distinguishes between the simple drive of "self-pride," the unschooled desire for ascendancy and regard, and what he calls the "other pride," pride in one's capacity for goodness, for self-sacrifice, the pride that recalls to us Grace's father. The morally complex "other pride" poses insidious danger to the social whole because the actions that it suggests indeed appear to operate generously. Yet their generosity is finally selfish, rejecting any possibility for mutual satisfaction in the insistence on individual identity. Lily Dale's language—"the good of you both" and "the infinite good of both of you"—attempts to interrupt Grace's relentless singular terms.

What Grace fails to see—and what Trollope emphasizes—is that in her circumstances, two parties' needs can be met if they cease to see each other as individuals. Maria Dobbs-Broughton's absurd cry to Conway Dalrymple, "'the sacrifices shall all be made by me!'" is, in effect, Grace's more serious position in a real, rather than imagined, situation (*LC* 481). Grace has turned her circumstances into the dilemma described by Colin Grant in his study of Christian ethics: "two altruists in the des-ert . . . pass a cup of water back and forth between them, each insisting that the other drink, until the water evaporates, and both die of thirst" (76). As Grant writes in response to this dilemma, which is also Grace's dilemma, "realism demands some scope for self-interest in life at its best" (76). In regard to this logical claim—a claim that in the 1880s would be Herbert Spencer's evolutionary argument for the preservation of the species through acts of measured egoism—Trollope stresses the idea that self-interest and other-interest do not have to exclude each other. At the novel's end when Mr. Crawley has been exonerated, his good-hearted, entirely unself-conscious cousin, Mr. Toogood, rejects the romantic idea that Crawley is a "hero," and describes him instead as an unnaturally selfless sort: "'But to find a man who was going to let everything in the world go against him, because he believed another fellow better than himself! . . . It's not natural; and the world wouldn't go on if there were many like that'" (698). The odd emptiness that Poovey has described as Crawley's absence of "true character" may well be Trollope's mode of evoking the alienated selfhood that is unusually susceptible to dreams of "unnatural" self-sacrifice (396).

A Marriage of Shared Interests

The Warden, as I have shown, ends with an ambiguous chiasm: Eleanor sacrifices her sacrifice and marries, while the warden makes his sacrifice and resigns. By contrast, *The Last Chronicle of Barset* is resolved in unified fashion. Mr. Crawley's name is fully cleared, he is promoted, and, of course, Grace is married off. Marriage in Trollope's novels is a complicated affair. Trollope envisioned marriage as a revealing testing ground for personal ethics and paired psychologies; thus it is often a site of terrible disharmony, misunderstanding, and mutual suffering, as *The Last Chronicle* dramatizes in its masterful treatment of the Proudies. That same novel also showcases the disparity in generosity between Mr. and Mrs. Crawley, where Mrs. Crawley's immense capacity for self-sacrifice seems only to allow Mr. Crawley's self-involvement to flourish undisturbed.

Yet Trollope's novels do not despair of marriage. In fact, I suggest that Trollope's good marriages operate as the antidote to self-sacrificial nihilism, marking a real difference between his novels and the work of many of his contemporaries, as well as the intertexts we have explored, Euripides' plays and the Book of Judges.[18] Trollope adapted the literary figure of marriage in a way that opposed a Victorian ethics focused on self-sacrifice without return. As John Milbank has noted, marriage can provide an ideal model where "enjoying and giving coincide" (59) in a state that is "no longer in need of any contractual re-establishment . . . marriage restores free but mutual giving in asymmetrical reciprocity, since in marriage there is no interval of debt between gift and return" (58). In this imagined state, the account book is gone. "Asymmetrical reciprocity" offers a new, debt-free model of continuous exchange in which the longevity and intimacy of relation make it difficult to distinguish between giver and recipient, between giving and enjoying. This is not the gift economy that merely mirrors commercial exchange but, for Milbank, something nearer the free gifts of grace.

While most marriages can only aspire to such conditions, the model helps us understand the comedic endings of *The Warden* and *The Last Chronicle of Barset* (endings at the far end of realism) in a new light. To be sure, these marriages often alienate contemporary readers in their re-establishment of what Poovey calls a "natural hierarchy of gender"; they also re-direct women's erotic self-imagining in restrictive ways (404).[19]

---

18. On marriage and the cultivation of sympathy in relation to the Victorian novel, see Ablow.

19. Two other excellent accounts of Trollope's relation to gender can be found in Wil-

Still, the marriages which close the novels can be read in heuristic terms to clarify the social vision I have been sketching here, one we might describe with Alan P. Fiske's term, "communal sharing." In discussing Fiske's ideas, Colin Grant notes:

> This is the most personal form of society, in which individuals interact directly to a large extent. . . . Such a social configuration encourages altruism in practice, but by that very token, renders the altruism identification itself virtually redundant. So natural is sharing in such a society that lines between self and others are vague at best. Self-interest, other-interest, and collective-interest are linked together in ways that preclude their identification. . . . [The communal sharing approach] takes altruism to be so natural and expected that it does not deal with altruism at its most distinctive, and even resists recognizing it as a moral or social ideal. (222)

In such a circumstance, altruism—self-sacrifice—goes on, but it goes on quietly, unselfconsciously. It does not look like altruism to its agents; it looks like ordinary living. In its smallest manifestation, we see it in *The Warden*'s bedesmen, early on in the novel, listening to music that they may not enjoy instinctively, but appear to enjoy because they know it gives their warden pleasure—and so it truly gives them pleasure, too. In a larger manifestation, it is the warden desiring that his daughter marry a man who has made his own life more difficult than it need be, because his daughter's happiness is his own. As Grant suggests, the intimacy of these relationships renders the identification of such acts superfluous and often impossible. No decisions are made to offer these kinds of gifts: if one were to ask the bedesmen or the warden whether they have made sacrifices to provide pleasure to their intimates, they would likely say no. Likewise, a marriage characterized by the ideal of "communal sharing" would be a quiet duet between people so well used to each other's desires and needs that gifts both large and small would be indivisible from the day-to-day, side-by-side march through time that is a shared life.

Although the extremity of Victorian moral judgment may have functioned to name a powerful ideal, it also rendered its claims beyond the scope of most human action. Trollope's fiction, in contrast, transformed a major Victorian ideal into the anticlimactic stuff of ordinary living. In quietly taking church politics as the ground for a serious reflection on

---

liam A. Cohen (1996) who considers the distinctions between male and female figures of property and ownership (159–90), and Kathy A. Psomiades (1999) who studies the anachronisms in Trollope's representation of gendered relations to self and property.

inherited Christian ethics, Trollope reconceived morally desirable action as mutually beneficial rather than purely altruistic; as automatic and unconsidered rather than deliberate or self-conscious; and as normative rather than extraordinary or impossibly idealistic.

That the Barsetshire series ends with a full-scale rejection of the ascetic ideal is not surprising. *The Warden* heralded the beginning of Trollope's own economic success. Trollope sold *The Warden* to Longman for the promise of half-profits, realizing from this promise less than £20 over two years. Still, he reflected in his *Autobiography:* "The novel-reading world did not go mad about *The Warden;* but I soon felt that it had not failed as the others [literary efforts] had failed" (98). Trollope was correct: though *The Warden* realized a paltry sum of money, it heralded the immense popularity and serious sales that he would enjoy for two decades.[20]

In the century's longest sustained period of economic optimism, Trollope, like his contemporaries, saw his novels of sympathy bring him exponentially increased material reward. At the same time, he hoped they would bring his readers spiritual reward. Under these propitious conditions, Trollope abandoned the unmixed evil of theft in order to explore the struggles between a right hand that dispensed and a left hand that sought sympathetic recompense.

---

20. For an account of Trollope as an aspiring professional writer, see Miller who suggests that Trollope embraced the commodity-form of the novel as few of his contemporaries did (*Novels behind Glass* 159–88). See also Nicholas Dames (2003) and Jonathan Freedman (2000).

CHAPTER 5

Collins' Writerly Sacrifice

o many modern readers, it is encouraging to see a "post-Victorian" horizon in Trollope's optimism that painful self-sacrifice might be replaced with mutual benefit and pleasure. Yet, as Trollope himself knew, the 1860s had not ushered in that utopian condition. Trollope's progressive vision of an altruism so thoroughgoing that it became the unrecognizable, yet vital medium of human relations took its inspiration from idealized versions of patriarchal marriage and a nearly feudal social structure based on patronage and the prerogative of charity. For Wilkie Collins, these institutions provided not solutions but ethical problems.

Keenly alive to the challenges of a society stratified by class and gender, and increasingly defined by the conditions of industrial capitalism, Collins sought an economic ethics recognizably rooted in Christian teachings, yet secularized enough to elude the hypocrisies and failures he associated with traditional Christian giving. He found this ethics, one that merged the ideal of sacrifice with the hoped-for outcome of mutual benefit, in the labor of professionalizing novelists writing for a public readership.

Collins' popular mystery novel of 1868, *The Moonstone*, systematically explores the way contemporary Britons, raised at the crux of the evangelical inheritance and the capitalist ethos, attempt and fail to transcend the marketplace logic of self-interest in their personal relations. As we saw in the previous chapter, in a system built on reward and punishment, all selflessness can be construed as selfishness. In a system founded on a "free gift" of grace, all recipients are certainly debtors and possibly thieves. By the standards of maximalist altruism, Christianity can hardly undo these paradoxes.

Mistrustful of the ethical pitfalls of Christian charity, Collins found himself in an extraordinary position, seeking an ethics that would be more authentically "Christian," that is selfless, than Christianity itself. Like many of his fellow intellectuals and writers, he lived an unconventional life and, by traditional Christian standards, a transgressive one. He never married, but supported and raised children with two women simultaneously over the course of his life. The outward forms of religion meant little to him. Still, in an 1852 controversy over the discussion of religion in journals, he could clearly assert, "I am neither a Protestant, a Catholic—or a Dissenter—I do not desire this or that particular creed; but I believe Jesus Christ to be the son of God" (*Letters* 1: 85–86). As Catherine Peters puts it in her definitive biography, Collins "took the life of Jesus to be the model for social behavior," like many free-thinkers of his time (108). His novels, like his life, refused any equation between what he called the "Clap-trap morality of the present day" and the "Christian morality which is of all time" ("Foreword," *Armadale*).

For Collins, in distinction from Trollope, the elusive Christian morality of all time seems to have been closely associated with what I have described as maximalist altruism: the sense that the smallest measure of self-interest rightfully discredited virtue. *The Moonstone* seeks such a maximalist altruism in the field of material exchange, dramatizing through a series of variations the seeming impossibility of the truly free gift. Gifts generally appear to be the most obvious material expression of altruism.[1] As theologian Stephen Webb puts it, they appear to come as a "lavish intrusion" into the world of objective, reciprocal exchanges (91). Yet Collins' repeated representation of gift exchange anticipates instead Marcel Mauss' theory that, despite appearances, gifts are nevertheless part of reciprocal exchange systems. One must always respond to a gift, on pain of punishment; the party who does not respond to a gift with a return is understood to evince signs of hostility. Further, insofar as a gift begs its own return and then some, it shares the structure of theft: an uninvited, unilateral act of demand or claim (note the term "intrusion" above).[2]

---

1. See Jill Rappoport's (2011) recent volume on gift exchange in Victorian culture for an insightful exploration of the ways women negotiated the tensions between assertion and altruism, as well as public and private spheres, through a gift economy.

2. See, too, Simmel, for an analysis that places theft and gift on the extreme end of a spectrum of exchange relations that reaches from more "subjective" to more "objective"

Collins' novel affirms the inescapable exchange circuit that Mauss' study describes, as we watch a spectrum of ostensibly generous economic exchanges disqualify themselves by claiming profitable returns. Exposed as thefts, bribes, or assignments of debt, the novel's gifts guiltily implicate their givers as self-serving aristocrats, imperial beneficiaries, and grasping Christians.

Yet Collins persists in seeking the truly "free gift" that might escape the reciprocal, self-interested logic of the market. If it was a common concern of conscientious Victorians of the middle classes to moralize the economy, for Collins and his fellow novelists of sympathy, such as Dickens, Eliot, and Trollope, the concern to justify material exchange was sharpened by the fact that the gospel of social generosity they articulated in their novels was an increasing source of material profit to them, especially in the 1860s.[3] While the correspondences of socially conscious writers indicate that they were elated by high earnings—as Collins wrote in a letter to his mother on 31 July 1861, "Five Thousand Pounds!!?!! Ha!ha!ha . . . nobody but Dickens has made as much"—their novels bore the burden of articulating a relationship between sympathy and potentially divisive wealth (*Letters* 1: 197). *The Moonstone* reflects a somber need to resolve individual benefit, especially benefit linked to textual production, with an ethics capable of rescuing generosity from the taint of self-interest.

Seeking to defend a secularizing and money-making profession as ethically vital, Collins represented literary production in his novel and his Preface as an arena of idealized, self-sacrificial exchange: an instance of maximalist altruism. Collins' ethically improved form of self-sacrifice promised to escape a circuit of necessary profit by embracing the realities of the literary marketplace Collins navigated. Always aware of the precarious nature of literary success, Collins saw his autonomous consumers, from publishers through the reading audience, positioned to assign the exchange-value of his product. Suffering from illness over the course of his career, and particular mental and physical strain during the composition of *The Moonstone*, Collins introduced his revised edition (1871) with a

exchanges. Simmel also explores the ways that reciprocal trade resembles theft and gift, helpfully complementing Mauss' analysis of the resemblance of gift relations to reciprocal exchange.

3. Daniel Hack (2005) claims that Victorian writers sought to be "in the marketplace," but "not necessarily *of it*" (84). Hack suggests that "rejection of the marketplace as the sole or ultimate index of value neither constitutes nor implies a complete disavowal of market competition and payment, let alone a modernist embrace of market failure as a source of artistic legitimacy" (84). I concur and go a step further, claiming that Collins considered market risk and hard-earned success as the source of his artistic legitimacy.

description of himself writing in uncertainty, to satisfy what he termed his
"duty" and "obligation" to the public:

> The novel completed, I awaited its reception by the public with an eager-
> ness of anxiety, which I have never felt before or since for the fate of any
> other writings of mine. . . . Everywhere the public favour looked over my
> faults—and repaid me a hundred-fold for the hard toil which these pages
> cost me in the dark time of sickness and grief. (*MS* 49)

From Collins' point of view, the writer could hardly be assured that his
costly sacrifice would come home to serve him, since so much depended
on others. In this case, his audience "repaid" him exponentially. Yet, cru-
cially, this outcome was merely fortunate and could easily have been otherwise. Collins thus imagined the vagaries of the marketplace as the force
that might free the self-sacrificial agent from the taint of working mechani-
cally for an assured reward. Commercial risk insured the authenticity of
writerly self-sacrifice.[4]

As we will see, in *The Moonstone,* the written texts offered from writer
to reader, texts born of painful, devoted, and, most important, possibly
fruitless sacrifice, are represented as the only free gifts. Posing the genuine
possibility of mutual benefit—the audience's pleasure and edification and,
simultaneously, the writer's spiritual and material success—the free gifts
of narrative offered Collins a resolution to an ancient ethical problem felt
with renewed force at the mid-century.

Christ's Free Gift: An Impossible Act to Follow

Like Trollope's first and last Barsetshire novels, *The Moonstone*'s plot
depends upon theft. Just as Trollope opposes theft and self-sacrifice to
reveal their underlying similarities, Collins suggests that the self-interest of
theft and the ostensible selflessness of gift stand in hidden and uncomfortable relation to each other. Collins' Moonstone, modeled on a number of
actual gems including the Koh-I-Noor Diamond that eventually became

---

4. On the social functions of risk for Victorians, see Elaine Freedgood (2006). She notes
the way capitalism is structured to defend big returns on the basis of the risks assumed by
investors. Collins' sacrificial sense of economic risk was coupled with the personal elements
of bodily pain and suffering that Gallagher (2006) has described in relation to nineteenth-
century theories of value.

Queen Victoria's, fantastically embodies an alternating history of theft and gift. In the novel, the Moonstone is taken by the British at the critical siege of Seringapatam in 1799 to resurface in a quiet Yorkshire estate where it is given as a bequest from uncle to niece. Within hours, a mysterious intrusion into the heroine's darkened bedroom results in the unrecoverable loss of the valuable gem.[5]

The looting of India and the symbolic violation of Rachel suggest a rapacity common to Victorian imperialist and patriarchal practices. While critics debate the manner in which Collins' novels relate to those structures, many agree that the novel represses its troubling inequities; that they are the unconscious of this novel, itself tellingly preoccupied with the untold, unspoken, and buried.[6] My focus here will shift away from reading the material transactions of the novel as large-scale, semi-allegorical expressions of the economic and social inequality that characterized imperial and patriarchal relations.

The many material exchanges of the novel demand an exploration of material exchange itself—giving, taking, owing, re-paying—particularly as shaped by a Christian genealogy of such terms. As we have seen throughout this study, the translation of social relations into terms of material exchange originated in Christian Scripture. Yet such metaphors of exchange came to seem so naturally suited to the social relations and moral psychology in Victorian novels that it became nearly impossible to recognize the particularly Christian inheritances that structured—and troubled—such descriptions. Collins, by contrast, renders the often-tense relationship between material and spiritual registers unusually visible.

When Collins focused on the difficulties that arose in translating from the material to the spiritual register, he was a late arrival to a long line of Christians who had wrestled with such problems. The earliest theologians noted that terms of exchange, especially excessive, non-reciprocal forms of exchange, structured the central narrative of redemption, with Christ dying between two thieves in a sacrificial gift to humanity that repays their debt

---

5. For the critical corpus on Collins and gender and empire, see the most recent bibliographic guide to Collins in Jenny Bourne Taylor, ed. (2006).

6. Tim Dolin (1997), for example, argues that "the invisible act at the heart of the mystery is a man's appropriation of his future wife's property" (83). Tamar Heller (1992) claims that Collins' radical political ideas are "buried" and "subsumed" (8). D. A. Miller's (1988) influential reading uses metaphors of vision rather than depth, yet arrives at similar conclusions about hidden truths: the novel masquerades as a dialogic text when, really, "the novel increases [the] power [of policing] in the very act of arranging for it to disappear" (50). Taylor (1988) provides an important exception to the "repression" readings, historicizing the novel's treatment of the unconscious.

of sin. The illogic of the "free gift" troubled theologians from Augustine to Aquinas to Anselm and eventually, Luther. How could Christ's sacrifice rightfully be a free gift of grace to a sinful humanity? Was not such a "free gift" simply another way of describing an unearned benefit that flouted personal justice and could resemble a form of theft or debt on the part of the recipient? To put it starkly, when the ordinary Christian benefited from Christ's death, why was he or she not considered a thief of grace? As John Parker has put it in his history of this problematic, "Christ had paid in humanity's stead; but this . . . leaves unspecified *how* Christians can partake of that payment, by what mechanism an undeserving sinner makes Christ's bounty his own" (124).

For Luther, the mechanism was famously faith rather than works; yet this innovation did not itself solve the economic difficulty. As Parker points out, the Latin term for faith was precisely the same term as "credit." Thus, John Henry Newman more than three hundred years later would address the same trouble in his sermon, "Sins of Ignorance and Weakness," preserving the sense of "gift," but pressing Christians to engage in personal expiation nonetheless:

> We are ever sinning; and though Christ has died once for all to release us from our penalty, yet we are not pardoned once for all, but according as, and whenever each of us supplicates for the gift . . . it is at our peril if we go on carelessly and thoughtlessly, trusting to our having been once accepted . . . at the very time of the death of Christ (as if then the whole race of man were really and at once pardoned and exalted). (95–96)

Newman's surprising ending here—his "as if" reminder that pardon is not automatic, that Christ's death assures nothing—reminds his listeners that the "free" gift of grace reflects God's freedom to give, rather than humanity's to receive. There is no way out of this particular relationship of imbalance. However much the Christian supplicates, denies him or herself, practices good works, he or she still can never *merit* the gift of salvation; it will always remain a gift.

Another way of saying this is to say that grace always remains an unpayable debt for the believer. Conscious of this burden, individual Christians might engage in acts of sacrifice and charity. Yet here the second paradox arises. As we have seen J. S. Mill worry, Christian charity is shown to be bedeviled by its inescapable effects: its givers automatically amass spiritual "credit" as they seek to do good for others: "God will render to every man according to his deeds" (Rom. 2:6); trust "in the living

God, who giveth us richly all things to enjoy; that they do good; that they be rich in good works, ready to distribute, willing to communicate; laying up in store for themselves a good foundation against the time to come" (1 Tim. 6:17–18). Though acts of Christian charity emulate the unapproachable ideal of selfless generosity embodied by Christ who died to redeem his people, they necessarily fall short. There is no charity without self-interest. Worse still, just as this form of charity threatens to turn people into objects, it can come to celebrate their misfortunes as the occasions for one's own responsive benevolence (Milbank 52). Collins' novel unfolds in the shadow of these difficulties, seeking a sacrificial sphere defined by a genuine generosity, heedless to personal cost, recompensed at the best of times by a mutual benefit that comes without coercion.

Bequest and Debt

Collins begins his exploration of the link between gift and claim at the novel's outset when Colonel John Herncastle, long ostracized by his family for crimes including the infamous theft of the Moonstone at the Siege, unilaterally resumes connection with his sister's family. He does so by bequeathing the stolen gem to his niece, Rachel Verinder, the novel's heroine, contingent on his sister's being alive at the time of his death:

> "I give the Diamond to her daughter Rachel, in token of my free forgiveness of the injury which her conduct towards me has been the means of inflicting on my reputation in my lifetime; and especially in proof that I pardon, as becomes a dying man, the insult offered to me as an officer and a gentleman, when her servant, by her orders, closed the door of her house against me, on the occasion of her daughter's birthday." (96)

The colonel's use of the gem as a "token of free forgiveness" sets up the novel's symbolic system in which moral life is materialized. At the same time, however, the word "token" poses the insurmountable problem of how these two systems of value might ever come into successful communication. With reference to a gem worth twenty thousand pounds, the diminutive sense of "token" emphasizes how exceedingly, distractingly valuable is the sign of forgiveness that the colonel has chosen.[7]

---

7. "Token" also suggests a representational relation. For an account that argues that the gem in this novel is always representational because of its relation to women's desire and property ownership, see Aviva Briefel (2004).

That the gem has been stolen from its rightful owners marks it from the outset as the novel's primary sign of violent appropriation, of non-reciprocal exchange. Moving between the national and familial frames of the novel, the colonel recapitulates the violent appropriation through bequest, rather than through theft. His act hearkens back to mythic structures of "the fatal gift, the present or item of property that is changed into poison" (Mauss 63). While the Indians believe that the gem brings misfortune and retribution to those who possess it through dishonest means, the novel's naturalized—that is to say, economic—expression of this curse is unpayable debt. That Herncastle bequeaths it to his niece contingent upon his sister's life suggests that the sister who rejected him is his desired exchange partner and that the desired object of the exchange is the unpayable debt merely carried by the gem.

The colonel's claim that the gem symbolizes the precious, yet unquantifiable, commodity of forgiveness is belied most obviously by the danger and indebtedness that must attend its receipt. Yet the superfluity of the phrase "free forgiveness," confirms the colonel's malice beyond doubt, for all forgiveness is "free" in the sense that it exceeds the strict measure of law. As the *Oxford English Dictionary* defines it, one who "forgives" abandons a claim against a debtor, pardons an offense, gives up resentment, and forgoes the opportunity to exact punishment or claim. In a system ruled by justice, one does not forgive an offence, but exacts its cost. In a system in which mercy plays its part, forgiveness is by definition free: it exacts nothing from its recipient. Operating as a self-canceling "double positive," the colonel's free forgiveness is anything but free.[8]

Herncastle's forgiveness and the gem together provide the novel's founding example of ethically problematic exchange because they function as what Mary Douglas has termed "so-called free" gifts: they preclude return and thus bring the relationship to a close. As Douglas explains, (elucidating Mauss' approach), "what is wrong with the so-called free gift is the donor's intention to be exempt from return gifts coming from the recipient. Refusing requital puts the act of giving outside any mutual ties. . . . A gift that does nothing to enhance solidarity is a contradiction" (vii).

---

8. For Collins, the ethical subject is the one who *asks* for forgiveness, not the one who grants it. While false forgiveness is characterized in the novel as a gift exchange (Miss Clack, too, "freely forgive[s]" Rachel after insulting her mother's memory, in Collins' sustained critique of the un-Christian tendencies of evangelicals [329]), true forgiveness is represented as a request, a favor one party "begs" from another when they feel remorse, as when Rachel begs forgiveness from her mother for distressing her (212) and from her aunt when she has spoken rudely (308). Rosanna begs forgiveness from Betteredge (220).

Thus while "free" gifts may not ever be repaid, they do exact a marked social price. The colonel's choice to leave Rachel the gem as a posthumous bequest rather than to give it as a gift emphasizes his desire to escape reciprocity. The death that transforms a gift into a bequest is as audacious as the diamond itself. The colonel gets the last word. He leaves the Verinders with a debt they cannot repay.

Gifts and Service

The initial exchange pattern of *The Moonstone*—theft, bequest, unpayable debt—offers an extreme version of self-interested exchange. Yet even when the novel represents more complex forms of social exchange, neither can those escape the taint of self-interest. At the outset of the novel, we encounter Lady Verinder, the sister of Herncastle. As characterized by Gabriel Betteredge, her loyal house steward, Lady Verinder is notable for her mercy, kindness, trust, and pity. In the novel's paradigmatic incident, Lady Verinder goes beyond "common justice" and welcomes into her home Rosanna Spearman, a reformed thief, crediting her with honesty even when the diamond disappears (417). (Later, this noble choice is recapitulated in Mr. Candy's employment of Ezra Jennings despite his troubled reputation.)

Lady Verinder's economy of mercy and credit is materialized in her many gifts, primarily to Betteredge, who has served the family over generations. Yet Lady Verinder's gifts to Betteredge, and his willingness to accept them, even when they press against his own nascent desires, define a friendship that is always also a form of service. As Betteredge alternates between referring to his situation as "my service" and "the service of my lady," the collapse of subject and object around the term and concept of service neatly reflects how much the servant merges his own interest with that of his mistress.

Betteredge unselfconsciously narrates the way that the mistress' gifts ultimately, if unintentionally, allow her to extract additional value from her subordinate in a way that more neutral exchange often precludes. If "friends make gifts," and "gifts make friends," the non-reciprocal gift exchange between Lady Verinder and Betteredge—she gives, he takes—solidifies a system of patronage (Sahlins 186). As Georges Bataille notes, for centuries, gift-giving functioned to confirm social hierarchies: "social rank is linked to the possession of a fortune, but only on the condition that the fortune be partially sacrificed in unproductive social expenditures such as festivals, spectacles, and games" (123). In the luxurious freedom to lose their wealth by giving it away in acts of charity or ostentatious sacrifice, aristocrats staged and exercised their power. Critical to this structure is the spectatorship or receipt of such "sacrifices" on the part of those at the bottom of the social ladder.

By the mid-nineteenth century in which the novel is set, the consolidation of wealth in the hands of a self-made middle-class had effaced the "fundamental obligation of wealth" to give itself away (Bataille 123). The social practice of giving impersonal charity, giving hierarchically, was yielding to the inclination to consolidate wealth horizontally, through exchanges among family and acquaintances. The events of *The Moonstone* are set in Yorkshire in 1848, a moment of high Chartist agitation and heated debate over the condition-of-England question. Tim Dolin has argued that to the extent that the novel treats this political context, it does so by blocking it out in a nostalgic "hanker[ing] after the imaginary genealogical continuity of landed wealth" (75).

Yet Lady Verinder's gifts to Betteredge reflect the historical moment, replete with its nostalgia and its attachment to old practices, and its semiconscious acceptance of and participation in the new. In fact, Lady Verinder's gifts exert such power over Betteredge because they function as both the "impersonal" form of charity dependent on social rank as well as the personal giving that goes on between intimates. In the twenty years spanning the setting of the novel and its composition, Gladstone's Reform Act had granted the vote to working-men in the towns, union reformation was under way, and new legislation had been passed on behalf of the rights of servants. Critics of these developments argued that good servants had become impossible to find as patronage was being replaced by "cold business arrangement[s]" (Dolin 75). Good servants were precisely the sort, like Betteredge, who responded to the hierarchy of the old structures and saw such relations as transcending business. The more they appeared to transcend business by resembling familial relations, the "better" the servant was likely to be.

Gifts were good business and never more so than when they emphasized a relation beyond business. In addition to the mistress' innocent, yet deeply ironic presentation to Betteredge of *Robinson Crusoe*, a book that he "[wears] out with hard work in [his] service" (61), the novel emphasizes one other gift in particular, a handmade waistcoat which Lady Verinder gives him on Christmas, 1847:

She remarked that, reckoning from the year when I started as page boy in the time of the old lord, I had been more than fifty years in her service, and she put into my hands a beautiful waistcoat of wool that she had worked herself to keep me warm in the bitter winter weather. (65)

The novel's specificity in noting that Lady Verinder gives Betteredge the waistcoat on Christmas, 1847, effectively establishes a division between the neutral exchange of commodities within a capitalist marketplace and the highly personal gift exchange within the extended "family" of the gentry. Between the 1830s and the late 1860s when Collins was writing, the ideology and celebration of Christmas underwent significant change. From having been a holiday marked by predominantly "vertical" gifts that "celebrated hierarchical structures of faction, patronage, and allegiance," Christmas became a largely familial holiday that marked the distinction between the worlds of commerce and the haven of home (Carrier 182). In the 1830s and 40s, however, this change was still to come and the gentry usually celebrated Christmas in the "old style, with a church service, a feast, and small presents to dependants and retainers" (187). By the 1870s, Christmas shopping had made its advent, bringing with it the problem of the relationship between gifts and commodities, and the overlap between the world of the family and the marketplace. As James Carrier writes, Christmas became the time of year "when people tell each other how warm the family is and how cold is the world outside" (189).

Lady Verinder's desire to give Betteredge a handmade gift that will "keep [him] warm in the bitter winter weather," and Collins' specification of its presentation on Christmas, a day whose celebrations increasingly divided gifts from commodities and familial from commercial relations, is correctly understood by Betteredge as a "magnificent present" (65). That the gift is clothing further underscores its intimacy. Quick to absorb the signs of both their human makers and wearers—sweat, smell, shape, and so on—clothes are highly personal objects that can emphasize the singularity of human beings.[9] Yet for all the intimacy of Lady Verinder's gift, for all her kind intentions, it cannot help but testify to the contrast between the hours that go into making a waistcoat and Betteredge's fifty years of service in "hard out-of-door work" (65). Like the colonel's "token" gift of the Moonstone, Lady Verinder's gift also marks disparity and non-reciprocity. As a reward, it depends on the hierarchical relationship for its force; it also perpetuates that relationship, re-charges it.

---

9. The other gifts the Verinders give Betteredge and his daughter—handkerchiefs and a dress—are cloth items as well.

For Betteredge, however, the waistcoat signifies only his lady's goodness. Indeed, the gift marks his mistress' desire to make another, more substantial gift. Lady Verinder has noted the effects of fifty years of service on
Betteredge and wants to relieve him from the hard labor of bailiff by trans-
ferring to him the easier tasks of steward. Ironically, however, Betteredge
perceives the gift as a "bribe," since his mistress accompanies the gift with
the request that he "take [his] ease for the rest of [his] days as steward in
the house": "It turned out however, that the waistcoat was not an honour,
but a bribe . . . to wheedle me into giving up my hard out-of-door work"
(65). Lady Verinder's "bribe," then, tricks Betteredge into doing what his
mistress wants, when what she wants would ostensibly be against her own
interests. Betteredge is lured into the "concession" of considering his own
needs before those of the household. It is only when the mistress appeals to
her servant's "weak side . . . she put it as a favour to herself," that Betteredge can agree to what is in his own self-interest (65).

The waistcoat is a truly meaningful gift, as is the substantial reward of
a comfortable end of days, yet Betteredge's understanding of it as a bribe
discloses the substitution of his lady's needs for his own. While the collapse of subjectivities elsewhere might be imagined as reflecting a deep and
mutual unity of interests (as Trollope might have seen it), here, the inequality of social position strains such a reading. Here, the collapse of subjectivities records the way that for a gift to function, a critical divide must be
preserved between giver and receiver. For Betteredge, this divide no longer
obtains and so gifts and "bribes" become oddly interchangeable. The final
result of this interchangeability is that Betteredge can barely imagine pure
pleasure in receiving a life-changing gift from his mistress because he owes
her infinitely. He takes in order to please her, when he can be persuaded
that it amounts to giving.

Betteredge criticizes the class structure only when he moves to describing the future master and mistress, Lady Verinder's daughter, Rachel,
and Franklin Blake. Rachel and Franklin seem blissfully unaware of the
gifts from which they benefit, Franklin occasionally borrowing money
from Betteredge without ever repaying it and generally living in debt, and
Rachel, blind to sufferings beyond her own romantic plot. In a telling passage concerning Franklin and Rachel, Betteredge gives voice to the distinctions between those who serve and those who are served. In response to
the resourcefulness of the rich and idle who fill their time with projects
that the serving classes must inevitably clean up, Betteredge says, in jest,
"It often falls heavy enough, no doubt, on people who are really obliged
to get their living, to be forced to work for the clothes that cover them, the

roof that shelters them, and the food that keeps them going" (106). Betteredge has worked a lifetime for the clothes that cover him, including the
waistcoat, and the roof that will shelter him. The gifts of a good mistress
ease that labor, no doubt, but they also prepare their own return.[10]

Charity and Theft

That Lady Verinder is the kindest of mistresses might mitigate the force
of such a structural critique as I have just offered. Yet, as if to re-focus the
reader on the problem of giving tempered by the self-interest of anticipated
return, Collins turns to evangelical Christianity which repeats those structures, only, on Collins' view, with much less good-will. Collins introduces
the unlovable, self-righteous spinster aunt, Miss Clack, as the embodiment
of all he detests about evangelicalism and false philanthropy, yet his critique goes beyond the opportunism of mere personal caricature.[11] Miss
Clack's narrative exposes the impossibility of pure giving, or perhaps giving at all, for the Christian believer.

In the "Narrative Contributed by Miss Clack," which Collins noted
as a favorite among his reading public, the financially-poor, spiritually-
rich Miss Clack desires to share her wealth by distributing her evangelical
tracts. Miss Clack's polite phrasing, "'will you *favour me* by accepting a
tract?'" (258, emphasis mine) unwittingly speaks the truth of the exchange,
as does the regular refusal of her tracts or the weary acceptance of the
readings only to "please" the giver (279). In a novel that does not hesitate
to express its themes through the names of its characters, the aural circularity of Miss Clack's name, CLC, may emphasize the circularity of gift and
return.

Miss Clack's moral paradox—the gift to others returning as the gift to
the self—is literalized when the novel describes her dissemination of tracts
as a kind of anti-robbery. When faced with a general lack of interest in
her offerings, Miss Clack packs up a carpetbag with the "choicest treasures" of her library and returns to the Verinder household (281). Mov-

10. See Lillian Nayder (1997) for an account of the way the young working-class women
of the novel articulate their oppression: Lucy Yolland predicts the day when "the poor will
rise against the rich" (*Moonstone* 248). Nayder argues that Collins "discredits their discon-
tent by characterizing it as female," but does not seem to be reading contextually, as even
Betteredge, with all his misogynist sentiments, recognizes the plight of Rosanna and Limping
Lucy (123).

11. See Jay (1979) on the portrayal of evangelicals in Victorian fiction.

ing from floor to floor, despite the "risk" she entails, she "slips" about the house (289), reminding the reader of the novel's other suspects in robbery, Rosanna Spearman, accused of "slip[ping] away to town" (182), and the housemaids who "steal" upstairs (177). After "slipping" a tract between the sofa cushions, Miss Clack moves to the window "unsuspected," and, "instead of taking away a flower, I added one, in the shape of another book from my bag. . . . In the drawing-room I found more cheering opportunities of emptying my bag" (289–90). In a parallel to Rosanna's removal of the nightgown linked to the Moonstone's theft, Miss Clack finds a dressing gown, but instead of removing it, she leaves it where it is and fills its pockets:

> It had a pocket in it, and in that pocket I put my last book. Can words express my exquisite sense of duty done, when I had slipped out of the house, unsuspected by any of them, and when I found myself in the street with my empty bag under my arm? (291)

In a novel that uses the word "pocket" over twenty-five times in dramatic reference to ownership and robbery—receipts, money, and letters are kept in pockets, pockets are "rifled" (261), and Godfrey Ablewhite's theft of the Moonstone is described simply as, "He put the Moonstone into his pocket" (530)—Miss Clack's link to "pockets," compounds the illicit— and commercial—nature of her activity.[12]

Miss Clack's narrative foregrounds the confusion among giving, getting, and owing; charity, theft, and fair pay. She begins her narrative by acknowledging a debt that is both longstanding and unpayable—"I am indebted to my dear parents (both now in heaven)" (255)—and the narrative in full meditates upon the problem of a status quo of debt. When one begins in debt, fair pay is hardly enough. Insufficient to meet the giver's bare obligation, fair pay begins to resemble robbery, gift-giving turns to fair pay, and true gift-giving simply eludes the realm of human relations. This structure is comically represented when, to aid a pious mission, Miss Clack indulges in the expense of a cab and pays the cabbie "exactly his fare. He received it with an oath; upon which I instantly gave him a tract" (280). To the cabbie, the tip is not a gift freely given, but part of the contract. Subsumed into requirement, its absence is experienced as a form of robbery. The cabbie has been shortchanged. Miss Clack's attempt to make

---

12. For a discussion of the gender politics attending "pockets" in Victorian dress, see Christopher Matthews (2010).

up the difference of the tip with a tract exposes the metaphoricity of her "true riches" (a difference she well understands or she would just as soon give him a tip) and the impossibility of translating from one economy to another. At the same time, the tract as currency also suggests just how economic the spiritual register is.[13]

Miss Clack's narrative roots the novel's moral economy—its "accounts" of "good and evil"—in Scripture (254). She begins reminiscing of a "happy, bygone time," "before papa was ruined," and describes her subsequent adult attempts to discipline the "fallen nature which we all inherit from Adam" (255). Default and the Fall come together (255). Imagining an Edenic period of solvency, before sin and before ruin, Miss Clack's narrative of adulthood describes working against an inherited debt that can never be paid off. Giving away her tracts allows her to feel temporarily "relieved in some small degree, of a heavy responsibility towards others" (258):

> When I folded up my things that night—when I reflected on the *true* riches which I had scattered with such a lavish hand, from top to bottom of the house of my wealthy aunt—I declare I felt as free from anxiety as if I had been a child again.

For a "blissful night," Miss Clack can sleep "Quite like a child again! quite like a child again!," pre-Fall and ruin (291).

Yet the repetition of the above phrases augurs not a sustained bliss, but inevitable return and re-beginning. The next day, the tracts come back to Miss Clack in a large parcel. At first, she wonders whether the parcel might be the "promised legacy" from her aunt which threatens to be "cast-off clothes, or worn-out silver spoons, or unfashionable jewellery," worldly objects whose value will not have withstood the test of time (292–93). For Miss Clack, such objects signify the vanity of earthly life. Of course, Collins' irony is that she well understands and covets the value that would attend new clothes, good silver, and fashionable jewelry. When Miss Clack opens the parcel, though, she discovers the return of her spiritually "precious" tracts. Her labor is canceled out, her debt re-confirmed, and her new day's work is obvious: "What was to be done now? With my training

---

13. Miss Clack's instinctive response, throwing another tract through the window of the cab as the cabbie heads off angrily, would also have alerted Victorian readers to the mix of spiritual and monetary pursuits, since tossing bills into cab windows was a popular mid- to late-century mode of advertising (Carrier 81). Collins' *No Name* features such an advertising moment.

and my principles, I never had a moment's doubt" (293). (Doubt here may
echo "debt.") And so she begins again, this time to copy the tracts into
letter-form.

We can understand Miss Clack's massively caricatured personality, the
ceaseless repetition of the same behaviors, the giving of her tracts, then
their return, then her renewed attempts at giving, as not only a commonplace jibe at evangelicals, but a consequence of her economy. Condemned
to work at a debt that a Christian can never pay, Miss Clack must repeat
and repeat. Planning to bequeath the forty-fourth edition of the aurally-
repetitive "Life, Letters, and Labours of Miss Jane Ann Stamper" (hear,
too, the pun: aunts tamper) to Rachel Verinder, Miss Clack offers to pass
on . . . debt.

Sale and Theft: Trade among Friends

Miss Clack's gifts expose the way that giving can come to seem like robbery in a Christian context inspired, but also depressed, by the unreach-
able ideal of Christ's freely given gift of grace. Collins turns to another
ethical context, friendship, to explore a related problem of debt among
human beings who see themselves as mutually responsible. In the context
of friendship, Collins asks whether it is possible for the mere retention
of one's own property to register as a kind of robbery. Moving toward a
more humanistic version of ethics, Collins suggests that the authenticity of
friendship—here, depicted among the working classes—depends on its difference from commercial practice.

In the aftermath of the theft of the moonstone, Betteredge and Sergeant
Cuff, the detective investigating the case, seek out Mrs. Yolland, a friend of
Rosanna's and a fisherman's wife. Mrs. Yolland retells her last encounter
with Rosanna, describing a moment of weakness in which she agreed to
accept Rosanna's money for a tin box and some old chains. Now, regretful
at having taken any of the "poor thing's little savings," notwithstanding
the "money's [being] welcome enough in our house," Mrs. Yolland asks
her visitors, Sergeant Cuff and Betteredge, to return the money to Rosanna:

> "Please say she's heartily welcome to the things she bought of me—as a
> gift. And don't leave the money on the table. . . . For times are hard, and
> flesh is weak; and I *might* feel tempted to put it back in my pocket again."
> (188–89)

Mrs. Yolland's belatedly willing spirit wishes to turn the commercial exchange retroactively into the gift exchange it should have been. Her request of Cuff to take the money off the table because "'times are hard, and flesh is weak; and I might feel tempted to put it back in my pocket again,'" casts the pocketing of her own money as a form of temptation and sin, rather than the justifiable choice not to give a gift and, instead, to take care of her own. Rosanna has bought the items from Mrs. Yolland. Sale is supposed to be a fair, neutral, and isolated instance of exchange in which nothing is owed and no follow-up transactions are necessary. Yet when commerce has gone on between friends, where it has no place, it is tainted by its association with theft. As with Miss Clack and the cabbie, in this episode, too, a free gift becomes the normative obligation.

Sergeant Cuff then intervenes to restore the norms of commercial exchange. Refusing to allow Mrs. Yolland to return the money to Rosanna, he argues that Mrs. Yolland "'charged her cheap for the things'" (189). In an inverse of the way we have seen tip become fair pay, here, in Cuff's economy, forgoing the acceptable proceeds of commerce merges with gift. At the price for which Mrs. Yolland sold them, Cuff says, the items are, "'clean given away! . . . I can't find it in my conscience, ma'am, to give the money back. . . . You have as good as made her a present of the things'" (190). From Cuff's perspective, the unnatural generosity of the commercial transaction has made it nothing short of a gift to Rosanna.

In the end, Mrs. Yolland cannot resist temptation. She takes the money back, but isn't converted to Cuff's way of thinking. Collins' description (narrated by Betteredge) suggests that she steals her own money:

> "Bother the money!" says Mrs. Yolland. With these words, she appeared to lose all command over herself; and, making a sudden snatch at the heap of silver, put it back, holus-bolus in her pocket. "It upsets one's temper, it does, to see it lying there, and nobody taking it," cries this unreasonable woman, sitting down with a thump, and looking at Sergeant Cuff, as much as to say, "It's in my pocket again now—get it out if you can!" (190)

Reminding us of the "hole in Mr. Franklin's pocket that nothing would sew up" (68), Franklin's propensity for debt, Mrs. Yolland puts the silver back "holus-bolus in her pocket" (190). Her pocket's hole and the ethic of Cobb's Hole is the hole made by gift, not debt. But the two are opposite sides of the coin in this novel. Among friends, gift is merely the appropriate recognition of debt.

Sacrifice and Written Text

The episode at Cobb's Hole provides a transition between the two dominant economies of the novel: the economy of gift, theft, and debt that we
have seen thus far, and the economy that the novel describes as "sacrifice."
With the exception of the originary gift of grace, gifts respond to a relationship of debt and register new debt. They demand a return as surely as
marketplace exchange, even if the passage of time between gift and return
obscures the compulsive reciprocity.

Against this backdrop, the novel introduces the free gift of sacrifice
as a form of non-reciprocal exchange, of gift-giving outside an economy
that mirrors the marketplace. Just as such a gift must elude the economic
structure in which return is necessary or automatic, in psychological terms,
sacrifice demands personal suffering on behalf of another without concern
for the self—without re-pocketing the money, so to speak. The two major
sacrifices traced by the novel are those of the servant Rosanna Spearman
and the privileged daughter of the house, Rachel Verinder, both of whom
sacrifice themselves for Franklin Blake. Rosanna gives up nothing short of
her life out of hopeless love for Franklin, calling him a man "worth dying
for" (248), and Rachel "sacrifice[s] [her]self" (273) for Franklin, giving up
her faith in him, her reputation, even the valuable Moonstone, all in order
not to charge him with the theft she believes he has committed: "'I spare
him, when *my* heart is breaking; I screen him when my own character is at
stake'" (417, emphases mine).

In the sections of *The Moonstone* that describe sacrifice, Collins again
merges the economic and the spiritual registers, this time to distinguish
sacrifice from the reciprocity of gifts. He achieves this distinction by limiting the applications of sacrifice to story and textuality. The one thing Collins can imagine successfully retaining its sacrificial character is a story
recorded as a written text, offered up by the writer to a highly valued other.
Though Rachel and Rosanna speak of sacrificing *themselves*, for Collins,
the sign of their sacrifice is the generation of a vital text, independent of
themselves.

Secrecy and Narrative

At the heart of the novel's concept of creative sacrifice is secrecy, an intentional silence that first produces a story and then renders it in text.[14] In sim-

_____

14. See Cohen for the related argument that Victorian fiction is marked by a dialectic

plest terms, this means that both Rosanna and Rachel offer their sacrifices in the form of not-offering information, keeping secret what they know, or think they know, in order to spare the beloved Franklin. Rachel produces mystery, doubt, and story out of her own longstanding tendency toward sacrificial secrecy, her willingness from childhood to "suffer . . . the punishment, for some fault committed by a playfellow whom she loved" without speaking a word then or later (109); as Betteredge notes, this is both a mark of integrity and an undesirable stubbornness. Rosanna's silence, by contrast, is less a choice than a reflection of her absolute lack of social capital. Deformed, poor, suspect, she is rendered silent from fear. In her late-discovered posthumous letter to Franklin, she writes, "Why didn't I speak to you! why didn't I speak to you!" and concludes, "I was frightened of you" (394).

The secrecy of these two women permits them to persevere in error. Both women believe Franklin to have stolen the gem. In fact, at the novel's end, we discover that his theft was committed unintentionally, as an effect of his having been drugged. Both women imagine that they are self-sacrificially protecting Franklin from the consequences of his action, although Franklin does not seek their protection since he is unaware that he requires it. Franklin is utterly unconscious of their painful offerings, though both women imagine that he must be silently conscious of them. The silence maintained by Rachel and Rosanna thus perpetuates the mystery of the theft, a mystery that would have been far more easily solved had they simply spoken.[15] In terms of the novel's structure, Rosanna is brought into the project of retrospective narration that makes up the novel only once the mystery is on its way to being resolved and then, by way of her posthumous letter which leaves sufficient mystery to allow the rest of the novel to proceed. Rachel is excluded altogether from the project of retrospective narration because she knows even more than Rosanna. Months later, when Rachel finally reveals to Franklin that she saw him take the gem, he upbraids her for the delay, suggesting that if she "had spoken out at the time," the truth would have been brought to light (417).

The sacrificial silences of Rosanna and Rachel thus reflect an author working within the constraints of his genre: the mystery of a crime and its prolonged resolution. The silences perpetuate the mystery and thus create

in which sexual secrets generously produce narratives, even as they are characterized as unspeakable.

15. D. A. Miller understands the novel's obsession with secrecy as upholding the value of privacy, "the determination of an integral, autonomous, 'secret' self" (162). My reading does not contest that position, but sees Collins as then working to imagine how those secret selves might come into communication.

the space in which Collins' novel can come into being. In the terms of narratology, sacrificial silence creates both story and narrative, *histoire* and *récit*: "the totality of the events narrated" and "the discourse, oral or written, that narrates them" (Genette 13). No sacrifice, no novel. Another way to put this is to say that the sacrifice internal to the novel now characterizes the production of narrative and the novel form itself. Yet, at the very same time that story and narrative come together as a creative product of sacrifice, the novel suggests that neither story nor narrative was necessary to begin with, that sacrifice itself is a kind of terrible delusion.

Narration seems to empty sacrificial gestures of much of their value, to make them fruitless in the worst way. Rosanna and Rachel have been protecting Franklin for nothing. The moment Rachel narrates, she discovers she has been the "victim of some monstrous delusion" (413). Rosanna dies on the basis of this delusion. The moment Rachel speaks—and the moment Rosanna would have spoken—their misperceptions come to light. Under the pressure of dialogue, keen questioning and answer, corrections are offered, understandings refined, mysteries dispelled or moved toward resolution. The sacrifice is revealed not to have mitigated the sum of human suffering, but to have increased and prolonged it. Just as the secret is no longer secret once it is told, self-sacrifice is no longer productively or justifiably sacrificial once it is conveyed to its intended object.

What then is the fate of sacrificial giving? Is the free gift empty at its heart, a delusion bearing only the compromised value of generous but misguided and ineffectual intention? If the novel is the product of sacrifice, is it then liable at any moment to betray its ethical irrelevance, its incapacity for fostering ethical human relations that limit suffering rather than increase it? I want to suggest that Collins preserves the possibility for sacrifice with a resolution that beautifully reflects his conditions and the conditions of many novelists at mid-century. He does this by slowing down the process of exchange and focusing on the in-between, the precarious, indefinite space between giving and receipt, a space of intention, where he locates narrative.

The Risk of Transmission: The Difference of Bodies and Texts

Thus far we have traced gifts that seem inevitably to demand return for the newly registered debt they produce. The inevitable return, however, depends upon the successful handing-off of the gift, a completed act of transmission, such as the quintessential finality of Colonel Hern-castle's bequest at death. Collins slows down this process to remind us of all the vicissitudes that ordinarily, in life, attend such transmission. The letter delayed or gone astray is the most transparent plot device known to melodrama.[16] Yet Collins differentiates his drama by depicting no deus ex machina phenomenon, but the simple human dilemma of sepa-rate consciousnesses. As we will now see, the sacrifice for Collins is the gift of immense, even self-destructive value that threatens to be met by its intended recipient with unconsciousness. The sacrifice is the precious gift intended and given, but given with no assurances of receipt. The value of sacrifice, I suggest, depends on doubt or risk.

For Collins, as a professional writer enmeshed in the Protestant Chris-tian tradition—a tradition characterized by the personal encounter with Christ's gospel—the most obvious form such a gift could take was textual. *The Moonstone* is made up of a variety of texts: narratives, "extracts" from letters, wills, and journals; solicited statements; shorthand notes; expan-sions of those notes; quotations from the novel *Robinson Crusoe*. Virtu-ally all these forms of text bear an intimate relation to those who have authored or transcribed them, yet Collins asks us to widen our focus to note both that intimacy and the critical distinctions between the texts and their writers. For Rachel and Rosanna, the letter form capitalizes upon the difference between a person and her textual self-representation. The letter signifies the difference between actual persons—bodily presences—and the traces of them in writing. More generally, both in the novel and in the con-text of his profession, Collins imagined and represented as sacrificial such texts that signified a difference between the immediacy of persons and the abstraction of language.

Rosanna's sacrifice is her life and her explanatory narration comes posthumously in the form of a letter written to Franklin, read only par-tially by him ("'I broke off in the reading of the letter'") because its reading becomes too distressing (385). With Rosanna's half-read letter, the novel simultaneously aligns and distinguishes Rachel and Rosanna. Both girls, we discover, have written letters to Franklin in sign of their sacrifice. While Rosanna's letter survives to tell us her side of the story, Rachel's has been torn up prematurely. We never read it and neither does Franklin. After all the novel's damage has been done, Rachel tells Franklin that a letter was the only way that she could imagine responding to his theft of the moon-

---

16. Though she attributes it only to the rule of coincidence in sensation novels, Winifred Hughes (1980) notes the recurrence of the "waste" phenomenon (22).

stone. She intended, she later tells him, to offer to pay the debts she thinks have motivated the theft. In order to do this without shaming either of them excessively, Rachel "'thought and thought—and I ended in writing to you'" (418). But the letter never reaches Franklin. In anger at what she perceives as Franklin's audacious offer to lead the search for the gem, Rachel rips up the letter.

Though Rachel imagines her letter as an agent that might *prevent* self-sacrifice, Rosanna right away recognizes the letter as the *sign* of self-sacrifice: the difference that will remain once she has sacrificed herself. Rosanna's letter faces a different fate than Rachel's, as does her body. In chiastic fashion, Collins has the privileged Rachel enact the sacrifice upon the letter and preserve herself, while Rosanna, the servant-girl, enacts the sacrifice upon herself, leaving behind the letter. Rosanna composes her letter knowing that either one or the other, her letter or herself, will survive, but not both: "'It would be very disgraceful to me to tell you this, if I was a living woman when you read it. I shall be dead and gone, sir, when you find my letter'" (380). More revealing than anything she could say in person, Rosanna's letter is written as an intentionally posthumous document, an assurance that if she cannot communicate with Franklin directly, he will still "'find out what I have done for you, when I am past telling you of it myself'" (398). While she writes, Rosanna expresses the hope that the decree may yet be reversed:

> "Why not believe, while I can, that it will end well after all? I may find you in a better humour tonight–or, if not, I may succeed better tomorrow morning. . . . Who knows but I may have filled all these weary long pages of paper for nothing? It has been hard, hard work writing my letter. Oh! If we only end in understanding each other, how I shall enjoy tearing it up!" (398)

Rosanna clearly equates the living letter with her dead self and the dead letter with her living self.[17] In similar fashion, Rachel, too, imagines the medium of the letter as a form of the self that is severed or alienated from the living person. Just as Rosanna sees the letter enabling her to say the things she cannot say in person, Rachel imagines writing a letter that would offer Franklin help without requiring them to acknowledge any

---

17. See Heller on "images of the unread" in Collins (161). Interpreting these images as representing contained female subversiveness and the repressed gothicism of sensation writing, Heller elides rather than marks the distinction between writing and body that is vital to my argument.

shame aloud: "'(not a word, mind, to be said openly about it between us!)'" (419). For both girls, letters emphasize the difference between a person and her textual self-representation.

Sacrificial texts, I suggest, depend upon this difference between a bodily presence and its written traces. This pattern resembles the Christian theology that understands God's Word as the result and sign of Christ's willingness to save a sinful humanity by dying on their behalf; Christ can be known now, saves now, through the gospel. In the novel's signal intertext, *Robinson Crusoe*, Crusoe describes this theology in the process of converting Friday and himself:

> nothing but divine revelation can form the knowledge of Jesus Christ, and of a redemption purchased for us, of a Mediator of a new covenant, and of an Intercessor at the foot-stool of God's throne . . . therefore the gospel of our Lord and Saviour Jesus Christ, I mean, the word of God . . . are the absolutely necessary instructors of the souls of men, in the saving knowledge of God, and the means of salvation. (Defoe 221)

Sacred revelation—"word"—is what is left when suffering flesh is gone.

In *The Moonstone*, the posthumous testimonies of two suffering souls, Rosanna and Ezra Jennings, come as the material signs of their sacrifices. Meanwhile, the people themselves, Rosanna Spearman and Ezra Jennings (a second physically marked social outcast), are the sacrificial victims. As René Girard has explained in his classic study, sacrifice is a symbolic system which deflects violence from a protected, valued object onto a "'sacrificeable' victim" (4). The defining feature of the "victim," however, whether animal, person, or thing, is that it

> bear a certain resemblance to the object [it] replace[s]; otherwise the violent impulse would remain unsatisfied. But this resemblance must not be carried to the extreme of complete assimilation, or it would lead to disastrous confusion. (11)

In the symbolic world of *The Moonstone,* Ezra and Rosanna are sacrificed for their privileged doubles, Franklin and Rachel.[18] While the novel uses

---

18. As Taylor notes, Ezra Jennings is easily read as the "negative reflection" of Franklin, as Rosanna is of Rachel (*Secret Theatre* 199). The pattern of similarity yielding to sacrificial difference is one of the ways Victorian novels critique the injustice of class structure. Rosanna herself remarks on the structure when she says, "Suppose you put Miss Rachel into a servant's dress, and took her ornaments off" (382).

such sacrifices to elucidate class injustice, here, sacrifice is also inseparable from textuality. Rosanna and Ezra's self-sacrifices are signified by the
documents they leave behind which become the novel's text. Rosanna's
letter and Ezra's diary—whose readings are both contingent upon their
deaths—resolve the mystery and lead to the comic ending of marriage and
regeneration. The similarity between Rosanna and Ezra's status as persons
sacrificed to text suggests a new application of Girard's theory. Collins'
novel establishes a sacrificial structure in which *persons* are the sacrificeable victims while *texts* are the protected, valued objects.

Though Rosanna and Ezra indeed die, sacrifice here need not mean
death. Collins' sacrificial texts are sacrificial primarily because when they
circulate in the absence of their authors, they approach the condition of
free gifts: objects that are offered but do not compel their own acceptance
nor consequently their own reciprocation. Collins explores this feature of
sacrificial textuality in a complicated passage narrated early in the novel by
Betteredge. Betteredge, an easy talker but an unpracticed writer, confronts
the possibility that Rosanna faces: that his work may not be read, that he
may expend a great deal of effort for nothing. This possibility shadows all
efforts at writing intended for an audience. Authorship, while authoritative, is only half the story. The success of writing depends also on the sustained willingness of readers.

In the following passage, Collins testifies to the author's simultaneous
power and subjection vis-à-vis his audience. The power comes from the
seemingly personal presence of the speaking author while the subjection
comes from his personal absence, and in its stead, the presence of written
words. Collins masterfully mixes these attributes in Betteredge's narratorial
self-presentation. Collins has Betteredge propitiate his audience anxiously
for their attention, even as he asserts his own freedom from the writerly
liability of non-personhood in authoritative commands and claims:

> Here follows the substance of what I said, written out entirely for your
> benefit. Pay attention to it, or you will be all abroad, when we get deeper
> into the story. Clear your mind of the children, or the dinner, or the new
> bonnet, or what not. Try if you can't forget politics, horses, prices in the
> City, and grievances at the club. I hope you won't take this freedom on my
> part amiss; it's only a way I have of appealing to the gentle reader. Lord!
> Haven't I seen you with the greatest authors in your hands, and don't I
> know how ready your attention is to wander when it's a book that asks for
> it, instead of a person? (83–84)

Here, the garrulous Betteredge sets himself apart from the "greatest authors," alongside his easily distractible fellow readers, even as he admits to being himself a "book." Like Collins, who attempted to replicate the language of conversation rather than literature in his essays and novels and dictated sections of *The Moonstone* ("Preface" *MS*), Betteredge first claims the privilege of talk rather than text, the immediacy of bodily presence rather than the mediation of text that always represents, rather than presents. The pause and break occasioned by the announcement, "Here follows the substance of what I said, written out entirely for your benefit," suggest that what has come before has somehow not been "written out," but has engaged the reader in a completely unmediated fashion.

Betteredge is unwilling to give up the immediacy of the speaking person to become the disembodied voice narrating the speech that once took place. What follows, he says, in a paradox of terminology, is the "substance," "written out." In fact, substance is the one thing that cannot be "written out"; substance, body, eludes text. In order to become a part of a text, substance—whether of the author or of the represented object—must be subsumed into words.

Victorian authors, particularly of serialized texts, experienced far more direct communication than many writers with their audiences. The blurring of the distinction between book and person, person and writer, person and reader, had its roots in lived experience. Accordingly, Betteredge's "speech" alternates between an insistence upon an equation of book and person, and the recognition that the narrating "person" no longer retains the full claims of personhood: "don't I know how ready your attention is to wander when it's a book that asks for it, instead of a person?" If the narrating person is not equivalent to an embodied, speaking person, Betteredge's imagined reader is not identical with the person either. As Garrett Stewart notes, the second person, "is a grammatical category in literature, not a receptive destination" (19). Yet the third and fourth sentences of Betteredge's exhortation use the second-person vocative to produce an implicitly gendered, living "listener": "Clear your mind of the children, or the dinner, or the new bonnet, or what not. Try if you can't forget politics, horses, prices in the City, and grievances at the club." The "you" is double, divided into he who cares for politics, and she who cares for children; he who is preoccupied by horses, and she, by dinner. But by the end of the fifth sentence, Betteredge has transformed listening persons into imagined readers: "I hope you won't take this freedom on my part amiss; it's only a way I have of appealing to the gentle reader." The "gentle reader"'s absence of marked gender further emphasizes Collins' representation of the reading being as the not-fully-person, the person without body.

The passage's conclusion—the necessarily rhetorical, because textual, questions, "Haven't I seen you . . . and don't I know . . . ?"—imitates dialogue between real persons, but simultaneously re-emphasizes the boundary between the interchange of real persons and the one-sided speech of literature. To whose advantage is this difference? While the writer appears to have the authority of address, it is the reader who ultimately chooses whether or not to listen. If, as Stewart argues, "the fictional text can only strive . . . to mandate, without ever being able to monitor your response," then it is a certainty that the fictional text, unlike a speaking person, cannot compel its "hearing" or reading, let alone the responses to it (19). Betteredge's series of powerful imperatives—"pay," "clear," "try,"—and his confident sense of offering readers a gift "entirely for [our] benefit," end in the recognition that despite having the authority of the page, even the "greatest authors," do not possess the privilege of persons to command being heard.[19]

Linear Narrative: A Space for Sacrifice

In Collins' essay, "The Unknown Public," he points to the prerogative of the reader when he declares, "I have only to ask . . . whether anybody waits to go all through a novel before passing an opinion on the goodness or the badness of it" (138–39).

The power of the reader to put down the book was constantly with Collins. And the fate of the next book lay just as significantly in the hands of the public, from editor to circulating library patrons to individual purchasers. If, as I have suggested, the risk attending the reception of laborious writing defined writing as Collins' free gift, as we will now see, the corollary to that proposition is that Collins' risk was expanded by the

---

19. My argument that speaking persons can compel their own hearing is limited to the comparison with texts. As *The Moonstone* and countless other nineteenth-century novels dramatize, the middle and upper classes could literally turn away people whom they did not wish to see or hear; this is one of the key functions of servants such as Betteredge. Still, that servants need to play this role indicates the difficulties of denying speaking persons in one's own bodily presence. In multiple places, Collins suggests that the more writers resemble persons and talkers, the more likely they are to be tolerated. See his representative comment that he seeks to address the public "with something of the ease of letter-writing, and something of the familiarity of friendly talk" ("Preface" 7).

necessary linearity of his chosen genre, the mystery novel. With expanded risk, came greater sacrificial value.

Collins' love for the documentary mode is reflected in *The Moonstone* which presents texts in multiple forms. Yet the novel divides between those texts assumed to be sacred that can be read in non-linear fashion, mined for gems of wisdom that merely shine the brighter when extracted from their original source, and those texts that require complete and linear reading for any gleam of latent value to emerge. The latter texts were an image of Collins' own writings, sacrificial texts demanding the "hard, hard work" not only of writing, but of sustained reading, too; relying on no assurance of their sacred status to command a reader's attention throughout (*MS* 398). By contrast, the former texts were associated for Collins with the threat of theft that defined both capitalist and Christian economics.

To the extent that Collins was concerned to retain his readers, he understood this challenge in the context of two predominating ways of thinking about and experiencing texts in the second half of the nineteenth century: as wholes and as extracts. Leah Price has detailed the complex ways in which the novel developed in relation to what she calls the "culture of the excerpt," as represented by the anthology form. Novelists came to write under the expectation, sometimes hopeful and sometimes chagrined, that the grand bulk of their novels would be pithily represented by quotation in reviews and by extracts in books that gathered "wisdom" in the form of decontextualized epigrams. Yet, at the same time, novelists were aware that the plot and dense detail that formed the medium for novelistic "wisdom" made novels less available to excerpting and quotation than the lyric or the essay. Summing up this conflict, Price suggests that

> Within the culture of the excerpt, the novel forms a test case. Few genres have been better placed to escape the anthology's sphere of influence. Sheer scale helps define the novel. So do the pace and duration of reading which that scale elicits. But the novel depends just as much on readers' resistance to those demands. Skipping (or anthologizing) and skimming (or abridging) have never been separable from a genre that cracks under its own weight. (5)

For Collins, the affiliation with linear reading came to define his work in terms of genre and ethical value.

At first, it seems surprising that Collins would embrace an affiliation with the linear model, since the extract model carried more cultural capital.

For instance, Price argues that in an age when the lyric and essay were the prime targets for anthologizing, the anthologizing of George Eliot served to elevate her to an exceptional status among novelists.[20] Collins, by contrast, was consigned to a category of novelists who were considered difficult if not impossible to excerpt and anthologize. Late in the century, in 1890, Edmund Yates criticized him on precisely these grounds, stating, "Collins's style is not a thing of literary beauty like Mr. Stevenson's, or a marvel of finish like Henry James's. It is jerky and absolutely unornamented. There are no elegant extracts to be got out of his stories; it would be no easy matter to compile beauties of Collins, and even birthday-book framers might be in difficulties" (qtd. in Price 139).

Yet, Collins' "unquotability" was as much a merit and feature of his appeal as Eliot's epigrams or James' finish. Earlier, in 1868, an anonymous reviewer for *Lippincott's Magazine* (December 1868) had pointed out just this quality, specifically as a feature of *The Moonstone:*

> Let the impatient reader, hurrying to reach the denouement, skip half a dozen pages. Instantly the thread of the story is broken, the tale becomes incomprehensible, the incidents lose their coherence. *The Moonstone* is a perfect work of art, and to remove any portion of the cunningly constructed fabric destroys the completeness and beauty of the whole. (qtd. in *Moonstone* 558–59)

While this reviewer prizes the plot or "thread of the story" as the mark of the novelist's art and Yates (responding to the changed aesthetic of the fin de siècle) devalued it, reviewers were agreed on the centrality of plot and linearity to Collins' work.

Within *The Moonstone,* Collins was concerned to represent the linear text as a sacrificial one. Ezra Jennings is the figure most fully associated with linear textuality, as he posthumously supplies the explanatory narrative necessary to the resolution of *The Moonstone* as novel and mystery. Mr. Candy, doctor to the Verinders, takes ill at the most inopportune moment, the day after secretly drugging Franklin Blake to prove the efficacy of medicinal courses to treat nervous sleeplessness. This trick produces Franklin's unconscious theft of the Moonstone which remains unrevealed due to Mr. Candy's illness. Ezra Jennings tends him in his delir-

---

20. It became the exceptional writer in genres outside of the lyric and the essay, whether Shakespeare or George Eliot, whose genius would be rewarded with inclusion in the anthology. Price notes that as their exceptional status seemed to firm up generic differences, their inclusion also transformed the genres in which they wrote (110).

ium. Sitting at his bedside, Ezra transcribes all Mr. Candy's incoherent, troubled ramblings and then ingeniously overcomes "the obstacle of the disconnected expression" by seeking "the thought which was underlying it connectedly all the time" (455–56), filling in gaps with his own words and weaving a "smooth and finished texture out of the ravelled skein" (456). The episode of the delirious Mr. Candy outlines the risks of a text produced only of extracts, absent all explanatory context, in a form—like the mystery novel—that desperately requires it.

Ezra's work toward a linear narrative evokes the very opposite of the skipping or skimming reading practice Price describes. Like the biblical Ezra, known as "Ezra the scribe," Collins' Ezra is likewise a devoted transcriber of others' texts. While Ezra Jennings never completes his own book on the nervous system and brain, and asks to be buried in an unmarked grave with a sealed package of his letters, diary, and the unfinished book, his own writing does not represent the fragmentary or excerpted so much as the cut-off and unfinished. The tragedy of his unfinished work reinforces his association with a sacrificial narrative linearity.

Collins' commitment to linearity is also evidenced by the novel's contrast between its own form and its two major intertexts, *Robinson Crusoe* and the Bible itself, two texts that shared immense cultural authority and easy availability for excerpting. As many critics have noted, *Robinson Crusoe* is a kind of secular Bible for Betteredge who calls the book "infallible" and "unrivalled" (535): "such a book as *Robinson Crusoe* never was written, and never will be written again. I have tried that book for years . . . and I have found it my friend in need in all the necessities of this mortal life" (61). The implicit comparison to Scripture reflects the massive influence of the novel on nineteenth-century readers who saw in it not only religious lessons of redemption, but the more secularized messages of self-help.[21]

In *The Moonstone*, Collins extracts quotations from both *Robinson Crusoe* and Scripture but then subsumes them to a linear narrative, as he

---

21. Peters (1993) makes this claim. See Susan Naramore Maher (1988) for one account of the novel and Victorian readers. Adaptations abounded, including evangelical ones. Ian Watt (1957), in his classic essay on the novel, describes Crusoe as a capitalist hero, the "embodiment of economic individualism" (63), and notes the novel's "reluctance to consider the extent to which spiritual and material values may be opposed" (83). The naïve harmonizing of spiritual and material progress in *Robinson Crusoe* might explain why the novel presented itself as an especially apt intertext for *The Moonstone,* where Collins committed himself to exploring both the troubling economic logic of Christian virtue, and the disharmonies and hypocrisies entailed in the meeting between Christian teachings of selflessness and the capitalist ethos.

does to other "documents" as well. As novelist, Collins becomes an anthol-
ogizer, but in a manner that subverts the organizing principles of anthol-
ogies and instead bolsters the ethical claims of the linear narrative over
those of the text open to being excerpted. Betteredge reads *Crusoe* in a
kind of bibliomancy, a reading practice based on the conviction that a text
produces "miraculous words" (536) with "prophetic" relevance (61) for
its reader, thus allowing him to read the novel piecemeal, "taking a turn at
it," rather than following it in linear fashion (65, 89). Likewise, Robinson
Crusoe himself reads the original sacred text, the Holy Scripture, by leaving out (the entire Hebrew Bible), repeating when he chooses, interrupting
or leaving off when he desires: "in the morning I took the Bible, and beginning at the New Testament, I . . . impos'd upon myself to read awhile every
morning and every night . . . as long as my thoughts should engage me"
(Defoe 77).[22]

These reader-determined modes of engaging texts would seem to shift
the power from text to reader, yet, paradoxically, Collins emphasizes the
authoritative nature of these texts in his representation of Betteredge's bibliomancy and Crusoe's perusal. While bibliomancy, for instance, appears
to depend on the special value of certain passages, it actually affirms the
sacred nature of the entirety of the quoted texts by the randomness with
which passages are selected: if *any* verse can have special value, then all
verses must. Even as Crusoe can elect to begin reading at the New Testament, rather than at Genesis, and to stop reading when his thoughts cease
to engage him, and Betteredge can likewise read the novel when and as he
wishes, still, these sacred texts announce their authority precisely by virtue
of their exceptional capacity to be excerpted, quoted, closed and opened at
will and whim of the reader, and still to be meaningful. The reader's role
becomes less powerful against the cultural authority of such a text and his
or her individual judgment less important to the standing of the text.

Where the dependency of author upon reader is minimal, the sacrificial effort of writerly communication is also absent. Collins thus asserts

---

22. Even beyond the practice of bibliomancy, the reading of the Christian Bible is rarely
a linear process. That the New Testament took its historical, material form as a codex in
distinction from the Hebrew Bible's form as a scroll underscores a reading practice particular
to Christianity. Since a verse in the Hebrew Bible is read to indicate its typological fulfillment
in the New Testament, a Christian reading does not consider either the Old Testament or the
New Testament solely as unfolding narratives. The force of a passage or episode borrows
much of its force from its unexpected indication of another passage. As Jeffrey Masten, Peter
Stallybrass and Nancy Vickers, ed. (1997) write, "Christianity deliberately cut into the Judaic
scroll to create a discontinuous practice of reading" (3). I am indebted to Peter Stallybrass
for first sensitizing me to these distinctions of form.

the ethical value of the contemporary novel and novelist against the sacred texts of Christianity and capitalist entrepreneurship, associating their "extracts" with theft rather than sacrifice. Collins achieves this association, I suggest, by analogizing the excerpt, the anti-linear text, to the novel's most contested object: the gem. When the jewel is first seen, Betteredge notes that "you could hold [it] between your finger and thumb," and yet, it lays "such a hold" on its observers that "when you looked down into [it], you looked into a yellow deep that drew your eyes into it so that they saw nothing else" (118–19). *The Moonstone* leaves its viewers no choice but to receive it. And it requires no extended process of reception. While a text is an "art of time," "never present as a whole in an instant of time," the gem is immediately apprehensible, with "no parts or sections, no areas or segments" (Fisher 21, 157). Unlike texts that must be read to be received, the Moonstone, as a discrete object, is perceptible instantaneously in its entirety: Betteredge describes Rachel "flash[ing] the jewel before my eyes" (118).

The Moonstone is, of course, the object in the novel most consistently associated with theft. Plundered in an imperial project, bequeathed within a family as a form of debt, pocketed, stolen unconsciously, re-stolen and re-stolen yet again, finally restored to the forehead of a god, the Moonstone's extraordinary value seems to consign it permanently to repeating cycles of theft and attempted restoration. Yet as it shifts back and forth from sacred to more obviously commercial sites and purposes, it cannot successfully separate these realms. I have argued here that *The Moonstone* is structured by the ethical difficulty of confronting an increasingly market and profit-driven set of social relations, especially in light of the inherited Christian aspiration toward the gift that demands no return and is, as such, sacrificial. Yet, I have also suggested that the Christian theology of the sacrificial free gift is not exclusively a foil to the market, but itself faces significant trouble as it is translated from Christ's super-human giving to the ordained Christian charity of ordinary people who cannot elude the structure of reward for virtue.

The "sacred" texts evoked by *The Moonstone*—the Bible and *Robinson Crusoe*—may thus be read to represent the Christian and capitalist ethos, and their merging. In Collins' novel, both participate in the structure defined by the near-inevitability of theft in their command of their own reception. In the age Collins was writing, they were always already sacred to their readers; no risk attended either their publication or their reading. Further, their reading did not demand a devoted, sustained attention but could be accomplished through random excerpting and quoting, in contradistinction from the novels Collins wrote which depended on the immensely challenging work of holding the reader's interest over time.

While Collins, like Dickens, highly valued the lessons of the New Testament, he understood much of the contemporary practice of Christianity to have devolved into a claptrap version of itself without any generosity of spirit. Collins thus set up the contemporary novel to stand in contradistinction from the already classic novel of capitalist virtue and even from a Scripture that could be read to "economize" human spiritual experience.

Literary Economics:
Profitable Sacrifice for Readers and Writers

In defining his own writing against the merging of Christian and capitalist ideals, Collins appropriated the realm of the sacred for the emerging novelist whose uncertain literary exchange might transcend self-interested economics. Yet this was a highly idealized version of his profession. In the novel's Preface, Collins described his relation to his audience in sacrificial terms, thanking them for "re-paying" him a "hundred-fold for the hard toil which these pages cost me in the dark time of sickness and grief" (*MS* 49). In this description of the work of writing, Collins excised all the commercial middlemen—publishers, printers, editors, booksellers, libraries—who allowed his book to reach the public, imagining an intense, unmediated relationship with his audience. In reality, Collins, like his fellow novelists of sympathy, was enmeshed in professional negotiations, securing the highest possible sale prices, considering the costs and benefits of multiple formats of publication, and protesting abuses of the absence of international copyright.[23]

The risk that had been ever-present in *The Moonstone*—that fair or generous exchange would inevitably be revealed as theft—was a condition of his professional life. In November 1869, Collins received a request from Dutch magazine publishers, the Belinfante Brothers, for permission to print a translation of his forthcoming novel, *Man and Wife*. The publishers offered the novelist a complimentary copy of their magazine in return for the rights. Replying that a free magazine was hardly tempting for an English novelist who did not read Dutch, Collins suggested the following alternative:

---

23. Not until the Berne Convention of 1887 and the American Platt–Simonds Bill of 1891 were writers legally protected against rampant international piracy.

Permit me to suggest that you might acknowledge the receipt of the right to translate "Man and Wife" in a much better way than by giving me the magazine. It is quite a new idea–you might give me some money. (10 November 1869, *Letters* 2: 328)

When the publishers expressed their reticence at commercial terms, Collins replied without a trace of humor:

I declare any publisher who takes my book from me with a view to use it in any form for his own benefit—without my permission and without giving me a share in his profits—to be guilty of theft. (18 November 1869, *Letters* 2: 331)

Rather than representing and depending on an extended relation with his reader, Collins' novel was now a valuable thing to be possessed, sold, bought, and, ruefully, stolen. His novel became an object that, in its solid entirety, was not unlike the brilliant, rocky Moonstone he wanted pictured on the cover of his novel to attract the attention of buyers (*Letters* 2: 345). Unlike Ruskin, who argued that the marketplace required its "martyrdoms," too, Collins limited the relation of sacrifice to a non-commercial sphere he imagined occupying with his readers (*Unto This Last* 24).

If Collins imagined his novel as a sacrificial offering to his readers but also as a commercial object that demanded fair exchange from those who brought it before his readers, we need not judge this a hypocrisy nor a mystification of the processes whereby privately penned texts become publicly circulating commodities. Instead, I suggest that the two conceptions depended upon each other, heightening the value of sacrificial exchange as they did so. That Collins needed the idea of the novel as a sacrifice par excellence and of the writer as the sacrificial agent and victim suggests just how ethically threatening the spread of marketplace values seemed to those middle-class writers who depended on that market to spread their message of social sympathy. It also teaches us that, in 1868, for an author involved in the largely secular pursuit of mystery and sensation novel-writing, sacrifice was still the most eligible and legible model available to suggest ethical rectitude.

Collins did not emphasize the fact that his writerly model of sacrifice carried with it a purified notion of gain, now collective and shared. As the 1860s had made novels more affordable and available to a larger audience than ever before and had, at the same time, granted novelists their highest selling prices, the mutual benefits of novels of sympathy were as material

as they were spiritual. Distinguishing the free gift of writerly sacrifice from
the theft he associated with so-called free gifts, Collins took steps to reconcile a moral economy and a profitable economy on an individual basis.
Imagining a wider basis on which to reconcile the two remained as vital as
it was elusive.

Robert Elsmere

The "True, Best Self"
and the Ideal of Mutual Service

Why is it that at the heart of this modern world, with all its love of gold, its thirst for knowledge, its desire for pleasure, there still lives and burns . . . this strange madness of sacrifice, this foolishness of the Cross?

—Mary Augusta Ward, *Eleanor* (1900)

*I*n the chapters preceding this one, I have investigated the ways that secularizing Victorian novelists at first seem to represent altruism and egoism as constituting an exhaustive moral polarity, only for their novels to grapple with the impracticability and undesirability of so elevated a moral ideal and so extreme a moral schema. These novelists—some tentatively, some confidently—forged an alternative ethic to individualist self-sacrifice in the shape of mutual benefit, an ethic rooted in the mid-century hopes that laissez-faire economics would produce shared plenty.

It would be simple enough to conclude this study by drawing a straight line from this early challenge of the self-sacrificial ethic to the "post-Victorian" sensibility that characterized the period between the century's end and the First World War. This sensibility found its métier in the repudiation of the "sordid necessity of living for others," as Oscar Wilde memorably put it ("Socialism"). Likewise, Lytton Strachey's *Eminent Victorians* charged that the values of renunciation had outlived their currency, while Friedrich Nietzsche mounted his attack on both Christian and humanist forms of altruism in a challenge to Enlightenment assumptions that continues to this day to find expression across disciplines: from evolutionary biologists who dispute the scientific possibility for altruism to economists who maintain that self-interest is the only reliable incentive by which to estimate human behavior to literary critics who approach past and contemporary religion and its humanist derivatives with a strong hermeneutic of suspicion.

I would like to leave aside more sweeping narratives to end more locally, in the late 1880s, with the phenomenon of *Robert Elsmere,* the best-selling novel of Mary Augusta Ward, a novelist considered by many to have inherited the mantle of George Eliot. I will suggest that this novel offers a new, historically particular harmonization of self-love and benevolence—a harmony experienced as so elusive to mid-Victorians—by imagining a pursuit of the common good dependent on the pursuit of the individual good.

A novel that went through seven editions in its first five months and sold over a million copies, *Robert Elsmere* occasioned wide discussion among those who "shared the deeper thought of the period," not least through William Gladstone's long review essay in *The Nineteenth Century* (Gladstone, "'Robert Elsmere'" 6). The novel's subject is what Ward calls "this transition England," in which "a religion which can no longer be believed clashes with a skepticism full of danger to conduct" (Ward *RE* 555, 600). At the same time, in its depiction of the poverty and suffering of London's East End dwellers, *Robert Elsmere* offers a portrait of the failures of laissez-faire liberalism to achieve benefits for all. The novel describes the social work and, in particular, the settlement movement that came as late-century responses to the realities of a new economy where joblessness, injury or illness often spelled disaster and where the goal of survival crowded out any more lofty ambitions. In the aftermath of the novel's writing, Mary Ward herself founded the Passmore Edwards Settlement in Tavistock Place.[1]

An unduly neglected novel (beloved of intellectual historians and philosophers, but not literary critics), *Robert Elsmere* compellingly narrates the loss and gain, the faith and doubt and then the abiding new faith of a sensitive, altruistic, intellectual Anglican minister who encounters the challenges of the German Higher Criticism as conveyed to him by a major philosopher destitute of nearly all social sympathy or tendency to altruistic action.[2] Robert, who is married to Catherine, a wife of a strong

---

1. Ward's other major project was the anti-suffrage movement.
2. Patricia M. Spacks (1995) attributes the fate of this novel to anxiety at the didac-

"ascetic temper," deeply rooted in orthodox Christian faith and the ideals of charity, painfully renounces his faith in a divine Christ, setting at
risk his nearest and widest social relations as well as his economic security (139). Giving up his parish and orders, and committed to blending a
modern faith in the teachings of a historical Jesus with embedded social
work, Robert moves himself and his wife to London's East End where he
embarks on what becomes a life-killing mission to share with working men
the redemptive force of Christ's example. Charismatic and talented at the
drama of sympathetic, evocative story-telling as few men are, practical and
idealistic both, Robert works tirelessly at this mission of inspiring men,
bringing about his early death from a tubercular disease that attacks his
fragile constitution. Ward assures us that his death does not end his work,
however, and his Brotherhood of Christ lives on in the hands of good men
who have absorbed his "incalculably diffusive" influence (*Middlemarch*
766). Even Catherine is brought to an understanding of Robert's inspiring
religious disposition, notwithstanding his heresy, and in the aftermath of
his death, she carries out his pledges of charity and becomes a presence at
the small chapel on Elgood Street even as she maintains her own faith, her
daughter alongside her.

   Robert Elsmere ostensibly poses a question for my project. The heroic,
efficacious death of the man Ward labels an altruist, in a novel all about
the transformative power of Christ's sacred example, seems to bespeak a
full embrace of the self-sacrificial ideal in an idiom barely changed from
the Christian orthodoxy it sets out to refuse. Can we not see the shadow
of Charlotte Yonge's Sir Guy Morville's death in Elsmere's? The former
death's immense spiritual meaning for Victorians and the equally affecting pathos of Sydney Carton's influence beyond the grave seem the direct
precursors to Elsmere's remarkable self-abdication, not to mention the
remarkable sales Ward's novel achieved. For the purposes of this study, is
there any indication that Ward succeeds George Eliot's tentative move to
justify an unsaintly life? or Trollope's refusal to credit self-sacrifice with
social efficacy? Can we reconcile Robert Elsmere's life-killing altruism with
Collins' concern that giving up is nothing but a mask for taking, that such
gifts may be no better than empty? In brief, did the narratives from which
I have made my case leave a mark?

   I suggest that Ward's novel does indeed register the efforts of mid-
century novelists and moralists to move beyond painful self-sacrifice to the

---

tic author's entry into private realms and the demand for readerly activity: "The didactic
novelist's pursuit and prying forbid passivity" they "insist . . . on how much is at stake for
everyone" (161).

ideal of mutual benefit. My account of the novel above paints it in terms of the problem of imagining religion for a modern world, yet the drama of the novel for at least one of its eminent Victorian readers, Gladstone, and I would venture to say, for some of its more invested twenty-first-century readers, is the challenge to Catherine and Robert's marriage and the inevitability of Catherine's compromises, compromises all the worse because they do not originate in her own spiritual and intellectual development, as Robert's do.[3] The gender politics of the novel are painful, as we watch Catherine forced to absorb the losses occasioned by Robert's changes of heart and mind. The submission she undergoes in watching her husband renounce his faith and remaining at his side is a terrible, almost punitive distortion of the Christian submission in which she believes so fully and in which she is so practiced.

Yet if Ward sacrifices Catherine to her didactic mission, it is not because she is female, but because of her ascetic temperament. In Catherine, Ward locates the old evangelical commitment to self-sacrifice in the forms we have already seen under critique. This self-sacrifice is shown up to be not only ineffective but harmful to others: it either demands too much of them in expecting equal commitment to one's own extreme ideal or alternatively coddles them in imagining that they cannot take care of themselves and thus require the sacrifices of others. Prideful and self-asserting, this old version of self-sacrifice breaks down social ties. Embraced by a self-selecting group of elite individuals, self-sacrifice divides rigidly and lastingly between those who give and those who receive, denying ordinary people the freedom and opportunity to exercise their own moral strength.

The novel explicitly invokes *Adam Bede* as an intertext, when a character compares the self-denying Catherine to Dinah Morris, calling her a "Quaker prophetess, a Dinah Morris in society" (577). Meanwhile, figures who resemble *Adam Bede*'s Mrs. Poyser and Lisbeth Bede offer ironic representations of the self-sacrificial ideal, as when Robert's mother responds to her son's aspirations by saying, "'Oh, I supposed you would insist on killing yourself. . . . To most people nowadays that seems to be the necessary preliminary of a useful career'" (78). Similarly, the local minister's wife bristles at Catherine's "pottering about orphan asylums" when she should be off getting engaged:

---

3. Spacks gives equal weight to Catherine's drama: the painful compromises of remaining married as her husband renounces the beliefs that undergirded their union. Jay (2001) describes Catherine as suffering the "subjugation of . . . intellectual independence to the requirements of nurturing a harmonious family" ("Women Writers" 263). On her view, Ward disallowed her heroines her own emancipation from orthodoxy.

Mrs. Thornburgh wholly denied, as she sat bridling by herself, that it was a Christian necessity to make yourself and other people uncomfortable. Yet this was what this perverse young woman was always doing. . . . No, Mrs. Thornburgh had no patience with her—none at all. It was all because she would not be happy like anybody else, but must needs set herself up to be peculiar. Why not live on a pillar, and go into hair-shirts at once? Then the rest of the world would know what to be at. (124–25)

Yet it will be Robert Elsmere himself, in a decidedly un-comic discourse, who introduces a new model of self-sacrifice that is inseparable from an ideal of self and other-fulfillment. It is too bad Dinah Morris could not have heard him preach.

In the novel's early pages, Catherine's ascetic character is set out against her "aesthetic" sister Rose, with Robert cast as the force to reconcile the two (8). In the years following her father's death and in place of her ineffectual mother, Catherine has served as the spiritual and practical head of the family, maintaining a loyalty to her father's austere evangelical commitments and his unworldly insularity. Catherine appears first in this novel just returned from tending to the sick, the dying, and the ignorant in her rural Westmoreland valley. Though Ward writes in praise of Catherine, to Rose, her sister's gentle charity is inseparable from "the most rigid self-repression, the most determined sacrificing of 'this warm kind world' with all its indefensible delights, to a cold other-world, with its torturing, inadmissible claims" (104). Worse, Catherine seems to ask "of all about her the same absolute surrender to an awful Master she gave so easily herself" (104).

Rose is hardly to be found on errands of compassion. We encounter her first via the sounds of her energetic violin practice: "In a stranger coming upon the house for the first time . . . the sense of a changing social order and a vanishing past . . . would have been greatly quickened by certain sounds which were streaming out on to the evening air" (7). Rose is the future. An exceptionally talented musician, she has been at odds with Catherine for years, avoiding her volunteer work in the local school because she has no talent for it, and wishing instead to devote herself to her music: "'When one can play the violin and can't teach, any more than a cockatoo, what's the good of wasting one's time in teaching?'" (17). Rose, beautiful, mischievous, and eager to enjoy the things of this world, rejects Catherine's relation to the world in the short, but all-expressive rejoinder: "'Duty! I hate the word!'" (84).

The novel opens with Robert's imminent arrival to assume the nearby

living at Murewell, a position he has accepted only because his ill health
and fragile constitution have unsuited him for the work he truly desires,
engaging in "the hardest pastoral labor and the worst forms of English
poverty" in the large towns (81). Still suffering under the "smart of his
own renunciation," Elsmere expects little in Westmoreland, but when he
encounters Catherine's pure, gentle, yet powerful presence, he falls in love
with her (88). Catherine, who has never envisioned a lover for herself,
comes to trust and care for him when he is able to address the "great problem of her life—Rose and Rose's art" (97). In her father's absence, Catherine has sought to keep Rose from the larger world that is inseparable from
any serious musical study. Catherine appeals to Robert:

> How was it lawful for the Christian to spend the few short years of the
> earthly combat in any pursuit, however noble and exquisite, which merely
> aimed at the gratification of the senses, and implied in the pursuer the
> *emphasizing rather than the surrender of self?* (97, emphasis mine)

To this painful problem, which will only metastasize for Catherine once
she marries Robert, Robert answers in a way which bridges Catherine's
evangelical zeal with Rose's aesthetic passion. Talking, as Ward says, in a
Kingsley-like strain, Robert tries to "lift her to a more intelligent view of a
multifarious world, dwelling . . . on the influence of beauty on character,
pointing out the value to the race of all individual development" and suggesting that God, "the Great Designer," would not have granted artistic
aptitudes unless He imagined a use and function for them in His world
(97, 98). Yet it is when Robert describes the "humanizing effect of music"
on the poor that Catherine comes alive to his words (98). Robert is an
unusually persuasive speaker, "And yet," Ward's narrator intones,

> as we all know, these ways of speech were not his own. He was merely talk-
> ing the natural Christian language of his generation; whereas she . . . was
> still thinking and speaking in the language of her father's generation . . . he
> was only talking the commonplaces of his day. But to her they were not
> commonplaces at all. (97–98)

Ward insists throughout the novel that however special Robert may be,
however deeply he may feel the truth of what he preaches, he is the product of his age. His age is no longer one of asceticism.

Ward explores the problems of asceticism by rehearsing arguments we
have seen before: the self-sacrificial ideal is shown to be needlessly and

stubbornly applied in cases where instead of one party suffering, all can benefit. It is also a cover for pride in Christian achievement. As in the case of Dinah Morris, marrying off Saint Catherine is not easy; as in the resolution of Dinah's case, Catherine, too, must ultimately sacrifice self-sacrifice. Yet in distinction from *Adam Bede,* Catherine's tragedy is that she will sacrifice herself in ways she could never have anticipated. Catherine has never considered marriage because she has devoted herself to the poor and needy. But she has been deterred even more powerfully because she has imagined herself bound to her two sisters and her widowed mother by a pledge to her father to keep them bound to the narrow path and bring them "safe to the day of account" (119). In an argument with Robert before he explicitly proposes marriage, Catherine warns him not to appeal to her. Her position emphasizes the claims of parents on children, who are typically all too ready to cast them off in their hour of need, so that "All the long years of devotion and self-sacrifice go for nothing"; Catherine insists that the grown child's "business first of all is to pay its debt, whatever the cost" (133). Robert, accusing Catherine of "making all life a sacrifice to the past," argues back:

> "[S]urely the child may make a fatal mistake if it imagines that its own happiness counts for nothing in the parents' eyes. What parent but must suffer from the starving of the child's nature? What have mother and father been working for, after all, but the perfecting of the child's life? Their longing is that it should fulfill itself in all directions. New ties, new affections, on the child's part, mean the enriching of the parent. What a cruel fate for the elder generation, to make it the jailer and burden of the younger!" (133–34)

While Robert sounds like J. S. Mill, arguing that asceticism is only desirable so as to prevent others from having to live with such privations, Catherine sounds like an Eliot heroine, at moments echoing Dinah Morris, at other moments, Maggie Tulliver and Romola. Robert's words, says Catherine, are "'all sophistry. The only safety lies in following out the plain duty. . . . There are many for whom it is easy and right to choose their own way; their happiness robs no one. There are others on whom a charge has been laid from their childhood'" (134). Catherine crowns this painful speech with the anti-utilitarian finality, "'We are not here only to be happy'" (134).

Yet Robert is no Stephen Guest and he is not arguing for a betrayal of others in favor of his own and Catherine's stolen happiness. To Robert, the holy bond of marriage makes for a blessing that runneth over. Like Rose, who is convinced that Catherine's commitment to her family is "'sacrifice run mad!,'" Robert refuses to credit Catherine's judgment that the situation requires one party's pain to produce another's happiness (137). Parties in sympathy can benefit simultaneously. Further, he appeals with the argument that in attempting to sacrifice oneself, one inevitably sacrifices others:

> "Life is not so simple. It is so easy to sacrifice others with oneself, to slay all claims in honor of one, instead of knitting the new ones to the old. Is life to be allowed no natural expansion? Have you forgotten that, in refusing the new bond for the old bond's sake, the child may be simply wronging the parents, depriving them of another affection which ought to have been theirs?" (135)

In a case like his and Catherine's, new claims may be "knit to the old" and then all may be fulfilled simultaneously, to a surplus of satisfaction. Should Catherine prevail and sacrifice herself, not only will she be guilty of leaving a potential new affection unrealized but she will actively harm the parent she wishes to honor.

Ward takes Robert's side in this argument, as she depicts Mrs. Leyburn, Catherine's mother, urging the marriage upon her daughter. This plot element allows for the critique of Catherine's sacrificial pride, a critique in this case self-inflicted by Catherine's austere judgment. In a comic, ironic turn, when the pastor's wife, Mrs. Thornburgh, alerts Mrs. Leyburn that Catherine is likely to deny Robert for her mother's sake, Ward describes Mrs. Leyburn moving very quickly from an initial shock and tremulous sense of loss to a well-gratified interest in Elsmere's successful career at Oxford and his new living at Murewell. With Mrs. Leyburn's conversion, the narrator's irony spills over to Catherine: "Alas, poor Catherine! How little room there is for the heroic in this trivial everyday life of ours!" (146). The novel is rarely ironic in this way when it treats Catherine who is always earnest, always self-scrutinizing, always good even when rigid, and finally tragic. As in Trollope's case, it is primarily the self-dramatization of sacrifice that calls out a kindly irony from Ward: "Catherine, in the heat of her own self-surrender, had perhaps forgotten that her mother too had a heart!" (147). And when Mrs. Leyburn begins to indulge herself, imagining the joys of Catherine as a bride, a wife and a mother, Ward more seriously attests to the truth of Robert's argument that love and filial devotion are forces of natural expansion and that Catherine truly would deny her mother in denying Robert.

The risk of self-sacrifice as self-posturing, a mask for pride and self-assertion, becomes explicit when Mrs. Leyburn confronts Catherine and suggests she might be pleased if her daughter were to marry Elsmere. Catherine can feel nothing but that she is not wanted, that her long-standing devotion has gone for nothing. When she shares her distress that her mother could say goodbye to her so easily, Mrs. Leyburn brightens and says, "'They say it is such a nice house, Catherine, and such pretty country, and I'm sure I should like his mother, though she is Irish'" (150). Yet, quickly, the narrator moves from the comic to the wholly sympathetic, as Catherine herself comes to contemplate her past with wide-open eyes, alive to the irony of it all: "It was the bitterest moment of Catherine Leyburn's life. In it the heroic dream of years broke down. Nay, the shriveling ironic touch of circumstance laid upon it made it look almost ridiculous. What had she been living for, praying for, all these years?" (150). Catherine has labored under the mis-apprehension that she is not only useful to her family, but indispensable. Now, with the scathing self-scrutiny that differentiates Ward's spiritual drama from Trollope's social comedy, Catherine feels herself to be

> humiliated before the world and before herself. Her self-respect was for the moment crushed. . . . She had been convicted . . . of an egregious over-estimate of her own value. . . . How rich her life had always been in the conviction of usefulness—nay, indispensableness! Her mother's persuasions had dashed it from her. And religious scruple, for her torment, showed her her past transformed, alloyed with all sorts of personal prides and cravings, which stood unmasked now in a white light. (152)

If Catherine has over-estimated her own value, the novel suggests that she has under-estimated the capacities of her family. Just as Spencer argued that extreme altruism would produce in others an undesirable weakness, Rose argues that Catherine's loving predominance has created circumstances where others have learned to be passive and dependent. Offering Elsmere a narrative of their family life from the time of their father's death, Rose describes Catherine's selfless care of others from the time she was sixteen:

> "[S]he did everything: she taught us . . . she did most of the housekeeping; and you can see for yourself what she does for the neighbors and poor folk. She is never ill, she is never idle, she always knows her own mind. We owe everything we are . . . to her. Her nursing has kept mamma alive

through one or two illnesses. Our lawyer says he never knew any business affairs managed better than ours, and Catherine manages them. The one thing she never takes any care or thought for is herself. What we should do without her I can't imagine; and yet sometimes I think if it goes on much longer none of us three will have any character of our own. After all, you know, it may be good for the weak people to struggle on their own feet, if the strong would only believe it, instead of always being carried. The strong people *needn't* always be trampling on themselves—if they only knew." (127–28)

Self-sacrifice deprives others of their freedom—to make choices different than those the agent might make; to develop their own strengths and their own independent characters, and to live in a fluidity of identities where they can move back and forth between the conditions of dependant and giver, rather than hardening into a single, limited role.

Catherine's eventual marriage to Robert moves the novel to explore a different ethic: a self-realization devoted to the realization of others.[4] As Robert enters into the comparative historical study which occasions his crisis of faith, he is brought up short by the problem of testimony: the unreliable facticity of reports originating in historical moments with different epistemologies and conventions of perception.[5] As Robert tries to find a new faith that can replace the belief in the literal understandings of the Gospels' account of the miracles of the Incarnation, the Resurrection, and Revelation, he finds a model in a lay preacher whom he first encountered at Oxford, Thomas Grey. Ward's character Grey was recognizable to educated Victorians as Thomas Hill Green (1836–1882), the liberal political reformer and idealist philosopher who from 1878 was Whyte's Professor of Moral Philosophy and to whom Ward dedicated the novel in honor of his "love of God and service of man." Opposed to utilitarianism, Green offered an alternative vision to the claim that the good was equivalent to a sum of pleasures, suggesting instead that the good had to be an abiding and absolute good for all men, irrespective of likes and dislikes. As I will explore, Green argued that "the true good must be good for all men, so that no one should seek to gain by another's loss, gain and loss being esti-

---

4. See Dixon's helpful account of *RE*. He describes Green's and Ward's attempts to merge idealism with altruism, a project rejected by Sidgwick as incoherent (254–63).

5. See Chadwick, *Secularization* 189–228. See Andrew Elfenbein (2008) for an account that focuses on Robert's relationship with the philosopher whose iconoclastic work influences him. Elfenbein argues for the influence of Ward's novel on Oscar Wilde's *The Picture of Dorian Gray*, which he calls an "erotically uncensored version of *RE*" (504).

mated on the same principle for each" (232). At the bottom of Green's philosophy was a practical understanding of the social challenges of his time
and the difficulty in aligning the interests of the poor and the rich so as to
limit the gulf between them.[6]

In Ward's novel, Grey/Green is nothing short of a hero, stepping in to
offer Robert spiritual sustenance at a breaking point, in a single case that
Robert knows has hundreds of analogues in the lives of other men: "Here,
indeed, was a man on whom his fellows might lean, a man in whom the
generation of spiritual force was so strong and continuous that it over-
flowed of necessity into the poorer, barrener lives around him, kindling
and enriching" (68). While Green had important counterparts in his day,
the historian Olive Anderson affirms "that among opinion-forming late
Victorians and Edwardians his name and words were venerated above all
others" ("Feminism" 686). Anderson attributes his influence to a confluence of three factors. First was his base at Balliol: "The enthusiasm, reverence and love he inspired in the brightest and best of those at Oxford in
the 1860s and above all in the 1870s, meant that for the next fifty years
many of those with influence in church and state spent their lives trying
to practise what they believed to be his teachings" (686).[7] Second, Green's
early death at age forty-five left his friends and colleagues bereft and,
in response, they engaged in a major effort to bring out all his writings,
thus multiplying the number of educated Victorians who came to know
his work. Finally, and perhaps most monumentally, Victorians at all levels
were introduced to his ideas in Ward's novel, which was published with
extracts of Green's Lay Sermons.

While T. H. Green's writings ranged from political economy and philosophy to Christian dogma, his *Prolegomena to Ethics* (1883), published
in the year that followed his death, gives us a glimpse of the moral theory
that appealed so to Ward in bridging the gap between the needs of the self
and the other, as well as past and present ethics. Robert's initial influence
upon Catherine is as a spokesman for the development of Rose's musical
talent. As we have seen, he links the value of human creativity to God's
gift of talents and to the social work of art. Later in the novel, he seeks to
explain to Catherine the marriage of reason and modern faith in the same

---

6. See Marcus G. Singer (1992) for a short but useful account of Green's position in
nineteenth-century ethical thought: Green and Mill were the "the great liberals of the age,"
united in their liberalism, opposed in their respective idealism and utilitarianism (71–73, 73).

7. See Collini on the shaping effects in Green's case (and others of the "partially pro-
fessionalized academic class") of "making one's role as a teacher central to one's identity"
(224–27).

way: "'Do you ever ask yourself . . . what part the reasoning faculty, that faculty which marks us out from the animal, was meant to play in life? Did God give it to us simply that you might trample on it and ignore it, both in yourself and me?'" (457). As Susan Mizruchi has noted, the German Higher Criticism "accorded enormous power to the interpreter. . . . Through its rigorous scholarly methods, the higher criticism transformed in the Bible into a living enterprise centered in the human consciousness" (95).

Robert's development of his own "reasoning faculty" is simultaneously an imperative of service and a personal quest. When Catherine asks him to set aside religious matters in order to protect what is left of his orthodox faith, he answers that he cannot because his commitment to the work is to himself, to God, and to others: "'No! . . . not till I have satisfied myself. I feel it burning within me, like a command from God, to work out the problem, to make it clearer to myself—and to others'" (456). When, at the end of the novel, Catherine presses him on his deathbed to reach out for "'the true comfort—the true help—the Lamb of God sacrificed for us!'" he merges her language of collective, religious truth with his own new language of selfhood, asserting that his "'true best self'" is in God's hands, that self he has strived to develop in the heat and press of the new truth made available to him in his historical moment (674).

The sense of self-development and improvement in the context of an immediate social world was central to Green's vision of moral duty. "For any truest idea of what is best for man that can guide our action is still a realisation of that capacity for conceiving a better state of himself, which we must ascribe to every child whom we can regard as 'father of the man' capable of morality" (Green 185). The capacity of man to compare his present self with a better self is, for Green, the engine of moral progress. And yet, in spite of his commitment to individual development and aspiration, Green's thinking could not be further from what Ward's Catherine decries as "a proud and tameless individuality, this modern gospel of the divine right of self-development" (240).[8] First, the capacity to

---

8. Collini characterizes Green quite differently than I do here, as a prophet of the "culture of altruism," or "anti-selfishness sensibility," whose philosophy found "something repugnant in even the hint of self-regarding actions" (83, 82). Collini argues that Green's philosophy was as successful as it was because of the widespread nature of those assumptions. I suggest that Green's commitment to sacrifice takes a very different mode of expression than mid-century theories that dispense with self-realization or development. See also Jil Larson's excellent 2009 study for further support of the distinction between mid- and late-century sensibilities. She explores the paradox of "reclaiming of the self through shifting the focus from self to the larger world of work and duty to others" (25). For Larson, the late-century

conceive one's better self is a gift: a "spiritual endowment . . . through which human life has been so far bettered" and through which people mark out the paths which they must follow to realize further their aspirations (Green 189). More important still, the self which contemplates its own development is never an isolated one and the development it contemplates is never individual:

> [T]he self of which a man thus forecasts a fulfillment, is not an abstract or empty self. It is a self already affected in the most primitive forms of human life by manifold interests, among which are interests in other persons. These are not merely interests dependent on other persons for the means to their gratification, but interests in the good of those other persons, interests which cannot be satisfied without the consciousness that those other persons are satisfied. The man cannot contemplate himself as in a better state, or on the way to the best, without contemplating others, not merely as a means to that better state, but as sharing it with him. (210)

For Green, other human beings can never be a means to the end, because the end is always a shared state, "a bettering of the life which is at one his and the society's" (256). Here, the conflict between reasonable self-love and benevolence recedes because both ideals prompt toward the same rule of action, "founded on one and the same quest for a self-satisfaction which shall abide, but which no man can contemplate as abiding except so far as he identifies himself with a society whose well-being is to him as its own" (249).

Green takes pains to distinguish his notion of well-being from a utilitarian idea of a sum or succession of pleasures. Instead, Green envisions the greatest happiness for the greatest number as "self-devotion to an ideal of mutual service" (262); "a life of self-devoted activity on the part of all persons" (309).[9] This devotion of self to mutual service means that each man recognizes his fellow as *"like himself* . . . having objects which it is their vocation to realise, which health is the condition of their realising, and which form part of one great social end, the same for himself as for

---

ethos was marked "not by a deontological escape from self or a paradoxically strong-willed refusal of choice but instead by anxious yet flexibly ethical searching, an openness to the surprising and unusual, and an ambivalence poised between regard for Victorian morality and attention to the ethical relevance of that which lies beyond morality's authority" (31–32).

9. See also Dinah Maria Mulock Craik's "What Is Self-Sacrifice?" (1875) for the distinction between self-sacrifice and self-devotion. Craik's sharp critique of the sacrificial sensibility focuses on women and takes up many of the objections to sacrifice that this study has explored in novels.

them" (254, emphasis mine). The valuing of each man as being like one-self—a vessel of a vocation, liable to spiritual health or sickness—recalls George Eliot's tireless work to articulate and to help her readers "conceive with that distinctness which is no longer reflection but feeling" that each human being has "an equivalent centre of self" (*Middlemarch* 193).[10]

For Green, this sympathy is not sufficient as a perception, but operates as a demand for action. It dictates the life one leads in pursuit of a social end dimly conceived, but imperative nonetheless: "What this [social] end is he conceives, like the rest of us, very dimly, though, but for the power which the idea of there being such an end exercises over him . . . he would not live the life he does" (254). In living the "life he does," each man develops his own potential as he invests in the potential of others; thus, Robert Elsmere honing his God-given capacity to speak, to teach, to feel, among the artisans and laborers of the East End who come, likewise, to a real-ization of their own possibilities: "The men present were evidently begin-ning to regard the work as *their* work also, and its success as their interest. It was perfectly natural, for not only had most of them been his support-ers and hearers from the beginning, but some of them were now actually teaching in the night-school or helping in the various branches of the large and overflowing boys' club" (620). For Green, the pleasure that was so critical to the utilitarians is not the aim of this pursuit. Though the pleasure of others *accompanies* the "fulfillment of his mission," it is the "comple-tion of [each man's] capacities" within this social context that defines the good (255).

Green's ideal was one we can identify with a movement of political altruism particular to late Victorian England. The 1880s, a period of eco-nomic recession, was one in which social reform of all sorts was on the rise.[11] An increasingly activist press raised new interest in the problems of urban poverty, the newly described phenomenon of unemployment, prob-lems of sanitation and housing, the particular plight of children and ani-mals, and the challenges of temperance. Even as charitable work in the slums became more common, in this era, altruism became a motive asso-ciated less with the generous impulses of individuals and voluntary asso-

10. Interestingly, Green credits utilitarianism with the radical teaching that each human being has an absolute value irrespective of class, creed, and other social distinctions. He suggests that it was this radical egalitarianism that occasioned the opposition with which utilitarianism was met (226).

11. Highly relevant is Ward's 1894 novel *Marcella*, set in the 1880s, concerned with the competing promises of socialism and more traditional paths to rectify the split between the rich and the poor.

ciations and more with a vision of the state as the appropriate force to address social ills (Dixon 232, 373). By the 1870s, liberal theory, as Owen Chadwick tells us, entered its

> collectivist phase. . . . A doctrine which ended in the slums of great cities could hardly contain all the truth. . . . Once, the aim of liberal theory was negative. . . . Now it became positive—to accept restriction for the ends of morality and justice. Liberty was henceforth seen more in terms of the society than of the individual: less as freedom from restriction than as a quality of responsible social living in which all men had a chance to share. (*Secularization* 46–47)

Altruism came in this period to be more and more closely associated with the terms "collectivism" and "socialism," and to characterize efforts on behalf of those "below one on the social scale" (Collini 83).[12]

In a fascinating semantic phenomenon, the linkage between collectivism and socialism, on one hand, and altruism, on the other, insured that the moral opposition between individualism and altruism would become more pronounced. As collectivism and socialism were the political antonyms of individualism, then altruism, so closely linked with the former political movements, was logically the ethical antonym of individualism (Dixon 237). In a political and social climate that understood altruism and individualism to be at odds, Green's formulation of an altruism that merged individual development with social conscience offered a reconciliation not otherwise easily available.

The reconciliation was certainly paradoxical—a self-denying self-development. Yet, to late Victorians across the spectrum of faith, one can imagine how much sense it would have made. After all, the scriptural teaching beloved of the mid-century Evangelicals, "he that loses his life . . . finds it," was still a powerful echo. To late Victorians, Robert Elsmere's commitment to his own "natural growth" did not oppose his self-denial (Ward 399): Ward's description of "the young enthusiast to whom self-slaughter came so easy" suggested not nihilism but heroic purpose, a passion to share with his East End fellows the sense that nothing mattered, "'so long as you feel

---

12. Dixon traces the language of altruism in this era: "'Altruism' . . . was a word that was in the right place at the right time—in a nation with a newly reawakened awareness of the suffering of the poor, a declining confidence in the beliefs and institutions of traditional Christianity, an urgent desire in some quarters to ensure that moral standards were not a casualty of the decline of orthodoxy, and an increasingly politically engaged population with an appetite for social reform" (234).

that you are *something* with a life and purpose of its own, in this tangle of a world'" (80, 621).[13] Robert's own particular gifts of performance and communication are not minimized, but made much of by Ward who, like Green, imagined each man's mission to be fulfilled "in whatever channel the idiosyncrasy and circumstances of the individual may determine" (Green 309). Self-development was unique and it served a social end.

Thus Green offered a recommendation for self-denial that was far more enticing than the vision of his fellow liberal but philosophical opponent J. S. Mill, who saw in it only the sign of an imperfect social world that might one day, in a more perfect state, be able to do without self-denial altogether:

> Though it is only in a very imperfect state of the world's arrangements that anyone can best serve the happiness of others by the absolute sacrifice of his own, yet so long as the world is in that imperfect state, I fully acknowledge that the readiness to make such a sacrifice is the highest virtue which can be found in man. (*Utilitarianism* 417)

For Green, sacrifice was an enduring and desirable condition of social relations. It was the domain not of the moral elite, but of all human beings. There was no absolute sacrifice, with a purity of separation between giver and recipient, but only sacrifices that necessarily reaped rewards.

Green's analysis of the importance of self-denial shared with Mill the basic Victorian assumption of its nobility: we admire the life of largest self-denial, he wrote, because "it implies a fuller realisation of the capacities of the human soul" (not because it renounces more pleasure) (294). Yet, insisting on the historical specificity of his discussion, Green moved from abstract to concrete, from philosopher to reformer (like Elsmere who expands his social mission after he gives up his living, rather than devoting himself to an uninterrupted scholarly life). Green contrasted the Greek ideal with his own, by noting that it was the wider "conceived range of claims to which the duty is felt" that enlarged the role of self-denial beyond its ancient role (220). In other words, in the modern world of Reform Bills and women's education, more people now *counted* as the neighbor on whose behalf one needed to sacrifice: "the recognition of new social claims

---

13. For a contrasting sense of nihilism, see the suicide of Laura Fountain in Ward's 1898 novel, *Helbeck of Bannisdale* ("because death puts an *end*" [462]) which, in this feature, shares a mood with other fin-de-siècle works. Note, too, the evolutionary sense of "tangle of a world," which evokes the potential nihilism often associated with a world absent of the divine.

compels its exercise in a new and larger self-denial" (293).[14] For Green, it was "the emancipation of the multitude, and the social situations arising out of it, that call forth the energies of the self-denying life as we now witness it" (295). When Ward details the success of Robert Elsmere's self-denying self-realization, she, too, moves into the present tense as she seeks to characterize the zeitgeist of "new forms of social help" (561):

> [A]s his aims became known, other men, finding the thoughts of their own hearts revealed in him, or touched with that social compunction which is one of the notes of our time, came down and became his helpers. . . . Week by week men and women of like gifts and energies with Elsmere spend themselves as he did, in the constant effort to serve and to alleviate. (568)

Robert Elsmere clearly possesses "genius" and a "brilliancy . . . none could rival" (Ward 680). Yet Ward's version of self-denying heroism dips into the cult of personality to transcend it with the Victorian ideology of that "Choir Invisible," as George Eliot put it. By passing on his talent for giving, Elsmere finds his immortality. For Ward, as for Green, sacrifice is always shared. It never falls to just one in its generation and it never disappears without effect upon generations beyond.

Finally, Green and Ward were linked by their conviction that "no one should seek to gain by another's loss, gain and loss being estimated on the same principle for each" (Green 232). We come here back to the utopian hope that the mid-century novelists associated with laissez-faire capitalism, the notion of a kind of economic "sympathy" in which shared pain would mean less pain for all and shared joy would mean more joy for all. This time, the aspiration is rooted more in a radical egalitarianism than a faith in economic miracles engineered by invisible hands. And yet, by the 1880s, Thomas Hill Green could both spell out the ideal and see clearly that the ideal was no more an imminent reality than it had been in the era of the Crystal Palace. Legislation needed to temper free trade and regulate the ownership of land since land was limited and its unfair acquisition or holding necessarily deprived others. And the principle of competition for private, material goods still denied the under-classes a share in the common good:

> Civil society may be, and is, founded on the idea of there being a common good, but that idea in relation to the less favoured members of society is

---

14. See Anderson (1991) on Green's feminist activity.

in effect unrealised, and it is unrealised because the good is being sought
in objects which admit of being competed for. They are of such a kind that
they cannot be equally attained by all. The success of some in obtaining
them is incompatible with the success of others. (263)

The "true good," by contrast, wrote Green, "must be good for all men"
(Green 232).

John Ruskin and Thomas Carlyle had also decried material competition and had imagined spiritual wealth and human value as the appropriate
ends and means of English glory, a glory built on pre-capitalist, paternalist
social and labor relations. Green and Ward saw a different resolution to
self-aggrandizing competition, a new faith which would embrace mutual
self-sacrifice as the basis for a social bond between poor and rich. As Robert Elsmere preaches to a skeptic,

> "[W]hat we *stand* to gain is a new social bond . . . a new compelling force
> in man and in society. What are you economists and sociologists of the
> new type always pining for? Why, for that diminution of the self in man
> which is to enable the individual to see the *world's* ends clearly, and to care
> not only for his own but for his neighbor's interest, which is to make the
> rich devote themselves to the poor, and the poor bear with the rich." (642)

Yet this capacity for disinterested self-sacrifice, argues Elsmere, is insup-
portable without the framework of religion, because the human will
is weak: "'Without religion you cannot make the will equal to its tasks.
Our present religion fails us; we must, we will have another!'" (642–43).
This new religion, however, promised no other-worldly rewards or private incentives; in that way, it eschewed the self-interested dimension of
Christian economics. Its sole reward was a new balance between oneself
and one's neighbors. "Love thy neighbor as thyself," now an imperative of
both duty and freedom.

Perhaps Elsmere's "religion" is most impressive because, in spite of
the novel's ending, it is a religion, as the Hebrew Bible says, "to live by"
(Lev. 18:5). The ancient rabbinic commentary on that oft-repeated verse is
simple: "and not to die by." While Elsmere's death served to indicate that
his institution would outlive his charismatic leadership, the novel does not
depend on it as its exemplary focus. Neither does his death retroactively
alter the meaning of what has come before. The real drama of *Robert Elsmere* as I have read it here is not its depiction of self-sacrifice unto death,
but its presentation of a transformative new moral. This moral did not

entail a total break from the culture of extreme altruism we have encountered over the course of this study, but shifted emphasis from individual suffering to collective growth.

If Ward's desire to maintain continuity with the culture of altruism seems disturbing, it is worth remembering that as punitive and harsh as the doctrine of self-sacrifice could be, it is also disheartening to imagine a literature or a society without an appreciation for what Dinah Maria Mulock Craik, herself a sharp critic of the mid-Victorian embrace of sacrifice, called the "strong affection which makes the welfare of the beloved of more importance to us than our own, or an equally strong devotion to a principle, which is merely an abstract form of the same emotion" (12). Ward, like her contemporaries and immediate predecessors, honored thorough self-devotion for a rightful cause.

Robert's death at the novel's end should not obscure for us Ward's innovation. As we saw most intensely in *Adam Bede*, mid-Victorian novels that privileged the collective over the individual had wrestled with the problem of individual costs that often underlay progress toward the greatest happiness for the greatest number. Novels such as *A Tale of Two Cities* and *The Moonstone*, which were premised upon the sacrificial logic that substitutes a victim (even a willing one) for beneficiaries of varying merit, could not avoid the tension between what Jan-Melissa Schramm has called expanded and restricted senses of personhood (36). This tension expresses itself in the limits to an economic thinking that presumes full fungibility among values. Sacrifice foregrounds both that fungibility and the necessary human singularity that makes of one figure a victim, and the other, a survivor or beneficiary. This irreducible singularity is inseparable from a sense of the sacred. Yet what about a human singularity that is itself capable of being made plural? A sacredness of economic logic that might help explain why theology has, since ancient times, turned to the economic to express itself in spite of the risks and difficulties that attend such analogies?

I have selected Ward as the end-point to this study because of her capacity to illuminate those questions that shape the novels of mid-century. Even as she turned to the tried-and-true Victorian mechanism of the sacrificial death to end her novel, she reconciled the ethical challenges of self-sacrifice in a powerful new way that accorded with the impulses and policies of increasing democratization. In the ethics she learned from Green—that the true good had to be a good for all men, that gain and loss had to be estimated for every individual on the same basis, that any life was at once an individual's and a society's—Ward embraced a radical egalitarian sense of the principle of substitution on which Christ's sacrifice had been founded.

We can see in this egalitarian sense of brotherhood a continuity with Ludwig Feuerbach (and other Higher Critics) whose ideas we read when considering Dickens' attempt to combat sin in the absence of an expiatory Christ. Economic logic can be seen here to serve a highly individualized moral program precisely because of its intimacy with fungibility, its availability to consider multiple—infinite—lives of equal, pressing value. In this aspirational vision, the one and the many might not be oppositional terms, but more focused and more extrapolated versions of the ethical landscape.

At the outset of this study, I claimed that the ethic of self-sacrifice yielded to an interest in mutual benefit. Mutual benefit, of course, is an outcome, rather than a strategy of action, as sacrifice might be described. As Charles Taylor has noted, mutual benefit is in fact the outcome of a market that negates collective action or agency, and, I might add, collective conscience (181). Classical market theory suggested that self-interest would bring about the greatest collective good, thus obviating and discouraging the need for collective agency. In such a schema, individuals do not need to aspire ethically nor balance the competing claims of self and others. An emphasis on intention yields to a focus on consequences.

But in the world of the novel, mutual benefit makes as little sense as Volume Two without Volume One, as little sense as characters with no names, no histories, no plots. The mid-Victorian novels of sympathy moved toward a version of mutual benefit differentiated from the world of the market by intention, agency, and the desire for ethical progress brought about consciously. The economic logic of substitution and exchange, as transmitted by Christian theology and classical political economy, came to serve an experimental contemporary ethics explored in novels that represented and evaluated strategy and outcome in tandem. Mutually tested for practicability and generosity, strategy and outcome were re-conjoined by novelists seeking an ethics and economics that would sustain life and sanctify it.

WORKS CITED

Ablow, Rachel. *Marriage of Minds: Reading Sympathy in the Victorian Marriage Plot.* Stanford: Stanford University Press, 2007.

Adams, James Eli. *Dandies and Desert Saints: Styles of Victorian Masculinity.* Ithaca: Cornell University Press, 1995.

———. "Gyp's Tale: On Sympathy, Silence and Realism in *Adam Bede.*" *Dickens Studies Annual.* Vol. 20. Ed. Michael Timko, Fred Kaplan, and Edward Guiliano. New York: AMS Press, 1991. 227–42.

Anderson, Olive. "The Feminism of T. H. Green: A Late-Victorian Success Story?" *History of Political Thought* 12.4 (1991): 671–93.

———. *Suicide in Victorian and Edwardian England.* Oxford: Clarendon Press, 1987.

Anonymous. Review of *The Warden* by Anthony Trollope. *Athenaeum*, 27 January 1855. 107.

Anonymous. Review of *The Warden* by Anthony Trollope. *Eclectic Review* n.s. 9 (1855). 360.

Appiah, Kwame Anthony. *Cosmopolitanism: Ethics in a World of Strangers.* New York: W. W. Norton, 2007.

Armstrong, Nancy. *Desire and Domestic Fiction: A Political History of the Novel.* Oxford: Oxford University Press, 1987.

———. *How Novels Think: The Limits of Individualism from 1719–1900.* New York: Columbia University Press, 2005.

Arnold, Thomas. *Christian Life, Its Course, Its Hindrances, and its Helps.* London: 1841.

Auerbach, Nina. *Communities of Women: An Idea in Fiction.* Cambridge: Harvard University Press, 1978.

Bailin, Miriam. "'Dismal Pleasure': Victorian Sentimentality and the Pathos of the Parvenu." *ELH* 66.4 (1999): 1015–32.

Baldridge, Cates. "Alternatives to Bourgeois Individualism in *A Tale of Two Cities*." *Glancy* 93–97.

Bataille, Georges. "The Notion of Expenditure" (1933). Rpt. in *Visions of Excess: Selected Writings, 1927–1939*. Ed. Allan Stoekl. Trans. Allan Stoekl et al. Minneapolis: University of Minnesota Press, 1985. 116–29.

Bentham, Jeremy. *An Introduction to the Principles of Morals and Legislation*. In *The Utilitarians*. Garden City, NY: Dolphin Books–Doubleday, 1961.

Berger, Courtney. "When Bad Things Happen to Bad People: Liability and Individual Consciousness in *Adam Bede* and *Silas Marner*." *Novel* 33.3 (2000): 307–27.

Binney, Thomas. *Is It Possible to Make the Best of Both Worlds?: A Lecture for Young Men*. London: 1853.

———. *Sermons Preached in the King's Weigh-House Chapel, London. 1829–1869*. London: Macmillan, 1875.

Birks, Thomas Rawson. "The Nature and Effects of the Atonement." *The Victory of Divine Goodness*. London: 1870.

Blake, Kathleen. *Pleasures of Benthamism: Victorian Literature, Utility, Political Economy*. Oxford: Oxford University Press, 2009.

Bodenheimer, Rosemarie. *Knowing Dickens*. Ithaca: Cornell University Press, 2007.

———. *The Real Life of Mary Ann Evans: George Eliot, Her Letters and Fiction*. Ithaca: Cornell University Press, 1994.

Boose, Lynda E. "The Father's House and the Daughter in It: The Structures of Western Culture's Daughter–Father Relationship." *Daughters and Fathers*. Ed. Lynda E. Boose and Betty S. Flowers. Baltimore: Johns Hopkins University Press, 1989.

Booth, Wayne C. *The Company We Keep: An Ethics of Fiction*. Berkeley: University of California Press, 1989.

Born, Daniel. *The Birth of Liberal Guilt in the English Novel: Charles Dickens to H .G. Wells*. Chapel Hill: University of North Carolina Press, 1995.

Bornstein, David, and Susan Davis. *Social Entrepreneurship: What Everyone Needs to Know*. Oxford: Oxford University Press, 2010.

Bowen, John. "Counting On: *A Tale of Two Cities*." In Jones, McDonagh, and Mee 104–25.

Bradstock, Andrew, Sean Gill, Anne Hogan, and Sue Morgan, eds. *Masculinity and Spirituality in Victorian Culture*. London: Palgrave Macmillan, 2001.

Brantlinger, Patrick. *The Reading Lesson: The Threat of Mass Literacy in Nineteenth-Century British Fiction*. Bloomington: Indiana University Press, 1998.

Bray, Charles. *The Philosophy of Necessity; or Natural Law as Applicable to Moral, Mental, and Social Science*. 2nd ed. London: Longman, 1863.

Briefel, Aviva. "Tautological Crimes: Why Women Can't Steal Jewels." *Novel* 37.1/2 (2004): 135–57.

Brontë, Charlotte. *Jane Eyre*. Ed. Richard Nemesvari. Peterborough, Ontario: Broadview, 1999.

Brown, Callum G. "A Revisionist Approach to Religious Change." Bruce 31–58.

Bruce, Steve, ed. *Religion and Modernization: Sociologists and Historians Debate the Secularization Thesis*. Oxford: Clarendon Press, 1992.

Budge, Gavin. "Realism and Typology in Charlotte M. Yonge's *The Heir of Redclyffe*." *Victorian Literature and Culture* 31.1 (2003): 193–223.

Butler, Joseph. *Fifteen Sermons Preached at the Rolls Chapel*. London: J. and J. Knapton, 1726.

———. *The Works of Bishop Butler*. Ed. S. Halifax. 2 vols. Oxford, 1874.

Carlyle, Thomas. *Sartor Resartus*. In *A Carlyle Reader: Selections from the Writings of Thomas Carlyle*. Ed. G. B. Tennyson. Cambridge: Cambridge University Press, 1988. 122–336.

Carpenter, Mary Wilson. *George Eliot and the Landscape of Time: Narrative Form and Protestant Apocalyptic History*. Chapel Hill: University of North Carolina Press, 1986.

Carrier, James G. *Gifts and Commodities: Exchange and Western Capitalism since 1700*. London: Routledge, 1995.

Carroll, David, ed. *George Eliot: The Critical Heritage*. London: Routledge and Kegan Paul, 1971.

Chadwick, Owen. *The Secularization of the European Mind in the Nineteenth Century*. Cambridge: Cambridge University Press, 1975.

———. *The Victorian Church*. 2 vols. London: W. & J. Mackay, 1966.

Chalmers, Thomas. "Introductory Essay." In *The Imitation of Christ: In Three Books* by Thomas à Kempis. Trans. John Payne. New York: Collins, Brother & Co., 1844. 13–21.

———. *Posthumous Works of the Rev. Thomas Chalmers*. Vol 2. Edinburgh: Constable, 1852.

Clinton, Bill. *Giving: How Each of Us Can Change the World*. New York: Knopf, 2007.

Cohen, William A. *Sex Scandal: The Private Parts of Victorian Fiction*. Durham: Duke University Press, 1996.

Coleridge, Christabel. *Charlotte Mary Yonge: Her Life and Letters*. London: Macmillan, 1903.

Collini, Stefan. *Public Moralists: Political Thought and Intellectual Life in Britain, 1850–1930*. Oxford: Clarendon, 1991.

Collins, Wilkie. *Armadale*. New York: Penguin, 1995.

———. *Letters of Wilkie Collins*. Ed. William Baker and William M. Clarke. 2 vols. New York: St. Martin's, 1999.

———. *The Moonstone*. Ed. Steve Farmer. Peterborough, Ontario: Broadview, 1999.

———. *My Miscellanies*. New York: Harper and Brothers, 1893.

———. "Preface." *My Miscellanies*. 7–8.

———. "The Unknown Public." *My Miscellanies*.

Colón, Susan E. "Realism and Parable in Charlotte Yonge's *The Heir of Redclyffe*." *Journal of Narrative Theory* 40:1 (2010): 29–52.

Courtemanche, Eleanor. *The 'Invisible Hand' and British Fiction, 1818-1860: Adam Smith, Political Economy, and the Genre of Realism*. New York: Palgrave-Macmillan, 2011.

Craik, Dinah Maria Mulock. *Sermons Out of Church*. New York: Harper, 1875.

Cruse, Amy. *The Victorians and their Reading*. Boston: Houghton Mifflin, 1962.

Dale, Peter Allan. *In Pursuit of a Scientific Culture: Science, Art, and Society in the Victorian Age*. Madison: University of Wisconsin Press, 1990.

Dames, Nicholas. "Trollope and the Career: Vocational Trajectories and the Management of Ambition." *Victorian Studies* 45 (2003): 247–78.

Daunton, Martin. *State and Market in Victorian Britain: War, Welfare and Capitalism.* Woodbridge: Boydell, 2008.

Davis, Todd F., and Kenneth Womack. "Preface: Reading Literature and the Ethics of Criticism." In *Mapping the Ethical Turn: A Reader in Ethics, Culture, and Literary Theory.* Ed. Todd F. Davis and Kenneth Womack. Charlottesville: University of Virginia Press, 2001. ix–xiv.

Defoe, Daniel. *Robinson Crusoe.* London: Penguin, 1965.

Dickens, Charles. *David Copperfield.* Ed. Jerome H. Buckley. New York: W. W. Norton: 1987.

———. *A Tale of Two Cities.* Ed. Stephen Koch. New York: Bantam, 1989.

Dixon, Thomas. *The Invention of Altruism: Making Moral Meanings in Victorian Britain.* Oxford: Oxford University Press, 2008.

Dolin, Tim. *Mistress of the House: Women of Property in the Victorian Novel.* Aldershot: Ashgate, 1997.

Dombrowski, Daniel A. "Back to Sainthood." *Philosophy Today* 33.1 (1989): 56–63.

Dooley, Allan C. *Author and Printer in Victorian England.* Charlottesville: University of Virginia Press, 1992.

Douglas, Mary. "Foreword: No Free Gifts." In Mauss vii–xviii.

Edwards, Ruth Dudley. *The Pursuit of Reason: The Economist, 1843–1993.* London: Hamish Hamilton, 1993.

Elfenbein, Andrew. "On the Discrimination of Influences." *Modern Language Quarterly* 69.4 (2008): 481–507.

Eliot, George. *Adam Bede.* Ed. and intro. by Carol A. Martin. Oxford: Clarendon, 2001.

———. *Adam Bede.* Ed. Stephen Gill. New York: Penguin, 1985.

———. *The George Eliot Letters.* Ed. Gordon S. Haight. 9 vols. New Haven and London: Yale University Press, 1954–74.

———. *Middlemarch.* New York: Bantam, 1985.

———. *Mill on the Floss.* Ed. A. S. Byatt. New York: Penguin, 1985.

———. Review of *The Natural History of German Life.* 1856. In *Selected Essays, Poems and Other Writings.* Ed. A. S. Byatt and Nicholas Warren. London: Penguin, 1990.

———. *Romola.* Ed. Andrew Sanders. New York: Penguin, 1980.

———. *Scenes of Clerical Life.* Ed. David Lodge. New York: Penguin, 1973.

Elliot, Kamilla. "Face Value in *A Tale of Two Cities.*" In Jones, McDonagh and Mee 87-103.

Ellis, Sarah Stickney. *The Mothers of England: Their Influence & Responsibility.* Fisher, Son & Co., 1843.

Ellison, Robert H. "The Tractarians' Sermons and Other Speeches." In *A New History of the Sermon: The Nineteenth Century.* Ed. Robert H. Ellison. Leiden and Boston: Brill, 2010. 15–58.

Euripides. *Iphigenia at Aulis.* Trans. Kenneth Cavander. Englewood Cliffs: Prentice-Hall, 1973.

"The Failure of Altruism." *Fraser's Magazine,* October 1879.

Feltes, N. N. *Modes of Production of Victorian Novels.* Chicago: University of Chicago Press, 1986.

Ferguson, Frances. "On Terrorism and Morals: Dickens's *A Tale of Two Cities*." *Partial Answers* 3.2 (2005): 49–74.

Feuerbach, Ludwig. *The Essence of Christianity*. Trans. George Eliot. Amherst: Prometheus Books, 1989.

Fisher, Philip. *Wonder, the Rainbow, and the Aesthetics of Rare Experience*. Cambridge: Harvard University Press, 1998.

Fiske, Alan P. "The Four Elementary Forms of Sociality: Framework for a Unified Theory of Social Relations." *Psychological Review* 99 (1992): 689–723.

Flint, Kate. *The Woman Reader, 1837–1914*. Oxford: Clarendon, 1993.

Foley, Helene P. *Ritual Irony: Poetry and Sacrifice in Euripides*. Ithaca: Cornell University Press, 1985.

Forster, John. *The Life of Charles Dickens*. 2 vols. New York: C. Scribner's Sons, 1907.

Fraser, Nancy. "Recognition without Ethics?" In Garber 95–126.

Freedgood, Elaine. *Victorian Writing about Risk: Imagining a Safe England in a Dangerous World*. Cambridge and New York: Cambridge University Press, 2004.

Freedman, Jonathan. *The Temple of Culture: Assimilation and Anti-Semitism in Literary Anglo-America*. New York: Oxford University Press, 2000.

Frymer-Kensky, Tikva. *Reading the Women of the Bible*. New York: Schocken, 2002.

Gagnier, Regenia. *The Insatiability of Human Wants: Economics and Aesthetics in Market Society*. Chicago: University of Chicago Press, 2000.

———. "The Uneasy Pleasures of Freedom, Determinism, and Hope in *Little Dorrit*: A Literary Anthropology." Address delivered at the International Dickens Conference: Uneasy Pleasures. Hebrew University, Jerusalem. 15 June 2009.

Gallagher, Catherine. *The Body Economic: Life, Death, and Sensation in Political Economy and the Victorian Novel*. Princeton: Princeton University Press, 2006.

———. *Nobody's Story: The Vanishing Acts of Women Writers in the Marketplace 1670–1820*. Berkeley: University of California Press, 1994.

Garber, Marjorie, Beatrice Hanssen, and Rebecca L. Walkowitz, eds. *The Turn to Ethics*. London: Routledge, 2000.

Gates, Barbara. *Victorian Suicide: Mad Crimes and Sad Histories*. Princeton: Princeton University Press, 1988.

Gay, Peter. "'The Manliness of Christ.'" In *Religion and Irreligion in Victorian Society. Essays in Honour of R. K. Webb*. Ed. R. W. Davis and R. J. Helmstadter. London: Routledge, 1992.

Genette, Gérard. *Narrative Discourse Revisited*. Trans. Jane E. Lewin. Ithaca: Cornell University Press, 1988.

Giffen, Allison. "Dutiful Daughters and Needy Fathers: Lydia Sigourney and Nineteenth-Century Popular Literature." *Women's Studies* 32 (2003): 255–80.

Gilbert, Sandra M., and Susan Gubar. *The Madwoman in the Attic: The Woman Writer and the Nineteenth-Century Literary Imagination*. New Haven: Yale University Press, 1984.

Girard, René. *The Scapegoat*. Trans. Yvonne Freccero. Baltimore: Johns Hopkins University Press, 1986.

———. *Violence and the Sacred*. Trans. Patrick Gregory. Baltimore: Johns Hopkins University Press, 1977.

Gladstone, William Ewart. *Church Principles Considered in their Result.* London: John Murray, 1840.

———. "'Robert Elsmere' and the Battle of Belief." *The Nineteenth Century* (May 1888). New York, n.d.

Glancy, Ruth, ed. *Charles Dickens's "A Tale of Two Cities": A Sourcebook.* London: Routledge, 2006.

Grant, Colin. *Altruism and Christian Ethics.* Cambridge: Cambridge University Press, 2001.

Graver, Suzanne. *George Eliot and Community.* Berkeley: University of California Press, 1984.

Green, Thomas Hill. *Prolegomena to Ethics.* Oxford: Clarendon Press, 1884.

Greiner, Rae. "Sympathy Time: Adam Smith, George Eliot, and the Realist Novel." *Narrative* 17.3 (2009): 291–311.

Gunn, Giles. *The Culture of Criticism and the Criticism of Culture.* New York: Oxford University Press, 1987.

Hack, Daniel. *The Material Interests of the Victorian Novel.* Charlottesville: University of Virginia Press, 2005.

Hale, Dorothy J. "Aesthetics and the New Ethics: Theorizing the Novel in the Twenty-First Century." *PMLA* 124.3 (May 2009): 896–905.

Hardy, Barbara. *The Novels of George Eliot.* London: Athlone Press, 1963.

Harpham, Geoffrey Galt. *The Ascetic Imperative in Culture and Criticism.* Chicago: University of Chicago Press, 1987.

———. *Getting It Right: Language, Literature, and Ethics.* Chicago: University of Chicago Press, 1992.

———. *Shadows of Ethics: Criticism and the Just Society.* Durham: Duke University Press, 1999.

Hawkins, Sherman. "Mr. Harding's Church Music." *ELH* 29 (1962): 202–23.

Held, Virginia. *The Ethics of Care: Personal, Political, and Global.* Oxford: Oxford University Press, 2006.

Heller, Tamar. *Dead Secrets: Wilkie Collins and the Female Gothic.* New Haven: Yale University Press, 1992.

Hennedy, Hugh L. *Unity in Barsetshire.* The Hague: Mouton, 1971.

Hennell, S. S. *Essay on the Sceptical Tendency of Butler's "Analogy."* London: John Chapman, 1859.

Herbert, Christopher. *Culture and Anomie: Ethnographic Imagination in the Nineteenth Century.* Chicago: University of Chicago Press, 1991.

———. "Filthy Lucre: Victorian Ideas of Money." *Victorian Studies* 44.2 (Winter 2002): 185–213.

———. *Trollope and Comic Pleasure.* Chicago: University of Chicago Press, 1987.

———. *War of No Pity: The Indian Mutiny and Victorian Trauma.* Princeton: Princeton University Press, 2008.

Hertz, Neil. *George Eliot's Pulse.* Stanford: Stanford University Press, 2003.

Heyd, David. "Supererogation." *Stanford Encyclopedia of Philosophy.* Fall 2008. http://plato.stanford.edu/entries/supererogation/. 12 August 2011.

Hilton, Boyd. *The Age of Atonement: The Influence of Evangelicalism on Social and Economic Thought, 1785–1865.* Oxford: Clarendon, 1986.

Himmelfarb, Gertrude. *Victorian Minds: A Study of Intellectuals in Crisis and of Ideologies in Transition*. New York: Harper Torchbooks, 1970.

Houghton, Walter E. *The Victorian Frame of Mind, 1830–1870*. New Haven: Yale University Press, 1957.

Hughes, Winifred. *The Maniac in the Cellar: Sensation Novels of the 1860s*. Princeton: Princeton University Press, 1980.

Hunt, Aeron. "Calculations and Concealments: Infanticide in Mid-Nineteenth Century Britain." *Victorian Literature and Culture* 34 (2006): 71–94.

Hutton, R. H. "Ethical and Dogmatic Fiction: Miss Yonge." *National Review* 12 (January 1861): 211–30.

Jaffe, Audrey. *Scenes of Sympathy: Identity and Representation in Victorian Fiction*. Ithaca: Cornell University Press, 2000.

Jay, Elisabeth. *Faith and Doubt in Victorian Britain*. London: Macmillan, 1986.

———. *The Religion of the Heart: Anglican Evangelicalism and the Nineteenth-Century Novel*. Oxford: Clarendon, 1979.

———. "Women Writers and Religion." In *Women and Literature in Britain, 1800–1900*. Ed. Joanne Shattock. Cambridge: Cambridge University Press, 2001. 251–74.

———, and Richard Jay, eds. *Critics of Capitalism: Victorian Reactions to 'Political Economy*. Cambridge: Cambridge University Press, 1987.

Keble, John. *The Christian Year*. Oxford, 1827.

Keen, Suzanne. *Empathy and the Novel*. Oxford: Oxford University Press, 2010.

Kendrick, Walter M. *The Novel-Machine: The Theory and Fiction of Anthony Trollope*. Baltimore: Johns Hopkins University Press, 1980.

Kertzer, Jonathan. *Poetic Justice and Legal Fictions*. Cambridge: Cambridge University Press, 2010.

Kincaid, James R. *The Novels of Anthony Trollope*. Oxford: Clarendon, 1977.

Knoepflmacher, U. C. *George Eliot's Early Novels*. Berkeley: University of California Press, 1968.

Koven, Seth. *Slumming: Sexual and Social Politics in Victorian London*. Princeton: Princeton University Press, 2006.

Krueger, Christine L. *The Reader's Repentance: Women Preachers, Women Writers, and Nineteenth-Century Social Discourse*. Chicago and London: University of Chicago Press, 1992.

Kucich, John. *Excess and Restraint in the Novels of Charles Dickens*. Athens: University of Georgia Press, 1981.

———. "George Eliot and Objects: Meaning as Matter in *The Mill on the Floss*." *The Mill on the Floss*. Ed. Carol T. Christ. New York: W. W. Norton, 1994. 557–75.

———. *Imperial Masochism: British Fiction, Fantasy, and Social Class*. Princeton: Princeton University Press, 2007.

———. "The Purity of Violence: *A Tale of Two Cities*." *Dickens Studies Annual* Vol. 8. Ed. Michael Timko, Fred Kaplan, and Edward Guiliano (1984): 119–37. New York: AMS Press.

———. *Repression in Victorian Fiction: Charlotte Brontë, George Eliot, and Charles Dickens*. Berkeley: University of California Press, 1987.

Lane, Christopher. *Hatred and Civility: The Antisocial Life in Victorian England*. New York: Columbia University Press, 2004.

Langford, Thomas A. "Trollope's Satire in *The Warden*." *Studies in the Novel* 19 (1987): 435–47.

Larson, Jil. *Ethics and Narrative in the English Novel, 1880–1914*. Cambridge: Cambridge University Press, 2009.

Ledger, Sally, and Holly Furneaux, ed. *Charles Dickens in Context*. Cambridge: Cambridge University Press, 2011.

Levine, George. "Dickens, Secularism, and Agency." In *Contemporary Dickens*. Ed. Eileen Gillooly and Deirdre David. Columbus: Ohio State University Press, 2009. 13–33.

———. *Dying to Know: Scientific Epistemology and Narrative in Victorian England*. Chicago: University of Chicago Press, 2002.

———. *Realism, Ethics and Secularism: Essays on Victorian Literature and Science*. Cambridge: Cambridge University Press, 2008.

Lyons, Paul. "The Morality of Irony and Unreliable Narrative in Trollope's *The Warden* and *Barchester Towers*." *South Atlantic Review* 54.1 (1989): 41–54.

MacDonald, Michael, and Terence R. Murphy. *Sleepless Souls: Suicide in Early Modern England*. Oxford: Clarendon, 1990.

Maher, Susan Naramore. "Recasting Crusoe: Frederick Marryat, R. M. Ballantyne and the Nineteenth-Century Robinsonade." *Children's Literature Association Quarterly* 13.4 (1988): 69–75.

Mansbridge, Jane J. "On the Relation of Altruism and Self-Interest." *Beyond Self-Interest*. Ed. Jane J. Mansbridge. Chicago: University of Chicago Press, 1990. 133–43.

Mare, Margaret, and Alicia C. Percival. *Victorian Best-Seller: The World of Charlotte M. Yonge*. London: Harrap, 1947.

Marx, Karl. *Karl Marx: Selected Writings*. Ed. David McLellan. Oxford: Oxford University Press, 1977.

Mason, Emma. "Religion." In Ledger and Furneaux 318–25.

Masten, Jeffrey, Peter Stallybrass, and Nancy J. Vickers. "Introduction: Language Machines." *Language Machines: Technologies of Literary and Cultural Production*. Ed. Jeffrey Masten, Peter Stallybrass, and Nancy J. Vickers. New York and London: Routledge, 1997. 1–14.

Matthews, Christopher Todd. "Form and Deformity: The Trouble with Victorian Pockets." *Victorian Studies* 52.4 (2010): 561–90.

Maurice, F. D. *The Doctrine of Sacrifice Deduced from the Scriptures: A Series of Sermons*. Cambridge: Macmillan & Co., 1854.

Mauss, Marcel. *The Gift: Forms and Functions of Exchange in Archaic Societies*. 1950. Trans. W. D. Halls. New York: W. W. Norton, 1990.

McCloskey, Deirdre N. *The Bourgeois Virtues: Ethics for an Age of Commerce*. Chicago: University of Chicago Press, 2006.

McKeon, Michael. *The Origins of the English Novel, 1600–1740*. Baltimore: Johns Hopkins University Press, 2002.

Michie, Elsie B. "Buying Brains: Trollope, Oliphant, and Vulgar Victorian Commerce." *Victorian Studies* 44.1 (2001): 77–97.

———. *The Vulgar Question of Money: Heiresses, Materialism, and the Novel of Manners from Jane Austen to Henry James*. Baltimore: Johns Hopkins University Press, 2011.

Milbank, John. "The Midwinter Sacrifice: a Sequel to 'Can Morality Be Christian?'" *Angelaki* 6.2 (August 2001): 49–65.

Mill, John Stuart. "Auguste Comte and Positivism." In *Collected Works of John Stuart Mill: Essays on Ethics, Religion and Society.* Vol 10. Ed. J. M. Robson. Indianapolis: Liberty Fund, 2006. 261–368.

———. "On the Subjection of Women." In *The Basic Writings of John Stuart Mill.* New York: Modern Library, 2002.

———. "Utilitarianism." In *The Utilitarians.* Garden City, NY: Dolphin Books, 1961.

———. "Utility of Religion." In *Collected Works.* Vol 10: 403–28.

Miller, Andrew H. *The Burdens of Perfection: On Ethics and Reading in Nineteenth-Century British Literature.* Ithaca: Cornell University Press, 2008.

———. *Novels behind Glass: Commodity Culture and Victorian Narrative.* Cambridge: Cambridge University Press, 1995.

Miller, D. A. *The Novel and the Police.* Berkeley: University of California Press, 1988.

Miller, J. Hillis. *The Ethics of Reading: Kant, de Man, Eliot, Trollope, James, and Benjamin.* New York: Columbia University Press, 1989.

Mizruchi, Susan L. *The Science of Sacrifice: American Literature and Modern Social Theory.* Princeton: Princeton University Press, 1998.

Nayder, Lillian. *Wilkie Collins.* New York: Twayne, 1997.

Newman, John Henry. "Moral Consequences of Single Sins." In *Parochial and Plain Sermons.* San Francisco: Ignatius, 1997. 756-65.

———. "Self-Denial the Test of Religious Earnestness" (1833). In *Selected Sermons.* Ed. Ian Ker. New York and Mahwah, NJ: Paulist Press, 1994. 86–94.

———. "Sins of Ignorance and Weakness" (1832). In *Selected Sermons,* 95–102.

Newton, Adam Zachary. *Narrative Ethics.* Cambridge: Harvard University Press, 1997.

Nunokawa, Jeff. *The Afterlife of Property: Domestic Security and the Victorian Novel.* Princeton: Princeton University Press, 1994.

Nygren, Anders. *Agape and Eros.* Trans. Philip S. Watson. New York: Harper and Row, 1969.

Osteen, Mark, and Martha Woodmansee, eds. *The New Economic Criticism: Studies at the Interface of Literature and Economics.* London and New York: Routledge, 1999.

Otto, Rudolf. *The Idea of the Holy.* Trans. John W. Harvey. Oxford: Oxford University Press, 1970.

Oxford English Dictionary. "Amends." *Oxford English Dictionary.* 2nd ed. 6 Feb. 1996. 11 August 2011.

———. "Forgive." *Oxford English Dictionary.* 2nd ed. 6 Feb. 1996. 11 August 2011.

———. "Sacrifice." *Oxford English Dictionary.* 2nd ed. 6 Feb. 1996. 11 August 2011.

Parker, John. "God among Thieves: Marx's Christological Theory of Value and the Literature of the English Reformation." Diss., University of Pennsylvania, 1999.

Paxton, Nancy L. *George Eliot and Herbert Spencer: Feminism, Evolutionism, and the Reconstruction of Gender.* Princeton: Princeton University Press, 1991.

Perkin, Harold. *The Origins of Modern English Society, 1780–1880.* London: Routledge and Kegan Paul, 1969.

Peters, Catherine. *The King of Inventors: A Life of Wilkie Collins.* Princeton: Princeton University Press, 1993.

Peterson, William S. "Gladstone's Review of *Robert Elsmere*: Some Unpublished Correspondence." *The Review of English Studies* 21.84 (November 1970): 442–61.

Piggott, Solomon. *Suicide and Its Antidotes*. London: J. Robins and Co., 1824.

Poovey, Mary. *Genres of the Credit Economy: Mediating Value in Eighteenth- and Nineteenth-Century Britain*. Chicago: University of Chicago Press, 2000.

———. *Uneven Developments: The Ideological Work of Gender in Mid-Victorian England*. Chicago: University of Chicago Press, 1988.

Pope, Alexander. "Essay on Man." London, 1891. Project Gutenberg. http://www.gutenberg.org/files/2428/2428-h/2428-h.htm. 1 April 2011.

Post, Stephen G. *A Theory of Agape: On the Meaning of Christian Love*. London: Associated University Presses, 1990.

Price, Leah. *The Anthology and the Rise of the Novel from Richardson to George Eliot*. Cambridge: Cambridge University Press, 2000.

Psomiades, Kathy Alexis. "Heterosexual Exchange and Other Victorian Fictions: *The Eustace Diamonds* and Victorian Anthropology." *Novel* 33 (1999): 93–118.

Rappoport Jill. *Giving Women: Alliance and Exchange in Victorian Culture*. New York and Oxford: Oxford University Press, 2011.

Richards, Thomas. *The Commodity Culture of Victorian England: Advertising and Spectacle, 1851–1914*. Stanford: Stanford University Press, 1990.

Robbins, Bruce. *Upward Mobility and the Common Good: Toward a Literary History of the Welfare State*. Princeton: Princeton University Press, 2007.

Robertson, F. W. "The Sacrifice of Christ." 23 June 1850. *Sermons Preached at Brighton*. London: Kegan Paul, 1884. http://www.gutenberg.org/files/16645/16645-h/16645-h.htm#VII.

Rosman, Doreen. *The Evolution of the English Churches, 1500–2000*. Cambridge: Cambridge University Press, 2003.

Rothschild, Emma. *Economic Sentiments: Adam Smith, Condorcet, and the Enlightenment*. Cambridge: Harvard University Press, 2001.

Rubin, Gayle. "The Traffic in Women: Notes on the Political Economy of Sex." *Towards an Anthropology of Women*. Ed. Rayna R. Reiter. New York: Monthly Review Press, 1975. 157–210.

Ruskin, John. *Sesame and Lilies*. Ed. Deborah Epstein Nord. New Haven: Yale University Press, 2002.

———. *Seven Lamps of Architecture*. In *The Works of John Ruskin, Library Edition*, ed. E. T. Cook and Alexander Wedderburn, 39 vols. (London: George Allen, 1903).

———. *Unto This Last*. Lincoln: University of Nebraska Press, 1967.

Ruth, Jennifer. *Novel Developments: Interested Disinterest and the Making of the Professional in the Victorian Novel*. Columbus: Ohio State University Press, 2006.

———. "The Self-Sacrificing Professional: Charles Dickens's 'Hunted Down' and *A Tale of Two Cities*." *Dickens Studies Annual* Vol. 34. Ed. Michael Timko, Fred Kaplan, and Edward Guiliano (2004): 283–99.

Sahlins, Marshall. *Stone Age Economics*. Chicago: Aldine, 1972.

Sandback-Dahlström, Catherine. "Be Good Sweet Maid: Charlotte Yonge's Domestic Fiction: A Study in Dogmatic Purpose and Fictional Form." Diss., University of Stockholm, 1984.

Schaffer, Talia. "The Mysterious *Magnum Bonum*: Fighting to Read Charlotte Yonge." *Nineteenth-Century Literature* 55.2 (2000): 244–75.

Scheffler, Samuel. "Morality's Demands and Their Limits." *Journal of Philosophy* 83 (1986): 531–37.

———, ed. *Consequentialism and Its Critics*. New York: Oxford University Press, 1988.

Schneewind, J. B. *The Invention of Autonomy: A History of Modern Moral Philosophy*. Cambridge: Cambridge University Press, 1997.

———. *Sidgwick's Ethics and Victorian Moral Philosophy*. Oxford: Clarendon, 1977.

Schramm, Jan-Melissa. *Sacrifice, Substitution, and Atonement in Nineteenth-Century Narrative*. Cambridge: Cambridge University Press, 2012.

Schultz, Bart, ed. *Essays on Henry Sidgwick*. Cambridge: Cambridge University Press, 1992.

Searle, G. R. *Morality and the Market in Victorian Britain*. Oxford: Clarendon, 1998.

Shuger, Debora Kuller. *The Renaissance Bible: Scholarship, Sacrifice, and Subjectivity*. Berkeley: University of California Press, 1994.

Sidgwick, Henry. *The Method of Ethics*. 7th ed. Indianapolis: Hackett, 1981.

Simmel, Georg. *The Philosophy of Money*. Trans. Tom Bottomore and David Frisby. London: Routledge and Kegan Paul, 1978.

Singer, Marcus G. "Sidgwick and Nineteenth-Century Ethical Thought." Schultz 65–92.

Singer, Peter. *The Life You Can Save: Acting Now to End World Poverty*. New York: Random House, 2009.

Smalley, Donald, ed. *Trollope: The Critical Heritage*. London: Routledge and Kegan Paul; New York: Barnes and Noble, 1969.

Smiles, Samuel. *Self-Help*. Oxford: Oxford University Press, 2002.

Smith, Adam. *The Theory of Moral Sentiments*. Ed. D. D. Raphael and A. L. Macfie. Oxford: Clarendon, 1976.

———. *Wealth of Nations*. Ed. Andrew Skinner. New York: Penguin, 1999.

Spacks, Patricia Meyer. *Boredom: The Literary History of a State of Mind*. Chicago: University of Chicago Press, 1995.

Spencer, Herbert. *The Principles of Ethics*. 2 vols. Indianapolis: Liberty Fund, 1978.

———. *Social Statics*. London: John Chapman, 1851.

Spurgeon, Charles Haddon, "Love's Commendation." 23 November 1856. *Sermons of the Rev. C. H. Spurgeon, 2nd Series*. New York: Sheldon and Co., 1869. 410–25.

———. "Satan's Banquet." 28 November 1858, *Sermons of C. H. Spurgeon, Fifth Series*. New York: Robert Carter, 1883. 270–88.

Stewart, Garrett. *Dear Reader: The Conscripted Audience in Nineteenth-Century British Fiction*. Baltimore: Johns Hopkins University Press, 1996.

Stewart, Susan. *On Longing: Narratives of the Miniature, the Gigantic, the Souvenir, the Collection*. Durham: Duke University Press, 1993.

Stocking, George W., Jr. *Victorian Anthropology*. New York: Free Press, 1987.

Strahan, S. A. K. *Suicide and Insanity: A Physiological and Sociological Study*. London: S. Sonnenschein and Co., 1893.

Strauss, David Friedrich. *The Old Faith and the New: A Confession*. Trans. Mathilde Blind. London: Asher and Co., 1874.

Sutherland, J. A. *Victorian Novelists and Publishers*. Chicago: University of Chicago Press, 1976.

Taylor, Charles. *A Secular Age*. Cambridge: Belknap Press of Harvard University Press, 2007.

Taylor, Jenny Bourne. *In the Secret Theatre of Home: Wilkie Collins, Sensation Narrative, and Nineteenth-Century Psychology*. London: Routledge, 1988.

———, ed. *Cambridge Companion to Wilkie Collins*. Cambridge: Cambridge University Press, 2006.

Templar, Benjamin. *The "Religious Difficulty" in National Education*. London: Simpkin, Marshall, and Co., 1858.

Thackeray, William Makepeace. *History of Henry Esmond*. 1852. Ed. John Sutherland and Michael Greenfield. London: Penguin, 1985.

Thompson, John L. *Writing the Wrongs: Women of the Old Testament among Biblical Commentators from Philo through the Reformation*. New York: Oxford University Press, 2001.

Tillotson, Kathleen. *Mid-Victorian Studies*. London: Athlone Press, 1965.

Trible, Phyllis. *Texts of Terror: Literary–Feminist Readings of Biblical Narratives*. Philadelphia: Fortress, 1984.

Trollope, Anthony. *An Autobiography*. Ed. Michael Sadleir and Frederick Page. New York: Oxford University Press, 1980.

———. *Can You Forgive Her?* Ed. Andrew Swarbrick. New York: Oxford University Press, 1982.

———. *The Last Chronicle of Barset*. Ed. Stephen Gill. New York: Oxford University Press, 1980.

———. *The Small House at Allington*. Ed. James R. Kincaid. New York: Oxford University Press, 1980.

———. *The Warden*. Ed. David Skilton. New York: Oxford University Press, 1981.

———. *The Warden*. Ed. and intro. by Geoffrey Harvey. Peterborough, Ontario: Broadview Press, 2001.

Vance, Norman. *The Sinews of the Spirit: The Ideal of Christian Manliness in Victorian Literature and Religious Thought*. Cambridge: Cambridge University Press, 1985.

Van Ghent, Dorothy. *The English Novel: Form and Function*. New York: Holt, Rinehart and Winston, 1953.

Vicinus, Martha. *Independent Women: Work and Community for Single Women, 1850–1920*. Chicago: University of Chicago Press, 1985.

———. *Suffer and Be Still: Women in the Victorian Age*. Bloomington: Indiana University Press, 1972.

Wainwright, Valerie. *Ethics and the English Novel from Austen to Forster*. Burlington, VT: Ashgate, 2007.

Walker, Margaret Urban. "Moral Understandings: Alternative 'Epistemology for a Feminist Ethics." In *Explorations in Feminist Ethics: Theory and Practice*. Ed. Eve Browning Cole and Susan C. McQuin. Bloomington: Indiana University Press, 1992. 165–75.

Walton, Susan. *Imagining Soldiers and Fathers in the Mid-Victorian Era: Charlotte Yonge's Models of Manliness*. Surrey: Ashgate, 2010.

Ward, Mary Augusta. *Eleanor*. New York: Harper and Brothers, 1900.

———. *Helbeck of Bannisdale*. New York: Garland Publishing, 1975.

———. *Robert Elsmere*. Chicago, New York, and San Francisco: Belford, Clarke, and Co., n.d.

Waterman, A. M. C. *Political Economy and Christian Theology Since the Enlightenment: Essays in Intellectual History*. Hampshire and NY: Palgrave Macmillan, 2004.

Watt, Ian. *The Rise of the Novel*. Berkeley: University of California Press, 1957.

Webb, Stephen H. *The Gifting God: A Trinitarian Ethics of Excess*. New York: Oxford University Press, 1996.

Weber, Max. *The Protestant Ethic and the Spirit of Capitalism*. Trans. Talcott Parsons. New York: Charles Scribner's Sons, 1958.

Wells-Cole, Catherine. "Angry Yonge Men: Anger and Masculinity in the Novels of Charlotte M. Yonge." In Bradstock et al. 71–84.

Welsh, Alexander. *The City of Dickens*. Oxford: Clarendon, 1971.

———. *George Eliot and Blackmail*. Cambridge: Harvard University Press, 1985.

Wilde, Oscar. "The Soul of Man under Socialism." Project Gutenberg. http://www.gutenberg.org/dirs/etext97/slman10h.htm. 1 August 2011.

Wilkes, Joanne. *Women Reviewing Women in Nineteenth-Century Britain: The Critical Reception of Jane Austen, Charlotte Brontë and George Eliot*. Surrey: Ashgate, 2010.

Williams, Raymond. *The Country and the City*. New York: Oxford University Press, 1973.

Winslow, Forbes. *The Anatomy of Suicide*. London: Henry Renshaw, 1840.

Wolf, Susan. "Moral Saints." *Journal of Philosophy* 79.8 (1982): 419–39.

Woloch, Alex. *The One vs. the Many: Minor Characters and the Space of the Protagonist in the Novel*. Princeton: Princeton University Press, 2004.

Wyschogrod, Edith. *Saints and Postmodernism: Revisioning Moral Philosophy*. Chicago: University of Chicago Press, 1990.

Yonge, Charlotte Mary. *The Heir of Redclyffe*. New York: Garland Publishing, 1975.

INDEX

Ablow, Rachel, 20n22, 123n32, 170n18
Abraham, Isaac and, 162–63
absolution, 90, 91–92, 99
abundance, need vs., 105
Adam Bede (Eliot), 11, 28, 30, 99–138, 225; abandoning sainthood in, 117–19, 122; adulthood in, 107; altruism in, 111, 122, 134; amends in, 128–30; biblical names in, 110n16; changeability and conversion in, 128; Christian charity in, 112–13, 115–16; class structure in, 133; communal good and communal property in, 107; compensation in, 125, 128–30; consequentialism and ethics in, 101–5, 123, 129, 132, 138; death in, 131–32; disavowals and myth-making in, 136–37; dramatization in, 132; duty in, 117–19, 122; "dying to know" paradigm in, 131–32; egoism in, 111, 119–22, 134; epistemological difficulty of, 123; exclusion of characters in, 132; exclusivity of enjoyment in, 105; family system of, 132; focalization in, 132; free indirect discourse in, 121, 128; guilt in, 122–28; imagination in, 121; individualism in, 122, 137; inequality in, 105; as intertext for *Robert Elsmere*, 210, 213; irony in, 121–22; joy in face of sorrow in, 132–38; knowledge in, 130–32; "love yourself as your neighbor" moral in, 112–17; marriage in, 105–12; metaphors in, 126, 129; moral thought in, 102, 121; narcissism in, 109; non-reciprocity in, 116; omniscient narrator in, 133; perfect justice in, 135; play in, 128; post-facto sacrifice in, 129; public and private spheres in, 110; reconception of plot of, 111–12; remorse in, 130; reparation in, 125; scarcity and competition in, 105–12; scripture in, 135–36; self-abnegation in, 115; self-aggrandizing hypocrisy in, 120; self-interest in, 120–22; selflessness in, 117; self-love in, 113; self-regard in, 116; sin in, 123, 128, 131; social redemption in, 123; status of women in, 110; sympathy in, 106, 120, 122–23; unblending human

father–daughter relations, 146–47, 151
fellow-feeling, 2n2, 20, 28
Feltes, N. N., 20n21
female characters, repression of, 51
female exchange, 145
female power, 54
female sacrifice: archetypal images of,
    152; de-valuing or naturalization
    of, 57
female self-sacrifice, 32
female subversiveness, 194n17
female writers, preacher role of, 34n3,
    109n14
femininity: definitions of, 51; Victorian,
    52n20
feminism, 34n3, 51n17, 52, 223n14
feminist criticism, 109–10, 154n12
feminist ethics, 21n25
Ferguson, Frances, 76n16
feudal social structure, 173
Feuerbach, Ludwig, 28, 66, 95–98, 148,
    226; *The Essence of Christianity*,
    3, 95
Fifteen Sermons (Butler), 14, 114
Fiske, Alan P., 171
Flint, Kate, 22n27
Foley, Helene P., 155
forgiveness, 180; false, 180n8; free, 180
Fraser, Nancy, 23
Freedgood, Elaine, 176n4
Freedman, Jonathan, 172n20
freedom: to alienate as proof of owner-
    ship, 155; to give oneself as proof of
    self-possession, 155
free gift, 175–76, 181, 189, 196, 198,
    206; of Christ, 176–79; of grace,
    174, 178; illogic of, 178; of sacrifice,
    190; written texts as, 176
free indirect discourse, 121, 128, 150–51
free trade, 19–20, 223; anti-monopolist,
    19; as new vision of community, 20
French Revolution, 4
French Revolution (Carlyle), 71
friendship, 188–89; authenticity of, 188
Frymer-Kensky, Tikva, 154n12, 162

fungibility, 225–26; of social life, 79

Gagnier, Regenia, 13n13, 23n31, 24,
    149n8, 163n15
Gallagher, Catherine, 13, 20n22, 23n31,
    176n4
Gaskell, Elizabeth, 13, 34–35; *The Life
    of Charlotte Brontë*, 32; *Mary Bar-
    ton*, 34; *Ruth*, 32, 34, 51
Gay, Peter, 57n23
gender: of Christ, 54–58; and Christian
    self-sacrifice, 32–61; differences
    of, 21; and empire, 177n5; natu-
    ral hierarchy of, 170; politics, 26,
    186n12, 210; narrative possibilities
    of, 58–59; of sacrifice, 51–54; as sec-
    ondary category, 55; societal stratifi-
    cation based on, 173
generosity: duty vs., 8; selfless, 179; true,
    140
Giffen, Allison, 145–46
gift economy, 170; feminine Christian,
    104n10
gift exchange, 174, 174n1
gifts, 174, 188–89, 192–93; as bribes,
    184; reciprocity of, vs. gifts, 190;
    and service, 181–85; textual form of,
    193. *See also* free gift
Gilbert, Sandra M., 52n20
Girard, René, 75, 84, 195–96
Giving (Clinton), 24n32
Gladstone, William, 9, 79, 80, 208, 210;
    Reform Act, 182
Goethe, J. W. von: *The Sorrows of
    Young Werther*, 69
goodness, 78–79, 88, 97; vs. asceticism,
    41; vs. happiness, 102
Gospels, 6
gothicism, 35n6, 83; repressed, 194n17
grace, free gift of, 174, 178, 190
Grant, Colin, 151n9, 171
Graver, Suzanne, 123
Great Exhibition, 18
greed, sacrifice as, 12

for sacrifice in, 198–204; speaking
person in, 197–98; symbolic system of, 179; theft in, 181, 185–88;
"token" in, 179, 183; trade among
friends in, 188–89; variety of texts
in, 193; young working-class women
in, 185n10
moral character, anatomizing of, 103
moral duty, 218
moral-economic thought, 121
moral-economic vocabulary. *See* economic-moral vocabulary
moral economy, 142, 187
moral education, 23
moral growth, fostering of, 103
moral heroism, 118
morality, 7, 90, 92, 98, 117n25, 125,
126n33; Christian, 14–18, 29, 139,
174; of individual intention, 101;
middle-class, 65, 93; of personal
benefit, 112; political economy not
hostile to, 18; public, 9; pre-eminence of in Victorian culture, 10;
rational, 88; reduction of religion to,
113; religious, 33; sexual, 69; transcendent, 28, 74; Victorian, 93–94,
218n8; vs. religious sensibility, 88,
92
moral perfectionism, 52n19
moral polarity, 160
moral progress, 218
moral psychology, 177
moral rectitude, 2, 121
morbidity, 158
Morris, William, 33
Morselli, Enrico, *Suicide*, 66n6
motherhood, 52
Mozley, Anne, 128
multicultural studies, 21
murder, biblical prohibition against, 65
Murphy, Terence R., 65–66
mutual benefit, 24, 30–31, 179, 207;
as alternative ethic to self-sacrifice,
207, 209–10; earnest pursuit of, 31;
economy of, 11–13; ethic of, 18,

139–72; free gifts and, 176; granted
to authors and readers, 29; harmony
and, 20; outcome of, 173, 226; possibility of, 176; as beyond self-sacrifice, 210; vs. painful sacrifice, 18
mutuality of existence, 139–40
mutual reward, from sacrifice to, 155–58
mutual service, ideal of, 207–26
mystery novel genre, 199, 205

narcissism: fear of, 109; marriage and,
109
narrative: and emptying of sacrificial gestures of value, 192; linear, 198–204;
moral exemplarity in, 52n19; possibilities of, 57–58; realist, 93; secrecy
and, 190–92
narrative gifts, inequality of, 112
narratology, sacrificial silence and, 192
narrator: merging of with narrated, 83;
omniscience of, 58, 133
narratorial self-presentation, 196
"The Natural History of German Life"
(Eliot), 20–22
Navigation Acts, 19
Nayder, Lillian, 185n10
need, abundance vs., 105
new economic criticism, 23
new ethics, 22n26
New Historicism, 23n29
Newman, John Henry, 7, 32, 37, 39,
126–27; "Sins of Ignorance and
Weakness," 178
Newton, Adam Zachary, 22, 22nn27–28
Nicholas Nickleby (Dickens), 71n11
Nietzsche, Friedrich, 207
Nightingale, Florence, 49n14
nihilism, 221, 222n13
The Nineteenth Century, 208
No Name (Collins), 187n13
non-reciprocity, 116, 183; forms of
exchange, 177, 180
"nova" effect, 74n14
novel-reading, 21n23

cide and self-sacrifice in *A Tale of Two Cities*, 62–98; suicide as, 65
sincerity, 120
sinfulness, human: as devaluation of self, 89
Singer, Marcus G., 217n6
Singer, Peter, 24n33
singularity: Christ-like, 80–87; heroism vs., 80; human, 225; tension between interchangeability and, 74–76, 78–80
"Sins of Ignorance and Weakness" (Newman), 178
Sleepless Souls (MacDonald and Murphy), 65–66
Smalley, Donald, 142n3
The Small House at Allington (Trollope), 141
Smiles, Samuel: *Self-Help*, 66
Smith, Adam, 14, 19, 77, 101–4, 139; invisible hand, 16, 19, 101–4; *The Theory of Moral Sentiments*, 101, 117–18; *The Wealth of Nations*, 15n17, 101–2, 102n5
social atomism, 12
social conflict, 100
social entrepreneurship, 24
social exchange, 181
social generosity, gospel of, 175
social good, 15, 100
social harmony, 29
social hierarchy, 132, 181–83
social ills, 221
socialism, altruism and, 221
social mobility, 76
social order, 19
social position, inequality of, 184
social redemption, 123
social reform, 220
social relations, 177; pre-capitalist and paternal, 224
Social Statics (Spencer), 126
social work, 208–9
Socrates, 65
The Sorrows of Young Werther (Goethe), 69

Southern Cross, 51n17
Spacks, Patricia M., 208n2, 210n3
Spencer, Herbert, 2, 41, 52, 53, 99n1, 113n20, 116, 122, 169, 215; *The Data of Ethics*, 11; *Social Statics*, 126
spiritualism, Christian, 153
spiritual vs. material register, 177
Spurgeon, Charles Haddon, 5, 17, 55–56, 90
Stallybrass, Peter, 202n22
Stephen, Leslie, 10, 11, 52
Stewart, Garrett, 196–98
Stocking, George W., 148n7
Strachey, Lytton: *Eminent Victorians*, 207
Strahan, Samuel A.K.: *Suicide and Insanity*, 66n6, 67, 68
Strauss, David Friedrich, 153n11; *The Life of Jesus*, 152
struggle, narrative possibilities of, 58
subjectivities, collapse of, 184
subjectivity: intercollective, 27; of sacrifice, 150
substitution, 72–74, 95; anti-sociality of, 77; and risks, 74–79; sacrificial, 28; self-abnegating, 73
subversiveness, female, 194n17
suffering, 101, 115, 120, 123, 135, 140, 176n4; active, 56; Christian ethic of, 105; and the good, 43; guiltless Christian, 48; individual, vs. collective growth, 225; joy vs., 139–40; mutual, 170; of others, 100; personal, 6, 104, 123, 190; sum of human, 192; this-worldly, 71; unjust, 105
Sugar Bill, 19
suicide, 12, 222n13; altruistic, 68; culpable, 27; and *felo de se* verdict, 69–70; fictional, 68–74; and insanity, 69; lovelorn and melancholy, 69; male vs. female, 70n10; and *non compos mentis* verdict, 69; pathological vs. Christlike redemp-

LITERATURE, RELIGION, AND POSTSECULAR STUDIES
Lori Branch, Series Editor

Literature, Religion, and Postsecular Studies publishes scholarship on the influence of religion on literature and of literature on religion from the sixteenth century onward. Books in the series include studies of religious rhetoric or allegory; of the secularization of religion, ritual, and religious life; and of the emerging identity of postsecular studies and literary criticism.

CPSIA information can be obtained
at www.ICGtesting.com
Printed in the USA
FFOW04n1840260916
27963FF